BUSINESS/SCIENCE/TECHNOLOGY DIVISION
CHICAGO PUBLIC LIBRARY
400 SOUTH STATE STREET
CHICAGO, IL 60605

D0806007

Environmental Policy
Concepts and
International Implications

PRAEGER SPECIAL STUDIES IN INTERNATIONAL ECONOMICS AND DEVELOPMENT

Praeger Publishers   New York   Washington   London

HC
110
,E5
U78

Reprinted from two issues of *Natural Resources Journal* devoted entirely to environmental policy, Volume 11, No. 3 (July 1971) and Volume 12, No. 2 (April 1972). *Natural Resources Journal* is published by the School of Law, The University of New Mexico.

PRAEGER PUBLISHERS
111 Fourth Avenue, New York, N.Y. 10003, U.S.A.
5, Cromwell Place, London S.W.7, England

Published in the United States of America in 1973
by Praeger Publishers, Inc.

All rights reserved

© 1973 by Praeger Publishers, Inc.

Library of Congress Catalog Card Number: 72-92896

THE CHICAGO PUBLIC LIBRARY
APP AUG 1 3 1973 B

Printed in the United States of America

R06007 17899

CONTENTS

	Page
INTRODUCTION	viii
ENVIRONMENTAL POLICY AND THE CONGRESS Senator Henry M. Jackson	3
ENVIRONMENTAL POLICY IN A HYPERTROPHIC SOCIETY Lynton K. Caldwell	16
THE ENVIRONMENTAL MOVEMENT: AMBIGUITIES AND MEANINGS Grant McConnell	26
POLITICAL AND SOCIAL ACCOMMODATION: THE POLITICAL PROCESS AND ENVIRONMENTAL PRESERVATION Norman Wengert	35
ENVIRONMENTAL POLICY AND POLITICS: VALUE AND POWER CONTEXT Daniel H. Henning	45
THE COORDINATION OF LEGISLATIVE POLICY AND THE REGULATION OF PRIVATE INTERESTS: SOME SUGGESTED PRAGMATIC PRINCIPLES FOR ENVIRONMENTAL POLICY Wolfgang E. Burhenne and William A. Irwin	53
THE ROLE OF LITIGATION IN ENVIRONMENTAL POLICY: THE POWER PLANT SITING PROBLEM David Sive	65
THE BUREAUCRATIC RESPONSE TO ENVIRONMENTAL POLITICS Geoffrey Wandesforde-Smith	76

ENVIRONMENTAL POLICY: PUBLIC PARTICIPATION
AND THE OPEN INFORMATION SYSTEM
Harvey Frauenglass   86

PUBLIC PARTICIPATION AND ENVIRONMENTAL QUAL-
ITY
Dean Arnold W. Bolle   94

INTERNATIONAL ENVIRONMENTAL MANAGEMENT:
SOME PRELIMINARY THOUGHTS
Thomas W. Wilson, Jr.   103

ENVIRONMENTAL POLICY AND INTERNATIONAL INSTI-
TUTIONAL ARRANGEMENTS: A PROPOSAL FOR RE-
GIONAL AND GLOBAL ENVIRONMENTAL PROTECTION
AGENCIES
Albert E. Utton   109

TOWARDS A NEW METHODOLOGICAL APPROACH IN EN-
VIRONMENTAL LAW
Dante A. Caponera   114

THE CHANGING STRUCTURE OF INTERNATIONAL POL-
ICY: NEEDS AND ALTERNATIVES
Lynton K. Caldwell   134

ENVIRONMENTAL POLICY AS A WORLD ORDER PROB-
LEM
Richard A. Falk   142

POLLUTION AND LIABILITY PROBLEMS CONNECTED
WITH DEEP-SEA MINING
L. F. E. Goldie   153

THE RESOLUTION OF UNCERTAINTY
Harold P. Green   163

THE HUMAN ENVIRONMENT: PROBLEMS OF STAN-
DARD-SETTING AND ENFORCEMENT
Dr. Ian Brownlie   168

GLOBAL POLLUTION AND HUMAN RIGHTS
Abel Wolman   176

THE INDIVIDUAL AND THE ENVIRONMENT
Christian de Laet and Susan Singh   192

CHANCES AND PROBLEMS OF INTERNATIONAL AGREE-
MENTS ON ENVIRONMENTAL POLLUTION
Dr. Klaus Boisserée   199

LEGAL RESPONSES TO POLLUTION PROBLEMS—THEIR
STRENGTHS AND WEAKNESSES
Andrew R. Thompson   208

NATIONAL SOVEREIGNTY IN INTERNATIONAL ENVI-
RONMENTAL DECISIONS
Charles R. Ross   223

THE DEVELOPMENT OF INTERNATIONAL ENVIRON-
MENTAL LAW AND POLICY IN AFRICA
J. D. Ogundere   236

THE CONSERVATION OF MIGRATORY ANIMALS
THROUGH INTERNATIONAL LAW
Cyrille de Klemm   252

THE LAW SCHOOL AND THE ENVIRONMENT
Frances Irwin   259

ABOUT THE EDITORS   267

INTRODUCTION

It was the best of times, it was the worst of times, it was the age of wisdom, it was the age of foolishness, it was the epoch of belief, it was the epoch of incredulity, it was the season of light, it was the season of darkness, it was the winter of despair, we had everything before us, we had nothing before us.

Tale of Two Cities

The world has reached a crossroads environmentally—a time of decision-making. The impact of human activity upon the environment in which we live makes it imperative that we take stock of where we are and where we are going. We are on a collision course with the vector of population growth converging with that of technological growth which not only generates more pollutants, but makes it possible for us to exploit nature in a way never before possible.

There has been much activity by the nations of the world to meet this challenge. In the United States on the federal level alone, there exist over eighty agencies with environmental responsibilities. Moreover, the majority of colleges and universities are now establishing some type of environmental program concerned with governmental policy. However, environmental policy is a relatively new field, and is still lacking a body of theory. This book hopes to contribute toward building a theoretical basis for environmental policy—hence, it is oriented along theoretical, conceptual and philosophical lines.

It is time to study and understand this relatively unexplored but important area of environmental policy which will affect our survival and the quality of our lives and the lives of our children. Study and understanding, however, require a theoretical basis for perspective and analysis.

In addition, environmental policy must not only be developed at the local and national tiers, but also at the international level, because pollution knows no political boundaries. Nothing short of international cooperation will suffice to meet intelligently many of the environmental challenges that we face in the remaining years of the 20th century.

Secretary General U Thant of the United Nations took a bold step down the right road by calling the 1972 UN conference on the Human Environment in Stockholm. There, representatives of the over one hundred nations of the world and many international organizations met to confront and discuss six major subjects: the planning and management of the environmental quality of human communities; the environmental aspects of natural resources management which includes animal, chemical and mineral resources; the identification and control of environmental pollutants; the educational, informational, social and cultural aspects of environmental issues; economic development and the environment; and the environmental implications for international organization.

It has been suggested that the Stockholm Conference was both too early and too late; too late to arouse public opinion, since this had already been accomplished, and too early to take decisive action, since most governments aren't ready and in many areas our knowledge is inadequate. This is perhaps true, but it is neither too late nor too early for a significant beginning to the serious consideration of the ways and means to control damaging transboundary pollution. We offer this book as a part of that effort.

DANIEL H. HENNING
ALBERT E. UTTON

Environmental Policy

ENVIRONMENTAL POLICY AND THE CONGRESS

HENRY M. JACKSON†

The law locks up both man and woman
Who steals the goose from us the common,
But lets the greater felon loose
Who steals the common from the goose

Anonymous English Poem

Over the past few years a very major change has taken place in the American public's perception of man's proper relationship to his environment.[1] Traditional economic indices are no longer viewed as the sole measures of progress. We are entering an era in which qualitative values and aesthetic factors are considered as important as material well-being. A new concern for values which cannot easily be translated into the language of the market place can be felt and seen in citizen efforts to save open spaces, parks, and natural beauty from the poorly planned construction of freeways, airports, reservoirs, and industrial plants. People are no longer complacent about the quality of their surroundings, the use of the environment, or the way in which public resources are administered. Public concern has moved many of these issues squarely into the arena of public debate and decision making.

This change in the public's perception of environmental values has enormous, but still largely unexplored, implications for public administration, for our judicial system and for the continued viability of traditional legal concepts which define individual and public responsibilities in the administration of the environment.

I

THE EMERGENCE OF ENVIRONMENTAL MANAGEMENT AS A PUBLIC FUNCTION

A. *Changing Needs and Values*

As the United States approaches her 200th Anniversary we are confronted as a nation by a circumstance that is totally new in human history. Man has rapidly completed the occupancy of the easily inhabitable areas of the earth while his numbers have continued to increase at an accelerating and exponential rate.[2] Simul-

---

†United States Senator, State of Washington, Chairman of Interior and Insular Comm.

1. For a discussion of the meaning and scope of the term "environment" *see* Comm. on Interior and Insular Affairs, A Definition of the Scope of Environmental Management, Comm. Print, 91st Cong., 2d Sess. (1970).

2. Comm'n on Population Growth and the Am. Future, Interim Rep. (1971).

taneously, unprecedented economic power[3] and advances in science and technology have permitted man to make enormously increased demands upon available resources and the environment. In no nation are these coincidential developments—especially man's mastery of science and technology—more dramatically evident than in the United States. And yet, many Americans still find it difficult to understand why environmental management should suddenly become "everybody's business"; why long-accepted values, traditions and ways of thinking and acting in relation to one's surroundings are now being called into question.[4]

At the time of the American Revolution the total population of the continental United States barely exceeded 3 million individuals. The resource and environmental demands of the American Indians and the colonists on the Atlantic seaboard were very light when contrasted with current extractions and pressures. By the close of the 20th century if the U.S. population approximates 300 million, which is entirely possible, the daily stress man places on the environment will, on the basis of numbers alone, have increased 100 times over.[5] Technology has alleviated some forms of stress (as on forests for fuel or on wildlife for food), but science, technology, man's mastery of sophisticated machinery, and tremendous consumption of energy and other resources has greatly increased environmental stress in general. The net result has been enormous and unprecedented demands upon the environment and on a finite resource base.

The rate at which the Nation has changed since 1890 when the frontier officially ceased to exist has been unexceeded by any other social transformation in history. Scarcely one long generation removed from the last days of the frontier, America has become an urbanized and automated society with publicly institutionalized values in social security, labor relations, civil rights, public education, and public health that only a few decades ago were considered utopian and radical.

Powerful new tools applying the discoveries in chemistry, physics, biology, and the behavioral sciences were put to work for improving the health, wealth, comfort, convenience and security of Americans. By utilizing the vast natural resources of the environment, the Amer-

3. Econ. Rep. of the President, H.R. Exec. Doc. No. 92-28, 92nd Cong., 1st Sess. 2 (1971).

4. For an indication of the growing citizen involvement in challenging the conventional wisdom of governmental resource allocation, see the growing volume of environmental litigation reported in Environmental Law Rep. published by Environmental Law Institute and the Judicial Section of Environmental Rep. published by Bureau of Nat'l Affairs.

5. See Special Rep. to the Senate Comm. on Interior and Insular Affairs, 90th Cong., 2d Sess., A Nat'l Policy for the Environment (Comm. Print 1968).

ican people have achieved substantial increases in our standard of living in a relatively short period of time. We are now coming to recognize, however, that our growth, our wealth and our productive technology have been accompanied by side effects which were not always foreseen. Experience has shown us that large social costs as well as benefits can flow from the careless application of technology. In the absence of a system for adequately assessing the consequences of technological change, who could have predicted the many ways in which applied science would transform the conditions of American life?

It is only in the past few years that the dangers of muddling through events and establishing environmental policy by inaction and default have been very widely perceived. Today, with the benefit of hindsight, it is easy to see that our governmental institutions have too often reacted only to *crisis* situations. We always seem to be calculating the short-term consequences of environmental mismanagement, but seldom the long-term consequences or the alternatives open to future action.[6]

The nation long ago would probably have adopted a coherent policy for the management of its environment had it been recognized that mismanagement of the environment incurs huge social and economic costs. This recognition developed belatedly for several reasons: environmental deterioration in the past tended to be gradual and accumulative, so that it was not apparent that any cost or penalty was being exacted; it seemed possible to defer or to evade payment either in money or in obvious loss of environmental assets;

---

6.   As a result of this failure to formulate a comprehensive national policy, environmental decisionmaking largely continues to proceed as it has in the past. Policy is established by default and inaction. Environmental problems are only dealt with when they reach crisis proportions. Public desires and aspirations are seldom consulted. Important decisions concerning the use and the shape of man's future environment continue to be made in small but steady increments which perpetuate rather than avoid the recognized mistakes of previous decades.

Today it is clear that we cannot continue on this course. Our natural resources—our air, water, and land—are not unlimited. We no longer have the margins for error that we once enjoyed. The ultimate issue posed by shortsighted, conflicting, and often selfish demands and pressures upon the finite resources of the earth are clear. As a nation, and as a world, we face these conditions:

A population which is doubling at increasingly shorter intervals;

Demands for resources which are growing at a far greater rate than population; and

A growing technological power which is far outstripping man's capacity to understand and ability to control its impact on the environment.

Senate Interior and Insular Affairs Comm., Rep. on Nat'l Environmental Policy Act of 1969, S. Doc. No. 296, 91st Cong., 1st Sess. 5-6 (1969).

and the "right" to pollute or degrade the environment (unless specific legal damages could be proved) was widely accepted. Exaggerated doctrines of private ownership and an uncritical popular tolerance of the environmental side effects of economic production encouraged the belief that costs projected onto the environment were costs that no one had to pay.[7]

Today, the American people and government at all levels are coming to realize that to enjoy the benefits of technological advance, the environmental costs of all that we do must be made a part of all products and all resource-commitment decisions. From now on "pay-as-you-go" will increasingly be required for insuring against the inherent risks involved when man manipulates nature.[8]

B. A Public Environmental Policy and Philosophy

Fulfillment of public responsibility for the environment means that government must break the shackles of incremental policy-making in the management of the environment. In order to make intelligent decisions which are not based in the emotion of conservation's *cause celebré* of the moment or in the error of simply perpetuating past practices, there is a very real need to develop a national capacity for constructive criticism of present policies and the development of new institutions and new alternatives for the management of land, air, water and living space. Developing this capacity will require the creative utilization of technology to improve environmental conditions and to prevent unanticipated future instances of costly abuse. It will also require that government, business and industry pay closer attention to a far greater range of alternatives and potential consequences when making decisions having environmental impact than they have in the past.[9]

In the 1960s there were sporadic, uncoordinated efforts to deal with various aspects of the "environmental problem." Most of these efforts, however, were responses to specific problems and did not attempt, let alone achieve, a coherent statement of policy or public

7. These notions are, of course, now being challenged on many fronts. *See e.g.,* S.1032, 92nd Cong., 1st Sess. (1971) which proposes a wide expansion of citizen remedies to protect environmental rights. For the background of this measure see *Hearings on S. 3575 Before Subcomm. on Energy, Natural Resources, and Environment of the Senate Comm. on Commerce,* 91st Cong., 2d Sess. (1970).

8. *See* the tax reform measures discussed in Message From The President of the U.S., Program for a Better Environment, H.R. Exec. Doc. No. 92-46, 92nd Cong., 1st Sess. 2 (1971).

9. During the 91st Congress active consideration was given to legislation to establish a Federal Technology Assessment Board. *See* H.R. 17046, 91st Cong., 2d Sess. (1970) *See also* NAS, Technology; Processes of Assessment and Choice 7 (1969).

philosophy with respect to man's relationship to his surroundings.[10] This awaited the 1970s.

On January 1, 1970, the "National Environmental Policy Act of 1969"[11] became law. Though few realized it at the time, this measure was about to make important institutional reforms and fundamental and far-reaching changes at all points in the Federal decision-making process which touch on environmental questions. Environmental values which had in the past been ignored with impunity were suddenly elevated as a matter of Federal law to the status of national goals. All Federal agencies were directed to consider environmental values in all of their actions. A three member Council on Environmental Quality was established in the Executive Office of the President to see that the statutory mandate was carried out and that environmental issues of national concern received the personal attention of the President.

Adoption of the Act constituted Congressional recognition of the need for a comprehensive policy and a new organizing concept by which governmental functions can be weighed and evaluated in the light of better perceived and better understood environmental needs and goals. A national policy for the environment was necessary to provide both a conceptual basis and legal sanction for applying to environmental management the methods of systems analysis that have demonstrated their value in universities, private enterprise, and in some areas of government.

The National Environment Policy Act declared that:

> ... it is the continuing policy of the Federal government, in cooperation with State and local governments, and other concerned public and private organizations, to use all practicable means and measures, including financial and technical assistance, in a manner calculated to foster and promote the general welfare, to create and maintain conditions under which man and nature can exist in productive harmony, and fulfill the social, economic, and other requirements of present and future generations of Americans.[12]

---

10. *See* Jackson, *Foreward: Environmental Quality, the Courts, and the Congress,* 68 Mich. L. Rev. nn. 13-19, at 1076-77 (1970) for a listing of federal legislative efforts to respond to a wide variety of specific environmental problems in recent years.

11. 42 U.S.C. 4321-47 (Supp. V, 1970). Upon signing the Act, President Nixon stated that:

> It is particularly fitting that my first official act in this new decade is to approve the National Environmental Policy Act. ... We are determined that the decade of the seventies will be known as the time when this country regained a productive harmony between man and nature.

6 Weekly Compilation of Presidential Documents, 11 (Jan. 5, 1970).

12. 42 U.S.C. 4321-47 (Supp. V, 1970).

The Act also set forth national environmental goals to the end that the Nation may—

> (1) fulfill the responsibilities of each generation as trustee of the environment for succeeding generations; (2) assure for all Americans safe, healthful, productive, and esthetically and culturally pleasing surroundings; (3) attain the widest range of beneficial uses of the environment without degradation, risk to health or safety, or other undesirable and unintended consequences; (4) preserve important historic, cultural, and natural aspects of our national heritage, and maintain, wherever possible, an environment which supports diversity and variety of individual choice; (5) achieve a balance between population and resource use which will permit high standards of living and a wide sharing of life's amenities; and (6) enhance the quality of renewable resources and approach the maximum attainable recycling of depletable resources.[13]

These goals are "man" oriented. They are concerned with humanity and man's relationship to his surroundings. By way of contrast, most Federal resource policies and laws are "object" oriented. Human values and aspirations tend to be submerged in programs and numbers, and the issues tend to become quantitative and objective. Qualitative, humanistic considerations are too often lost in legislative and administrative efforts to adjust or redefine man's changing relationship to his environment.

Passage and implementation of the National Environmental Policy Act was begun in an atmosphere of public attention—almost a competition for primacy in advocating environmental causes.[14] This atmosphere has had beneficial as well as detrimental effects upon achievement of the Act's objectives. Public support undoubtedly has greatly accelerated the implementation of the new mandate by the various Federal agencies.[15] It has also resulted in making the Council

---

13. *Id.*

14. For a comprehensive review of legislative measures introduced in the 91st Congress. Congress *see* Environmental Policy Division, Library of Congress, Rep. to Senate Comm. on Interior and Insular Affairs, 91st. Cong., 2d Sess. Environmental Affairs of the 91st Congress (Comm. Print 1971).

15. I noted in remarks prepared for an address before the New Jersey Academy of Science in April, 1970 that:

> Untold numbers of decisions are being influenced by the Act; the Secretary of the Treasury, for example, announced on March 5 that he will not approve use of Federal funds for additional runways at John F. Kennedy International Airport in New York pending the results of an environmental study. Citing the Environmental Policy Act, Secretary Volpe said:
>> 'I am not going to approve the use of Federal funds for these airports and corridors unless and until I am satisfied that the price of this additional mobility is not irreparable damage to the quality of the environment.'

on Environmental Quality a focal point of Federal decision-making.[16] The importance assigned to the Council by the White House has greatly strengthened the Council in its relations with other agencies[17] and has enabled it to achieve stature and influence throughout the Executive establishment in an incredibly short period of time.

Along with attention, however, have come pressures which have made the transition to comprehensive environmental management more difficult. The President has looked to the Council for day-by-day guidance on current environmental issues and the Council has consequently been preoccupied with paper work and with short-term crises.

The Council's preoccupation with environmental "brush fires" has detracted from other major responsibilities assigned to it under the Act. The Council, for example, has made little progress toward developing procedures for measurement and evaluation of environmental indicators.[18] It has thus far made little contribution to the tremendous job of improving policies and procedures and developing an analytical methodology for making the hard tradeoff decisions between preservation and development that will measure our ultimate success in environmental management.[19]

The contemplative consideration of general directions, the anticipation of emerging problems, and the design of new decision criteria are critically important; though they are not dramatic and, thus, seldom newsworthy. Fulfilling these functions does not capture public attention the way the latest pronouncement on mercury poisoning, the SST, a major oil spill, or the proposed trans-Alaska oil

---

Similar announcements have been made in recent weeks on Federally funded highway projects and, earlier, on the super jetport in the Everglades.

Perhaps the most dramatic illustration of the great changes that the Act has made on Federal activities is that on April 2 the Corps of Engineers, often viewed as a despoiler of the natural environment, held its first major press conference in the Corps' 146 year history. The subject of the conference was the Corps' responsibilities under the NEPA.

16. *See* Council on Environmental Quality's First Annual Rep., Environmental Quality 1 (1970).

17. The Council on Environmental Quality played a key role in preparation of the President's Environmental Message and his environmental legislative program for the 92d Congress. Message From The President of the U.S., Program for a Better Environment, H.R. Exec. Doc. No. 92-46, 92d Cong., 1st Sess. 2 (1970).

18. 42 U.S.C. § § 4321-47 (Supp. V, 1970) [originally enacted as Pub. L. No. 91-190, § 204(2)]. *See also* Senate Comm. Rep. on Pub. L. No. 91-190, especially analysis of § 302(a) of S.1075.

19. To provide a Federal institution capable of making trade-off decisions efficiently and with full awareness of their impact, the Administration has proposed the establishment of a Department of Natural Resources. S. 1431, 92d Cong., 1st Sess. § 3 (1971).

pipeline does. In the final analysis, however, man's ability to survive on this earth and to enjoy quality social, cultural, and aesthetic conditions and experiences will not turn upon government's handling of a single contaminant, or decisions on a particular oil spill. It will turn upon government's ability to develop policies and decision-making models which integrate environmental concerns along with the full range of other important human values.

II
IMPLEMENTING ENVIRONMENTAL POLICY

A. Recent Institutional Changes

In addition to adoption of the National Environmental Policy Act, other changes have been made in the Federal establishment to improve responsiveness to the new importance of environmental concerns. The President, by the submission of Executive Reorganization Plans, has established two new Federal agencies which are primarily concerned with environmental matters. The first was the National Oceanic and Atmospheric Administration within the Department of Commerce.[20] This reorganization involved the transfer of a number of existing resource and environmental agencies to better consolidate the nation's oceanographic effort.

The second reorganization created a new independent agency, the Environmental Protection Agency (EPA).[21] This important Federal reorganization involved the consolidation of existing agencies and programs for water, air and solid waste pollution, and it also removed these agencies from the Executive Departments and created a new independent entity in government. EPA has developed its own constituency and its own institutional viewpoint which are now no longer directly influenced by the divergent and often developmental interests and responsibilities of their former parent departments. EPA provides a new center of activity and source of influence in environmental affairs, and it is a particularly potent one because it commands a large and growing technical staff, a significant budget, and some of the nation's strongest regulatory and enforcement environmental programs.

B. Proposed Institutional Changes

Even with the establishment of the Council of Environmental Quality and the reorganization of many of the Federal agencies, it is

20. Message From The President of the U.S., Reorganization Plan No. 4, H.R. Exec. Doc. No. 365, 91st Cong., 2d Sess. 7 (1970).
21. Message From The President of the U.S., Reorganization Plan No. 3, H.R. Exec. Doc. No. 364, 91st Cong., 2d Sess. 7 (1970).

evident that there is a need for a highly skilled and competently staffed organization to provide a continuing interdisciplinary, professional service in environmental policy analysis.

To fill this need legislation has been introduced in the Senate to establish a National Environmental Policy Institute.[22] The Institute would perform many of the important long-range functions which were recognized in the National Environmental Policy Act, but which have not received adequate attention because of the pressing, more immediate demands being placed upon the Council's resources and personnel.

Some of these long range needs include:

—designing a uniform and comprehensive system of national and worldwide environmental monitoring;
—subjecting available data on urban problems and on domestic natural resources to analysis;
—developing proposed methods for anticipating future and emerging environmental problems before they reach crisis proportions (air and water pollution and the introduction of chemical agents such as lead and mercury into the environment provide classic examples of problems which could have been largely avoided if they had been perceived as a "problem" at an early enough point in time); and
—providing in-depth policy analyses, using systems analysis techniques, of alternative solutions for dealing with environmental problems.

Establishing new national goals and priorities and reevaluating governmental policies for environmental management has led to proposals to restructure existing institutions in order to better facilitate achievement of environmental objectives. The primary target of these reorganizational considerations in the area of environment has been the Department of the Interior. It has long been recognized that duplication and conflict which results from the involvement of a variety of government agencies in environmental concerns could be better dealt with if programs of agencies related to environmental control were brought together in one Federal department.[23] On March 26, 1971, the President proposed a Department of Natural Resources (DNR) to meet this need.[24]

The proposed DNR would merge all of the existing functions of the Department of the Interior with the land use and land manage-

22. S. 1216, 92nd Cong., 1st Sess. (1971) and see Senator Jackson's introductory statement in 117 Cong. Rec. 3110-3118 (daily ed. Mar. 12, 1971).

23. See Mister Z, *The Case For A Department Of Natural Resources,* 1 Natural Resources J. 197 (1961).

24. S. 1431, 92nd Cong., 1st Sess. 3 (1971).

ment functions of the Department of Agriculture including the Forest Service, together with a number of other Federal efforts and functions related to water resources management and energy development. The proposed DNR would have five major divisions: Land and Recreation Resources; Water Resources; Energy and Mineral Resources; Ocean, Atmospheric and Terrestorial Sciences; and Indians and Territories.

C. The Need For A National Land Use Policy

While great strides toward introducing environmental values into all governmental decisions have been made, the nation has not developed institutional machinery and specific laws and policies at the State level to do a comprehensive, coherent job of land use planning and management.

To a very great extent, all environmental management decisions are intimately related to land use decisions. All environmental problems are outgrowths of land use patterns. The collective land use decisions which the nation makes in the future will dictate our success in environmental management; and the land use decisions of today will shape the environment future generations will enjoy.

Presently, land use planning and decision-making, with the exception of Federal lands, is a constitutional function of State government. Most of these decisions at the State and local level, however, are dictated by private decisions following private motives but are influenced, for better or worse, by governmental action. In the past, most of these decisions and actions have been unrelated to environmental values. Clearly, absent fundamental changes, many of them will continue to be dictated by private objectives—very often economic objectives.[25]

The basic authority and responsibility for regulating private land use actions rests with the State governments. States have traditionally applied public standards to private lands through zoning, property taxes, and regulation by delegation to local jurisdictions. Some of the States, notably Hawaii and Colorado, have begun to implement statewide land use planning.[26]

Often, funds to collect data and build a technical staff are lacking. In some states, the resistance to "planning" in any form is difficult to surmount. In every state, the tremendous influence of Federal activities such as highways, water resource projects, airports, and military establishments is largely beyond the control of the State

25. R. Babcock, The Zoning Game (1964).
26. Hearings on S. 3354 Before the Senate Comm. on Interior and Insular Affairs, 91st Cong., 2d Sess. (1970).

government. For these reasons, a national land use policy is needed.

A national land use policy can provide a framework within which the spectrum of proposals to utilize environmental resources can be balanced against one another and measured against the demands they collectively impose upon the government. A common structure is needed within which the public can compare alternative proposals to achieve environmental goals.

Legislation has been introduced in the Senate which is designed to make some basic changes in the Nation's management of its land resources. S.632, the "National Land Use Policy Act of 1971," has three major provisions.[27] *First,* it establishes a grant-in-aid program to assist State and local governments in improving their land use planning management capability. *Second,* States are required to exercise "State Rights" and develop and implement a state-wide "environmental, recreational and industrial land use plan." *Third,* the Federal government's responsibility for coordinating Federal land use planning activities, for improving Federal-State relations, and for developing data on land use planning activities, trends and projections is enlarged and centralized.

The continued initiation of Federally financed public works within a state would, under S.632, be contingent upon performance of the state's land-use planning responsibilities. When a state-wide plan has been completed and reviewed by the Federal coordinating body, the Federal agencies would be obliged to act in conformity with it unless compelling reasons of national policy justify exceptions.

III
CURRENT DEVELOPMENTS AND THE NEED
FOR A BALANCED ENVIRONMENTAL POLICY

As the national will to preserve a quality environment grows, it is essential that the nation not lose sight of the actual meaning and intent of a national environmental policy. Environmental policy, broadly construed, is concerned with the maintenance and management of those life-support systems—natural and man made—upon which the health, happiness, economic welfare and physical survival of humanity depend. Environmental policy should not be confused with narrow, single purpose efforts to preserve natural or historical aspects of the environment in a perpetually unaltered state. Environ-

---

27. S. 632, 92nd Cong., 1st Sess. 2 (1971) and see statement by Jackson in 117 Cong. Rec. at 905-19 (daily ed., Feb. 5, 1971). The present Administration has also proposed national land use legislation. *See* S.992, 92nd Cong., 1st Sess. 2 (1971). The background of this measure is found in CEQ, First Annual Rep., Environmental Quality 1 (1970).

mental quality does not necessarily mean indiscriminate preservation, at the cost of achieving other national objectives, but it does imply a careful examination of all alternative means of meeting legitimate human needs.

Environmental policy is concerned with the total environmental needs of man—ethical, esthetic, physical, and intellectual as well as economic.

In recent months there has been a growing tide of hysterical incantations by some environmental extremists who attribute *all* of the nation's environmental ills to economic growth and to America's large gross national product. These prophets of doom advocate that the adoption of a policy of "no growth" is necessary if environmental problems are to be resolved.

Many of those who advocate a "no growth" policy have themselves flourished in America's growing affluence. Thus they seldom appreciate the consequences that adoption of a "no growth" policy would bring. A policy of "no growth" ignores the interests of millions of Americans for whom the struggle to attain job security and provide the necessities of life for themselves and their families leaves little time for pursuit of abstract notions of environmental aestheticism.

There is a very real danger that the "either-or" tactics of some environmental extremists may jeopardize the whole movement for a liveable environment. Excluding all other alternatives, they ask the country to choose between preservation and progress, between technological advance and environmental degradation. Their dogmatic approach has put economic growth and environmental quality on a collision course.

Those who advocate this point of view are already alienating support that the environmental quality movement can ill afford to lose. By ignoring the interests of millions of Americans for whom job security and the prospect of the good life are decent aspirations, they are turning the fight for environmental quality into a confrontation between the "haves" and the "have nots." The poor people of this country want good jobs and decent housing. They aspire to the material goods and comforts enjoyed as a matter of course by more affluent Americans. Understandably, they do no want to be volunteered as the first victims of some state-backed program of Spartan rigor.

One of the most disturbing aspects of this no growth approach is the tendency to hold science and technology responsible for all of our environmental problems. It takes little effort or imagination to trace almost any environmental problem to some scientific, technological or engineering development. The indispensable contribution of science, technology and engineering to our well-being is however, easily forgotten, when unreasoning extremists attempt to sacrifice economic growth and public well-being on the altar of ecology. Also, conveniently disregarded is the fact that it is not science and technology, but the way in which they are used that has damaged our environment in the past and constitutes a major threat to the future of environmental quality.

Establishment of a no growth policy accompanied by major cutbacks in areas of scientific and technological advance would soon make this nation a technological Appalachia at a time when we need our best scientific and engineering talent as never before. For now and in the future we must rely heavily on this talent to solve major environmental problems—to provide clean energy, to devise pollution-free manufacturing processes and transportation systems and to develop new techniques for recycling and reusing our resources. The solution to these problems is not to halt economic growth or the development of science and technology, but rather it is to develop responsible programs and policies to guide their use.

CONCLUSION

Our national ability to develop a comprehensive, balanced and effective environmental policy in the months and years ahead will be a vital factor in the future achievement of other important national goals. The concept of "environment," like that of "economics," cuts across the full fabric of our national life and today is becoming a major influence on a broad range of resource allocation decisions in areas as disparate as transportation, national security, foreign policy, energy consumption, employment, technology development, and many others.

The environmental problems generated by years of corporate greed, by lack of governmental concern, by selfish capitalism and the misguided use of technology reflect fundamental flaws in our governmental institutions and in the laws and procedures by which we sort out the rights and duties of organizations and individuals in our society. Resolving these problems for human ends—to improve the quality of our life—is, in major respects, the most challenging task facing the legal profession in the last one-third of the century.

ENVIRONMENTAL POLICY IN A HYPERTROPHIC SOCIETY

LYNTON K. CALDWELL†

The tendencies of contemporary American society to inordinate and uncontrolled growth are fundamentally incompatible with the objectives of the environmental quality movement, as expressed in the National Environmental Policy Act.[1] Certain short-term, partial, or incremental improvements in environmental conditions may be compatible with unrestricted growth. But the sheer magnitude of the problems created by ever-increasing numbers of people, goods, and services, and the mobile interactions among them, will frustrate all efforts to create or maintain quality environments.

Paradoxically, the science and technology that have made possible the run-away growth of contemporary industrial society have also made possible the environmental quality movement. Men today know, should know, or may know, the consequences of their environmental impacts. Science enables them to learn what is happening; and technology, in many instances, could correct or alleviate the ill-effects of environmental abuse. But technology seldom is adequately applied to protect or enhance the environment. Equally in free-enterprising or socialist societies, technology is applied only when, in some sense, it pays someone to apply it. The payoff is usually economic; other possible payoffs—in health, safety, esthetics, ecological stability, and the continuing renewability of resources— being unperceived or discounted by most people and their political leaders. And there are also serious problems of man's environmental impacts for which technology has no apparent answers. Unending expansion of human populations and technologies entails an inexorable overstressing of the biosphere which no perspective technology can overcome.

The obvious explanation of this paradox is that science and technology have been applied toward the realization of goals and ambitions that have not been subjected to scientific scrutiny. Science has been commandeered to serve purposes that scientific analysis might reveal to be dangerous, improvident, or self-defeating. These negative aspects of applied science (of "pesticides" for example) characteristically affect men in the aggregate, often gradually, and only acutely at some future, and usually imprecise, point in time. Mean-

†Professor of Political Science, Indiana University; Chairman, Commission on Environmental Policy, Law, and Administration of the International Union for Conservation of Nature and Natural Resources.
1. 42 U.S.C. § § 4321-47 (Supp. V, 1970).

while, the government, the political party, the corporation, the local community, or the individual may "benefit" from action that poisons, degrades, or impoverishes the environment. Individuals do not readily see the harmful consequences of science applied to human purposes in agriculture, manufacturing, medicine, and transportation.

To object to the effects of hypertrophic affluence is widely condemned as self-centered ill-taste. Those who would contain growth are reminded that there are fifty million poor people in America who need more, not less, of everything. Many political "liberals" and free-enterprising businessmen find themselves agreeing that selfish environmentalists want to create an ecologically ordered world at the expense of the poor. Efforts to preserve open space and endangered wildlife, to conserve scenic beauty, and to prevent pollution are attacked from both "right" and "left" by critics for whom unqualified procreation and material consumption comprise all that is important in life.

In the technological society, the demands of ordinary people upon their environments exceed those of pre-industrial monarchs. The self-indulgent, materialistic, mass consuming society of democratic America proclaims every man a "king" and every woman a "queen." But the monarchial prototype is neither sober, hard-working Frederich William of Prussia, nor urbane, philosophic Marcus Aurelius—it is the "I'll take mine now and to hell with the consequences" Bourbon Louis XV, who, however, had the prescience to declare *"Apres moi le deulge."*[2]

The not so obvious explanation of the failure of society to be guided by the knowledge that science makes possible is that men in the mass are incapable of directing their own destinies. The overgrowth of modern society may, from this viewpoint, be treated as pathological. The hypertrophic society has fallen victim to a social "disease," an "endocrine failure" followed by run-away metabolism and accelerating growth.[3] The negative feedback and homeostatic mechanisms that contain and protect a stable self-renewing society have been supplanted by the self-generating impetus of positive feedback. The hypertrophic society embarks upon an ever-accelerating cycle of self-stimulation; development feeds development, growth

---

2. The consequences of the fusion of hedonism, individualism, and equalitarianism in the dominant ethos of contemporary America have been analyzed at length by A. Hacker, The End of the American Era (1970).

3. Leo Marx in an article generally paralleling the analysis presented in this paper, cites several writers and scientists who have developed the concept of malignancy as the characterizing aspect of America's reckless, uncontrolled growth: Marx, *American Institutions and Ecological Ideals,* Science 945-52 (1970).

grows upon growth. The pace of events moves faster and faster—the rate of expansion and change outrunning the capacities of increasing numbers of people to adjust. Disequilibriums, discontinuities, incompatibilities, and conflicts mount. Tension becomes pervasive. Minor disasters and intimations of impending catastrophies disturb the more perceptive observers but have no significant effect upon the headlong rush of "progress."

Technological development increasingly ties the economy into a "total system." Interdependicies increase. The autonomy of the individual is simultaneously increased and decreased, but the fate of the individual is increasingly bound-up with the fate of mass society. The farmer and frontiersman of America's past could make their own accommodation with nature; the multi-millions of contemporary America cannot. If their man-managed systems fail, many, perhaps most, of them will shortly meet Malthusian fates. Although these systems are visibly becoming more vulnerable, few people perceive them as less reliable than the systems maintained by nature. The city water main seems more reliable than the river which man has rendered unfit for many uses.

Unfortunately for the reliability of man-managed systems, societal hypertrophy is accompanied by social tensions and antagonisms. As with John B. Calhoun's rats, social war seems endemic in the situation.[4] As hypertrophy approaches advanced stages, the self-destructive tendencies inherent in the disease become evermore apparent. There may be a point beyond which the disease is fatal. Whether this point, if it exists, has been passed in contemporary societies cannot be determined by any analysis now available. There are observers, however, who believe that this point has been passed by more than a quarter-century and that nothing can avert the collapse of existing social structures over large areas of the earth. Whether this "collapse" is gradual and sporadic, or whether it may come as a sudden crash, cannot be foreseen. The internal weakening of the social structure that supports the system may be occurring progressively while a society achieves such hypertrophic triumphs as the SST, the John Hancock Building, and a trillion dollar GNP. Then, suddenly the "structure" begins to falter, the society is unable to mobilize its resources for a remedial response, failure of critical aspects of the life-support system follows rapidly, and the social system collapses into a state of chaos.

Socio-ecological bankruptcy, if and where it occurs, does not necessarily imply the total dissolution of society nor the end of civilization. But a reconstituting of the society would necessarily

4. *Population Density and Social Pathology,* Scientific American, Feb. 1962, at 139-48.

follow; no aggregation of people can live for long in anarchy. The artificial systems that modern technology makes possible must continue somehow to be operated if the lives of large numbers of dependent people are not to be forfeited. Under the more probable conditions following socio-ecological collapse, this restoration would be highly authoritarian and be backed by the summary use of force with the involuntary acquiescence of the threatened and frightened survivors.

This gloomy scenario is not a prognosis for all societies in the modern world. René Dubos may be right in foreseeing the gradual adaptation of men to progressively worsening ecological conditions. Those societies in which populations have not outrun adequate supplies of uncontaminated food and water, and in which concentrations of populations are not so large as to be totally dependent upon the uninterrupted functioning of mechanized supply systems, might effect a gradual correction of course that with watchfulness and enforced restraint might lead in time to self-sustaining stability. Hypertrophic societies, however, suffer from a malignancy rather than from the chronic degenerative diseases of ecological deterioration pervasive in less-developed countries. The ever growing complexity and vulnerability of megalopolitan conurbations such as a greater Tokyo, London, or New York increases the possibilities of sudden, disastrous breaks in their life-support systems. The effects of sustained deprivation of water, food, electricity, or police protection from the hypertrophied megalopoli of the late 20th Century has yet to be observed. Experiences in cities under attack in World War II are not in most cases relevant.

For a variety of reasons, a concomitant (and contributory cause) of socio-ecological collapse is social war. In European cities under siege during World War II, notably London and Leningrad, external threat united the beleaguered inhabitants to self-sacrifice, cooperation, and support of the civil and military authorities. Sabotage could receive summary treatment; but a city under siege from within, unremittingly harrassed and disrupted by guerrilla tactics, and pervaded by massive disaffection, disloyalty and distrust, presents an utterly different case. Life in London under air attack was grim but hopeful, touched with a feeling of heroic struggle. Life in a megalopolis, corrupted by seemingly hopeless ecological decay and laid open to unpreventable sabotage by unidentifiable individuals could rapidly become insupportable. The antagonisms within the undigested ethnic mix of great American cities makes them especially vulnerable to this type of disruption. The attitudes, assumptions, and behavior patterns of modern Americans greatly complicate their coping with circumstances of this character. Remedies in any direction would require changes in American society that appear to be beyond the bounds of probability. The slim prospect of spontaneous remission should not be ruled out, but there is greater probability that societal hypertrophy will run its destructive course, and that the historical continuity of American society will be broken before the end of the century.

Objectors to this prognosis of "decline and fall" may argue that, if one must indulge his fancies in so gloomy and "un-American" a direction, he ought also to consider whatever preventive measures there may be to avoid or mitigate disaster. And "what boots it with incessant care" to try to save the environment of a society inexorably headed for destruction? One's response may depend upon his acceptance of a moral imperative. That imperative is based upon two propositions: First, there is neither justice nor wisdom in presumptuousness, in professing certainty where one cannot be sure; second, the essence of human dignity, for the individual and for society alike, is to live so that if disaster comes, its advent will have been undeserved. We may paraphrase the words of the Spanish philosopher Unamuno who, paraphrasing Etienne de Sénancour, wrote: "And if it is nothingness that awaits us, let us so act that it shall be an unjust fate."[5]

To these propositions a third may be added: He who wills the end must will the means. One does not truly will the attainment of a healthful, self-renewing, self-correcting society unless he wills the means to its attainment. Those who, genuinely desire an ecologically sound society, but act as though "wishing would make it so," are guided by no moral imperative. They invite the contempt of anti-conservationists who rightly discount the effectiveness of individuals who are merely indulging their esthetic sensibilities. Those who would effect a cure for malignant societal hypertrophy, and its concomitant environmental effects, must look at his task with a goal-centered objectivity comparable to a physician attempting to arrest disease. Cure may be inconvenient, expensive, and painful. Where many individuals are involved; and where capabilities fall short of needs, choices may be required that, from some perspectives, may be unjust. Few people, and almost none in public life, will admit in theory what they acknowledge in practice—that choices in life are rarely between the just and unjust, but are almost always among varying degrees and conditions of injustice.

To acquiesce in the present dominant trend of society will effect the great injustice of condemning the entire society to environmental

5. Miguel de Unamuno, The Tragic Sense of Life in Men and Peoples 263 (1926).

degradation and ultimate societal collapse. But effective counter-measures entail their own lesser injustices, and these should be honestly faced and alleviated so far as consistent with the larger purpose. But the effort to create an ecologically viable society should not be constrained by demands that it adhere to standards of justice and equity that present societies have never observed. This is not to say that the ends justify all means, it is merely, frankly, to recognize that all of the choices available to us are in various ways painful. One may suffer pain from an automobile accident and from surgery, but the latter may be understood as controlled or purposeful pain, a regrettably but unavoidable consequence of an effort to save life. Environmental administration that is effective in today's world entails this kind of pain, but democratic society, unlike the voluntary patient, has not committed itself into the hands of doctors who would cure it. Nor, in the opinion of some otherwise hopeful observers, is it likely to do so until "stampeded" by hysterical reaction to ecological catastrophe. By then, the time for cure may have passed, but from among those who personally survive disaster may come forth the architects of a new social order.

What manner of men would be required for this task? Their counterparts, uncommon anywhere, are especially inconspicuous in contemporary society. They will be men of a renaissance perhaps more profound than that initiating the beginning of modern times. Collectively, they will need to embody the qualities of mind and outlook represented by Machiavelli, St. Francis, and da Vinci. Other-directed exemplars of the Great Society will not do for tasks that must actively involve real people but cannot be guided by anticipations of public opinion. Extrapolation of present styles of political leadership into the future can only lead to the conclusion that it is futile to expect effective leadership toward a reconstruction of social values, priorities, and institutions. The type of politics that has, heretofore, prevailed has not prevented and, at least in part, is accountable for the environmental crisis that is impending. Political leadership of the conventional sort cannot realistically be expected to guide the way toward remedial measures.

To meet and surmount what he calls the world crisis of transformation, John R. Platt calls for the large-scale mobilization of the intellectual resources of the Nation.[6] He suggests task forces made up of scientists and other citizens from all sectors of society. He offers a method for determining priorities for investigation, using a classification of problems and crises by estimated time and intensity. But he provides no program for putting this effort into effect.

---

6. Platt, *What We Must Do*, Science 1115-21 (1969).

Declaring that the only possible conclusion to an assessment of the difficulties of modern society "is a call to action," he asks:

> Who will commit himself to this kind of search for more ingenious and fundamental solutions? Who will begin to assemble the research teams and the funds? Who will begin to create those full-time interdisciplinary centers that will be necessary for testing detailed designs and turning them into effective applications?[7]

Answers to these questions do not come forth because Platt's crisis of transformation, of massive, accelerating change, is accompanied and partially caused by a crisis of mind and spirit, of will and rationality.[8] To speculate beyond how the technical or behavioral problems of man-environment relations might be attacked, brings one to a level of discourse upon which few scholars are willing to enter. This is the level of social theory, hitherto largely the domain of philosophers and reformers. Modern social science has penetrated the area at a few peripheral points, but the data and methodology of social science in its present state have not been adequate to answer the big questions concerning the behavior of societies. For this reason no one can be sure of the course and consequences of the environmental quality movement. Conjectures concerning possibilities point toward conclusions that appear to be either utopian or threatening to important sectors of present society. To illustrate the point, three possible courses for environmental policy will be indicated, each in its own way ungratifying.

The first possibility, predicted by critics of "environmentalism," is that the public will not accept the constraints and self-denials necessary to cope with environmental degradation. This outcome is widely prophesied by spokesmen for business enterprise, for technological innovation, and for the poor. This "realistic" assessment is resigned to the inevitable attrition of natural environments. Human adaptability and technological innovation are counted upon to overcome effects in the environment that are harmful to society, and there is often doubt expressed that conditions are really as bad as ecologists would have us believe. Spokesmen for this viewpoint remind us that man has survived great ecological catastrophes caused by nature, citing volcanos, earthquakes, and floods; and they ask rhetorically how society has been hurt by the extinction of the passenger pigeon and the dodo bird. This projected course assumes little change in present attidues or practices: reasonable control of pollution, yes!

7. *Id.* at 1121.
8. Caldwell, *A Crisis of Will and Rationality,* Environmental Education 1970, at 18-19 (1970).

but no! to measures that would seek an idealized static environment at the cost of economic growth and technological "progress."

The second possibility, held by the more optimistic environmentalists, is that people can, and will, change when they understand the situation. From this viewpoint, education and new laws may be relied upon to change social priorities and behavior. But this view assumes that people *will* be moved by information to take right action. Unfortunately, experience offers little support for this assumption. Knowing and believing are two quite different states of mind. "Deductions," as Cardinal Newman observed, "have no power of persuasion. . . . Many a man will live and die upon a dogma: no man will be a martyr for a conclusion."[9] To change people through education may require strategies and methods not available to formal schooling in pluralistic or democratic society. Knowledge in itself cannot be relied upon for action. Linked to a purpose toward which a coherent plan of action is programmed, knowledge may have a powerful reinforcing effect. Thus, the expectation of voluntary social acceptance of environmental quality goals implies the rise of an action-oriented ideology, a system of belief in which knowledge is joined to moral conviction. Until an imperative toward environmental quality motivates society sufficiently to force action, John Platt's questions are unlikely to receive adequate answers.

A third possible course combines elements of the two preceding propositions: first, that the society will not pay the price of environmental quality and, second, that knowledge, although an essential element of environmental action, will not in itself induce action. The third possibility is that public opinion will fail to arrest man's headlong rush toward ecological disaster and that, in consequence, a demoralized and distraught society will belatedly accept environmental policies that would be rejected under less compelling circumstances. This eventuality would imply the emergence of a coherent, action-oriented ideology for man-environment relationships and a leadership group, an elite, ready and willing to do whatever may be required to put society on course toward ecological solvency.

How this outcome would relate to the values and practices of liberal, representative democracy, as it has been understood in North America and Northwestern Europe, is also conjectural. To the extent that consensus existed regarding the quality of life and environment, the course of societal restructuring would be eased. But let there be no mistake, the events and conditions attending ecological catastrophe may not be conducive to sweet reasonableness or regard for all interests and values affected. Studies of ecological disasters under-

9. John Henry Newman, Discussions and Arguments on Various Subjects 295 (1897).

taken at the Hudson Institute encourage the belief that man may survive circumstances of severe environmental stress, but they would not support the confidence that survival could occur under business-as-usual arrangements.[10] Man-made eco-catastrophes may be far more widespread and severe than any natural events that have yet occurred in history, and their impact could be especially severe if it fell upon densely populated, highly interdependent megalopoli. A considerable displacement of traditional human rights by new rights and obligations would probably occur. Several major sectors of the economy would disappear or be thoroughly transformed.

Most Americans, and perhaps most people everywhere, would probably prefer that such transformation be orderly, gradual, and predictable. But this preference does not reflect the way in which societies normally change directions or alter course. Duress has been the most reliable mover of men. If some major restructuring is required for the solution of environmental problems, the previous structure must be reoriented or reorganized so that it does not obstruct or retard the development of the displacing system. In a democratic society, this task can most easily be performed if and when the established system is threatened with collapse from internal stress. The constructive reorientation of society along ecologically rational lines would not be easily accomplished at any time, but conditions of extreme social disorder would be especially unfavorable. But it may be that the established way of managing the economy would have to be weakened to a point at which the "public" and its political representatives be prepared to revise priorities and to consider alternative ways of managing the nation's economic and political affairs. Realization of the need for fundamental institutional and behavioral changes probably will require more than intellectual conviction. For the mass of men, experience may be the only convincing teacher. Even for the best informed, an emotional impetus is needed to reinforce the knowledge that man's behavior in relation to his environment must change. As James V. Neel has well said: "To some of us, this realization carries with it the need for a philosophical readjustment which has the impact of a religious conversion."[11]

Fortunately, representative democracy contains the potentiality of self-correction. Socio-ecological collapse does not seem to be an inexorable end for the hypertrophic society—at least its probability

10. J. Ingersoll, Historical Examples of Ecological Disaster, Part I, HI-242-RR/A 2-3 (1963) and Part II, HI-303-RR/A 1-2 (1964) (on file at Hudson Institute, N.Y.). *See also* R. Ayres, Special Aspects of Environment Resulting from Various Kinds of Nuclear Wars, Part III, HI-388-RR, ch. 4 (Nov. 30, 1964) (on file at Hudson Institute, N.Y.).

11. *Lessons from a Primitive People,* Science 819 (1970).

cannot be proved, and the art of political leadership in our time should be directed to insure, as best we may, that does not occur. All social and political systems change, and the constructive task of politics is to speed the transformation of the present system into a more stable and self-renewing society. The task is to cure the patient of the "disease" of societal hypertrophy, not to eliminate the symptoms by killing the patient. And, if in spite of our best efforts, we are unable to avoid disaster, some moral satisfaction may be gained by the knowledge that our failure was not a failure of nerve or will. If man is inherently unequal to the task, the outcome may be tragic; but it will be neither disgraceful nor absurd. To blunder into ecological disaster through the hypertrophic tendencies now in momentum, would be both.

THE ENVIRONMENTAL MOVEMENT: AMBIGUITIES AND MEANINGS

GRANT McCONNELL†

The mercurial rise of the present movement to rescue the environment is one of the most striking social phenomena of recent times. It is also one of the most confusing. The evidence of confusion is abundant. The supporters of "ecology" (not the least element of confusion is the varied use of this word) are a very mixed lot; they include individuals and groups from both the left and the right, as well as from the amorphous center. On the one hand the "establishment" is being roundly denounced for a vast range of environmental sins, and on the other hand no few leaders of that same establishment are loudly lending their voices to the general clamor—rarely, it is true, to proclaim their own guilt and repentance, but still vigorously and passionately. Republicans and Democrats vie to identify themselves with the cause. Even the young and the old are willing on occasion to sit together in strategy sessions to plot new campaigns.

On the face of things, it would seem reasonable to suppose that a movement with such impressive diversity of support carried a message of the greatest clarity. Certainly clarion calls are heard; they are innumerable and unending. But together they make a din that is utter cacophony. Some of the calls are to save this spot or that on the landscape. Others are to preserve some species of wildlife or some bit of flora. Still others demand the instant end of practices into which great ingenuity and great resources have been poured, insecticides, chemical fertilizers and so on. New groups form on the national scene, in states and, increasingly, in localities to oppose carefully nurtured plans to build an arctic pipeline, manufacture an SST, drain a swamp, or provide housing for a growing population. Each has its own demon to denounce, the AEC, the automobile industry, the fur trade, developers of all kinds. And beyond all these are the true Jeremiahs, the generalizers to whom we might be grateful if they would only agree on what is afoot. But they don't agree, even on the nature of the evil. It is a general waste of the common substance; it is the need for better use of resources; it is the population explosion; it is technology; it is imminent danger of human extinction.

Faced with this confusion, the ordinary citizen may perhaps be forgiven if he retreats into an uneasy cynicism, regarding all the talk

---

†Professor of Politics, University of California, Santa Cruz, California.

and agitation as simply the latest manifestation of a turbulent time, one in which all manner of certainties are being challenged. Looking at the civil rights movement, then the antiwar movement, perhaps even recalling earlier waves of radicalism, he may feel justified in dismissing the current crusade as one of those fast moving tides that occasionally appear, one succeeding the other, but all destined to recede as rapidly as they appeared. If there is a difficulty in that this tide, unlike the others in the present series, has caught up a puzzling diversity of supporters, there is the ready explanation that a crafty establishment is using it to break the force of the other more danger- ous movements in the series. In this light, the environmental move- ment is really conservative and marks the turn back toward a placid normalcy.

In face of all these claims, counterclaims and suspicions, is there anything that can reasonably be said to explain this movement? At the outset, there is a problem that is both obvious and seldom noted: why has this movement emerged with such seeming vigor at this particular moment? Very nearly every feature of the crisis that is currently being proclaimed has been with us for a long time. Pollu- tion was without doubt the central feature of those dark satanic mills cursed by English poets long ago. Preoccupation with the prob- lem of a growing population was what placed the tag of "dismal" on the science of economics, and this too dates from the nineteenth century. And so it is with virtually all of the evils which have come under the current maledictions. Things may well have reached a state worse than before, and yet even this is not obvious to everyone involved; very probably few individuals really believe that survival is at stake in any immediate sense, and in any event if the issue is survival of the race, how many of us can remain excited for long about that? However much we may subscribe to current revulsions, the problem remains, and it goes directly to the question, what is the movement really about?

To approach this question it is worth while to glance back at some of the sources of the present movement. Contrary to the impression that might be derived from some of the present cries of alarm, the movement did not spring full-panoplied from the brain of Jove in the year 1970. It had a gestation period of some length and a compli- cated one. Its geneology is diverse, even contradictory, and it needs recalling.

The immediate source of the current movement is the "conserva- tion movement." This term properly deserves the quotation marks, since it was a deliberate coinage. It was in 1907, if we are to take the testimony of Gifford Pinchot, that the idea for the label first appeared and it was by his efforts beyond any question that it was popularized. For a brief few years it must have been the most conspicuous feature of the domestic political scene dominated by Theodore Roosevelt. Pinchot's efforts began with the forests of the nation, the target of some of the most egregious exploitation in history. Although others before Pinchot had been alarmed by the rapid devastation which was overtaking the northlands of the United States, Pinchot had just the right political gifts and appeared at just the right moment to be effective. His primary achievement was creation of a dedicated branch of the federal government, the U.S. Forest Service, of which he became the first chief. However, he went on from that to call for the public control of railroads, coordination of government agencies, better rural schools along with the conservation of soil, water, and people. His movement thus became steadily more diffuse as one cause after another was added to his list and as the various conservation conferences and congresses multiplied. Ultimately, however, he overreached himself and without the support of a popular President, was forced to withdraw from the position of prominence he had so flambuoyantly enjoyed. His followers continued to carry his flag for a long time thereafter and to achieve occasional successes, but conservation was never the same.

On the face of things it would seem that the story was a simple one, a force of righteousness belatedly rising to halt a categorical evil and then waning as the cause was substantially won. The reality, however, was considerably more complex. "Conservation" to Pinchot and his era was not only a miscellany of particular causes, but a mixture of ideas whose relationship to each other was never thought out and which were in fact the set which had come together in the general atmosphere of Progressivism. Beyond the very simple urge to stop the destruction of the forests, there was, first, the idea that waste should be avoided. Certainly the devastation of the forests was wasteful, but only a few individuals had been concerned about this hitherto. Another idea, a very different one, was imbedded in the conservation movement that Pinchot invented. This was the deeply-felt sense that it was wrong the forests should be exploited for only a few buccaneering robber barons. The lands which became National Forests were public lands before the reserves were created, part of the national domain. And with the public domain there was a long history of scandal. As the frontier disappeared in the eighteen-nineties, the land predators appeared in the forested areas of the west and great fortunes were made by a large range of devices that did not exclude simple theft of publicly-owned timber. It is probably not too cynical to say that had the spoils of forest destruction been available on an equal basis, the conservation movement of the early nineteen-hundreds would have had little force or impact. This is not to say that Pinchot and his lieutenants would have been satisfied with any such a simple solution at the expense of continued devastation, but they were as much the children of their era as others and they shared fully in the mild egalitarianism of the Progressive period. Pinchot reiterated that the benefits of the forests were for all the people, and like other leaders of the time, he saw those benefits as very nearly wholly economic.

This ambiguity, fundamental as it was, however, does not itself explain the full complexity of the seemingly simple notion of conservation in this period. The apparently obvious idea of avoiding waste was itself loaded with the baggage of the time. Samuel P. Hays has elaborated on the meaning of this theme; in his eyes it was the heart of "conservation" which was "the gospel of efficiency." And once again, efficiency is an idea of disarming appearance. Hardly anyone in the Progressive era asked the question, efficiency toward what end? The implicit answer in that time would have been, in all probability, toward the end of maximizing output of economic goods per unit of human labor. This end was so much to be taken for granted in the era that to have asked the question would have appeared absurd. This was the time of economic growth and development *par excellence;* it was also the time of Taylorism and scientific management in both the private and the public spheres. Progressivism, of which the conservation movement was so much a part, was deeply imbued with this theme.

In this very same time there was a second strain of thought relating to the environment. It was older and in some respects more fully developed than that of the conservation proclaimed by the Progressives. It was from this that the first warnings about the destruction of the forests had been sounded, but as the new century approached the end of its first decade it was cast into deep shadow by the political pyrotechnics of Pinchot and his friends. This was a vision of the wholeness of Nature perceived by a small group of individuals, most of them scientists. If this group had needed any prophet, it would have been George Perkins Marsh, whose great work appeared during the Civil War. In many eyes it will seem odd that this group of men most of whose life work centered on the search for understanding through the disciplined pursuit of science became the guardians of a set of values thoroughly alien to the men of the conservation movement just discussed. It is only a partial exaggeration to characterize this set of values as religious. Indeed, the language of religion was recurrently used in the writings of some of the scientists, including those of Marsh.

It would be risky to construct a statement of the philosophical system shared by the individuals of the second group. Occasionally one or another of them spoke in highly teleological terms, but even this may have been no more than a figurative use of language. At most it is possible to note two elements. First was a largely intuitive sense of the interrelatedness of things. This was that vision of wholeness. Second was a feeling of awe and wonder. It would appear to have been rather similar to the deism of the eighteenth century except that it was far more charged with emotion. Inevitably, the sense of awe and wonder had an aesthetic dimension. The beauty of the wild places of the earth was probably as much of a magnet as any need to explore them and place names upon empty spaces of the map, to catalogue new varieties of plants or to understand those freaks of nature which were unknown in the civilized regions. For the most part, however, this was hidden under the standard justifications of science, and sometimes, of economic development.

These two currents, profoundly different as they were, came together during the Progressive era. Some scientists such as Charles Van Hise, for example, accepted the economic materialism of the Progressive movement, but the difference of outlooks did not disappear. Nevertheless, there could be agreement on such policy matters as halting destruction of the forests and general avoidance of conspicuous waste. The fundamental difference remained submerged until the second decade of the century. It came to the surface over the conflict on the building of the Hetch Hetchy Dam in Yosemite. This was an almost perfectly symbolic statement of the basic issue, for it not only pitted economic development against the protection of aesthetic values but it also brought the two most articulate spokesmen of the two strains of conservation into personal collision, Gifford Pinchot and John Muir. The victory of the dam builders seemed to settle the issue of what were the first values of the environment in America—if, indeed, there was any widespread doubt. The Hetch Hetchy Dam was for a public purpose, the water supply of San Francisco, and there could be little effective charge that the benefits of the dam would not be widely shared. With that issue absent, the dominant current of conservation was satisfied. It subsequently became possible for Pinchot's descendents to insist that conservation did not mean anything so simple as preservation, but something quite different, something they were not altogether clear about, but something that was definitely not "sentimental."

With the close of the Progressive era, the conservation movement might almost be said to have ended. However, the word "conservation" remained in currency, a word of righteousness to which no one could be opposed. Moreover, it had the quality, as should be evident, of being able to suggest a great variety of contradictory things. The institutional monument of the movement, the U.S. Forest Service, prospered and came to enjoy both prestige and power. But this was very nearly all that remained of the onetime "conservation movement." And this was the condition that prevailed until after World War II. At the end of that conflict there was a renewal of concern that the resource base of the economy was being dissipated. To this fear, a presidential commission responded reassuringly in 1952 that it was a fallacy to believe that "physical waste equals economic waste," and that with a bit of prudence things were going to be all right. Conservation meant "something very different from simply leaving oil in the ground or trees in the forest." It might have been written by Pinchot.

In that very decade of the 1950s, however, something curious happened. The term "conservation" was captured by the spiritual heirs of John Muir. The strain of thought they represented had never disappeared. It had, in fact, achieved a few minor victories of its own, the creation of a small federal agency, the National Park Service, for example. And it had sometimes enjoyed the conservation label despite the historic clash with Pinchot. That was all ancient history, however, and a new crusade for "conservation" got underway, but led this time by the enthusiasts for wilderness, parks, and wildlife—the "birdwatchers," the "sentimentalists," as their opponents tagged them with intended ridicule. Affecting an attitude of tolerant contempt, proponents of dams, reclamation projects, logging, mining and a host of schemes for economic development sought to brush aside the "unrealistic" demands of the new crusaders. On the face of things it should have been easy. But it proved otherwise. Very real advantages lay in the hands of the unrealists. First, there was the availability of that wonderful word, conservation; it was firmly appropriated by the crusaders, although probably more from confusion than by any Machiavellianism. Second, the battlegrounds chosen for the new war were such as to provide the maximum drama and to create the greatest public sympathy. Again, these battlegrounds were not picked with any sense of general strategy, but were the critical spots which must be saved before all else, the parks, and the scenic climaxes of the nation. To the surprise of nearly everyone, a substantial victory came to the conservationists in the mid-fifties' battle against the proposed Echo Park Dam on the Colorado River. This was a turning point of historic significance.

The large consequences of this victory was a reassessment in many minds. Conservationists suddenly found their ranks swelled by formerly passive sympathizers who had to this point despaired of ever seeing effective opposition to massive projects undertaken in the name of economic development. A few alert political leaders also began their own reassessments. And among the conservationists, euphoria mounted and plans for a grandiose expansion of the crusade were drawn up. A Wilderness Bill to protect a vast acreage of public lands from any economic exploitation and to establish a wholly new public policy was drawn immediately after the Echo Park victory. And at the Wilderness Conference of 1956 serious attention was given to population problems. In many localities, sharp attacks began to be mounted on pollution of air and water. The objective condition and the general trend of environmental deterioration, however, had not changed, and the euphoria quickly vanished. Conservationist energies seemed to be dissipated in a seven-year struggle for the Wilderness Act, a much more abstract and much less dramatic campaign than one to "save Echo Park" or some other scenic climax. Nevertheless, even the Wilderness Act was passed,[1] although in highly diluted form. Thereafter came a series of battles over specific spots of great beauty threatened by economic exploitation. The climax came in the fall of 1968, when concurrent victories were won on the fate of the Grand Canyon, the Redwoods and the North Cascades. They were all very qualified victories, but that was much less important than the fact that they occurred at all. Not the least interesting feature was that "conservationists" won against proponents of reclamation and intensive timber management, groups that had supposed themselves the real heirs of the conservation cause.

To this point it could be said with some accuracy that the conservationists of the new wave were a small group, an elite in some eyes. The recent dramatic conflicts, however, had elicited a degree of public support that astonished many Congressmen. They had also emboldened many individuals to leave the sidelines and to fight battles against evils that had long been before their eyes. There is no way of knowing how many individuals went through the experience of awakening to a generalized vision of environmental degradation from a start with outrage at some specific problem, but it was fre-

---

1. 16 U.S.C. § 1131 (1964).

quent. The large result was that the political base of conservation was enormously broadened. It became a popular movement.

In this development, scientists have once more played an important role. One after another has spoken out in plain language to sound the alarm on potential consequences of one form of development after another. One of the consequences is ironic. Even while many scientists are thus declaring themselves, hostility to science as such is growing as a result of the common contemporary identification of science with technology. But there is an even larger irony present than this. It is to be seen in the current headlong effort to mobilize technology to "clean up the environment." This is most evident with campaigns to reduce or eliminate air and water pollution. Plainly there are many important tasks for technologists to perform on this score. The implicit assessment of "the environmental crisis," however, is mistaken. Many of the evils which are now the objects of rising public wrath will not readily yield to technological solutions. Thus, more efficient exhaust attachments or new automobile engines may conceivably reduce air pollution to acceptable levels, but they will not affect other problems associated with a culture in which decisions to provide total mobility of automobiles at any and all costs have been permitted to determine the shape of cities, the uses of rural lands, and to affect virtually all aspects of life. The questioning of the values associated with an automobile-ridden society will continue and probably expand. And this is but an example of the nature of the Pandora's box that has been opened.

What light does this review of a not particularly prominent bit of history cast on the questions posed in the opening of this discussion? The first point to be noted is that a concern with the quality of the environment is not new. It is of long standing with a past minority, one that has occasionally acted with some effectiveness, although necessarily on small points of critical importance. It has also been long associated with an ecological point of view.

Second, there is a profound ambiguity in the movement we now see before us. Its roots in the conservation movement appear again and again as groups with the most contradictory objectives seek to declare themselves the true keepers of the faith. On the one hand, a very substantial faction is found proclaiming that the goals of economic growth and development are over-riding, provided only that benefits are not monopolized. It is willing to concede a minor importance to abatement of some of the most conspicuously adverse effects of past and present economic development. Insofar as a noisy minority is making demands for new parks and wilderness, a policy of appeasement should be followed, but not so far that it interferes in any substantial way with the serious economic business of life. This faction enjoys entrenched positions in both government and business. On the other hand, another and rapidly growing faction is demanding that first importance be recognized in an expanding range of policy decisions for the quality of the environment. By the same token, it seeks relegation of economic considerations to secondary status. The conflict is sharp and it tends to be argued out with the special intensity which charges of heresy arouse.

Third, the environmental movement is unlikely to disappear. It has a long history and its emergence as a substantial force is sudden in appearance only. It has been gathering strength over a period of at least two decades; what is new is that it has just recently achieved the critical mass necessary to command serious public attention. This is not the entire explanation, but it is sufficient to suggest that, although some of the stridency may subside, the widespread concern for the environment will continue in being and will probably continue to grow in effectiveness. The defeat of the SST in Congress is likely to prove a harbinger.

Beyond this, it is evident that today's environmental movement is both new and old. In one sense it has a past that has had a significant effect in helping to bring about a massive change of outlook, one that is rejecting the total primacy of economic materialism. On the other hand, the movement is itself partly the product of that change of outlook. That change is also the result of other forces, some of which are still obscure. But the trend is evident: while the emphasis of American society upon material values is unlikely to disappear, it may well be progressively curtailed as a search for alternative values becomes increasingly prominent. This change of outlook, far more than the very real deterioration of the objective environment is what the environmental movement will probably prove to be about.

POLITICAL AND SOCIAL ACCOMMODATION: THE POLITICAL PROCESS AND ENVIRONMENTAL PRESERVATION†

NORMAN WENGERT††

Accommodation, in the minds of many, has a negative connotation, suggesting compromise, and watering down what is thought to be right, proper, correct, and just. To compromise what has been determined by "rational" processes appears to encourage the non-rational; to make accommodations altering the efficient implies that a wasteful alternative has been developed. To accommodate the interest, views, and positions of others seems to be departing from concepts of professional integrity and violating professional ethics.

Yet, the political process as we know it in America rests strongly on the recognition of the plural values, the differing perceptions, and the multitude of goals of the population generally, and of the groups into which it is organized. It rests, also on the recognition that most programs and policies are never fully "right" or completely "true." Our most effective stance has usually been one of pragmatic modesty which accepts the tentativeness of much of life and the problematic character of societal action.

In part we are trapped by our own terminology and are victims of our own rhetoric. But to understand, and perhaps to maintain a viable system, we need to dispel stereotypes with respect to accommodation as a social process, emphasizing the dynamics of synthesyzing programs from many values, and suggesting a more reasonable approach to "rationality."

The mental set which involves hostility to accommodation and compromise, (frequently found among highly specialized technicians) clearly rests on assumptions with respect to the validity and correctness of particular positions. It tends to demand a single correct solution to each problem. There is much in our educational experience that supports the view that information generated by "rational" processes is absolutely valid and unquestionable. At the same time, much in present-day social science stresses the complexity of the goal or value structure, and emphasizes the contextual as well as the pragmatic relationships between ends and means. It also emphasizes the tentative and partial nature of much knowledge. Plan-

---

†Parts of this article were delivered at a conference in September 1969, sponsored by the Political Science Department of Colorado State University and the U.S. Army Corps of Engineers.

††Professor of Political Science, Colorado State University.

ning represents a kind of rationality in relating ends to means, but in this frame of reference the stress is on instrumental rationality and not on absolute sets of principles or conclusions.

More attention should be directed to questions of *what* ends are being sought, *whose* ends, *how* have these ends been determined.

Such a focus, in turn, often has the effect of requiring ends (goals) to be spelled out in more specific terms. It also directs attention to consequences and effects flowing from the pursuit of particular ends—costs and benefits to whomsoever they accrue in the broad terms of the original language of the 1936 Flood Control Act.[1]

A part of the problem, however, is that too often societal ends are short-range and limited in scope especially when dealing with resources and the environment. We pay lip service to the importance of long-range points of view, but our crystal balls are clouded, and we need to keep reminding ourselves that we are dealing with a tremendous number of variables and that the simplistic structure of analytical models may be far from reality. We need also to be reminded of our limited ability to analyze and predict future consequences.

By definition, the processes of deciding for the future (planning) and the techniques of program analysis require ignoring some variables and emphasizing others. The selective process goes on constantly as we look at data, trying to determine which are the relevant data that should be included, which weights to give, and so on. For those of us immersed in environmental planning these choices are often so automatic that we forget that we are making them. Moreover, it is very easy to develop habitual ways of approaching problems so that we become insensitive to the need to innovate in our approaches to a particular range of problems.

Let me illustrate how conventions with respect to data may restrict our understanding and interpretations of that data. Most of us have become accustomed to thinking about population problems of the world and of our nation in terms of birth rates. We have, therefore, been relieved to note that in the last three years or so, the number of births per year in the United States has been declining. We hope that the problem in the U.S. is taking care of itself. But is it really? Birth rates may not be the significant measure. More important and obviously of determining significance is *not* birth rate but the number of offspring per female. In other words, the present decline may simply be a short term effect, an effect that will be lost in the long pull, if American women continue to have three plus children during their entire child-bearing years. Clearly the ultimate

1. 33 U.S.C. § 701a-f, 701n (1964).

effect on total population is the same if a woman has four children in five years, or four children in twenty years. Spacing of children may be desirable; it might have important consequences for society as well as for the individual mother. But the effect on total population is identical.

To take another example, the market place model in economics is obviously useful in analyzing resource problems, although it may often be mistaken for reality. It is useful just because it eliminates or holds constant most of the operative variables of real life (where would economic analysis be without "ceteris paribus").

Thus, the analyst may use an extremely rational decision-making model for resources allocation, in which demands, supply and price are the chief variables operating in an assumed context of complete information.

If rationality is a difficult concept, *motivation* is even more difficult in relation to both individual and to organizational decisions. In the process of building alliances and alignments, and mobilizing support for programs or plans, which are all necessary characteristics of the way in which our political system functions, we may easily lose sight of what we had presumed to be "rationally" determined goals, substituting success in manipulating the system for success in achieving program goals and social purposes. Or alternately, achievement of program goals and social purposes as we define them takes on a higher value than relating them to public desire and more broadly defined integrative values.

Multiple or plural motives are usually involved, and the political system does not always provide for effective reconciliation and coordination of these pluralistic motives. Those involved in achieving particular program goals often overlook two facts: (1) that among those favoring a program is a range of intensity of support; and (2) that the reasons for support for a particular program or project will not necessarily be the same in the case of each supporter.

This may be difficult for those who are deeply involved in a particular program to accept. It is not easy to recognize that John Q. Public or particular officials may not have a burning interest in the environment, that their hierarchy of values may be different and in some cases, even though some may support a program to protect the environment, the reasons for which they do so may be different from ours. Depending upon how a program is defined, motives for support will generally include a mix, ranging from highly idealistic, goal-oriented support to support based simply on personal or political advantage.

Many of us respond most clearly to economic stimuli. To

illustrate—one of the most significant population movements in history occurred in World War II when we were able to mobilize and move people all over this country in the interest of war production. We did it, not the way the Russians did by loading workers in boxcars with their machines and shipping men and machines across the Urals. We did it by making it financially attractive to become mobile and to move to the far reaches of the country. Our system worked effectively by using economic incentives (individual, group and community) as stimuli to action, and this is, in a sense, "buying support."

The point to stress is that people support a program for their own reasons which may have no direct relationship to program objectives. A good example is the lawyer who runs for the school board not because he has a burning interest in education (in fact he may not have thought much about education) but in order to advertise himself. The legal code of ethics is very rigid in prohibiting advertising by lawyers, so the only way a lawyer can advertise is to get involved in other activities which give him visibility, running for the school board, serving on a local water board, etc. His interests in the primary program, education, water or what have you, may not be high. His initial concern is how he can get his name before the public. To be sure, the lawyer may not be highly deliberate in setting forth his reasons for behaving as he does. Many of his decisions are made by small, incremental bits and pieces, and in the process he reationalizes that what he is doing is socially significant and useful.

A little history may usefully illustrate how rather crass political goals may merge with socially desirable goals in creating programs having long-range constructive benefits. The decisions to enact the Homestead Act,[2] the Land Grant College Act,[3] and the Act creating the U.S. Department of Agriculture (all passed in 1862)[4] were essentially political, and in fact these statutes were not passed until the Southern Democrats had left Congress, giving the Republicans a clear majority. None would doubt that these laws resulted in much substantive good, but they also contributed to Republican dominance of national politics for four decades after the Civil War.

To the politicians these national enactments may well have been regarded primarily as devices to continue the Republican party in power, and they did have this effect especially through the vehicle of the electoral college, in that the creation of new states where these legislative programs had particular appeal regularly gave Republican

2. Act of May 20, 1862, ch. 75, 12 Stat. 392.
3. 7 U.S.C. § 301-305 (1964).
4. An Act to Establish a Dep't of Agriculture, 5 U.S.C. § 511 (1964).

candidates support. In terms of the popular election returns, Republican successes were often by close margins. In one election, they won because of the negotiated settlement of the Hayes-Tilden deadlock, and in another situation they actually had a minority of the popular vote but carried the electoral vote. The deciding factor often was the electoral votes in the new (and less populous) states, many of which were admitted to statehood in 1889 and 1890. That the Republican program for agriculture enacted in 1862[5] appealed to the people of the new states and contributed to their settlement is clear, and the new states tended to vote Republican in most Presidential elections (the depression of 1891-93 represented a temporary shift to the Democratic-Populist cause, but by 1896 most of the electoral votes of the new states were back in the Republican column).

This is not to suggest that the only basis for support of the Homestead program, the Land Grant College program, and the U.S. Department of Agriculture was political advantage. The record is clear that many Americans supported these programs on their merits, but political motivation cannot be overlooked.

A motive often present in political decisions is "being good to the home folks." This emphasis on local constituency is important to many political decisions, and is a vital aspect of American democratic processes. Today many speak of "participatory democracy" although the meaning of this term is not always clear. Political philosophers, academics and planners have not yet incorporated these values effectively in their thinking about public policy processes. The emphasis in recent years on national economic growth has, in fact, seemed to challenge the ethical validity of an emphasis upon locality and constituency. Application of "efficiency" as a test for the national consequences of public policies and programs has created the impression that failure to meet the efficiency test means the program or project is wasteful and represents a misapplication of government funds. ("Pork barrel" is not simply an epithet; its evil aspects are now presumably supported by sophisticated economic analysis.) Thus, the advocates of local programs have been put on the defensive, although to the elected official the local constituency remains of primary importance.

Clearly, the problem of reconciling local, regional and national interests remains a continuing one.

Redistribution of wealth, although not often mentioned explicitly

5. An Act to Establish a Dep't of Agriculture, 5 U.S.C. § 511 (1964); An Act Donating Public Lands to the Several States and Territories Which May Provide Colleges for the Benefit of Agriculture and Mechanical Arts, 7 U.S.C. § § 301-05 (1964); Act of May 20, 1862, ch. 75, 12 Stat 392.

by political leaders, is certainly another important social value at the root of many current program proposals. Taking from the rich and giving to the poor has political appeal (if one is not rich). A more viable and less inflammatory concept is the once popular term of taxing on the basis of *ability to pay,* which of course means redistributing the wealth, or shifting costs and benefits. This is a frequent consequence of many public programs, but the decision to so design public programs is often made not in terms of standards of equity and justice, but rather in terms of support and even group and personal enrichment. At the same time, how burdens will be distributed is not made explicit.

Another area of motivational analysis focuses on the benefits that may be considered *side-effects* of program decisions. I deliberately used the word side-effects rather than secondary benefits or other terms (externalities, spillover) which are associated with economic analysis, because I think we have to develop a new language since it may be too hard to give new meaning to old words. The rejection of secondary benefits by economists as a basis for project justification is sound only so long as the goal is national economic growth. In any case, however, secondary benefits are often very important sources of individual and community enrichment. Decisions on airport locations may disregard secondary economic benefits when made in Washington, but to the man who owns the land next to the proposed airport, secondary benefits are of crucial, if not sole importance. A great deal of local politics in the resource field is concerned with the distribution of secondary benefits. If politics is defined as "who gets what, when where and how," it must deal with secondary as well as with primary benefits. In many cases, local politicians could probably care less what effects particular programs or actions may have on the national economy. They may have neither the intellectual equipment nor the time to be concerned with what to them are remote issues, when they are dealing with pressing day-to-day problems right at their doors.

Another recent line of analysis which suggests the extent to which our dominant analytical structures (models) to a large extent determine the kinds of questions we ask, the kinds of problems we seek to solve, and the kinds of data we collect, has been proposed a few years ago by Bertram Gross in connection with proposals to develop a system of "social indicators" as a basis for assessing the impact of public programs, Commenting on current development concepts, Gross pointed out that most approaches were like single entry bookkeeping, and he suggested that better policy decisions might result from a system (double entry in character) in which negative consequences might be offset against alleged benefits from particular programs. As an example, he used the development of the New Jersey meadows for industrial purposes. Such developments have usually been measured simply in terms of benefits to the economy, such as increased employment, greater productivity, etc. But these gains are not usually compared to what society might be giving up in abandoning a portion of this still relatively wild area on the doorstep of Manhattan. Nor does present social accounting permit an assessment of the costs of highway and living congestion, air pollution, etc. which may result from development.

Moving to another perspective, it is clear that a critical problem for all planning in the United States is how to relate what planners do to theories, concepts and values of democracy. There are many facets to this problem—majority rule, consensus, participation, groups, social power, influentials, representation, time spans, and others.

Space permits me to deal only superficially with a few. But my purpose is not simply to raise interesting philosophical questions, but rather to suggest how theories and concepts vis-a-vis democracy may vitally affect the way in which we make environmental decisions.

It is not hard to accept the idea of majority rule in selecting a legislator, a mayor, a governor, or even a President. We take majority rule for granted in the functioning of legislative bodies and associations. And at one time, the referendum was regarded as the most democratic method for making public decisions. But today, given our deep concern for minority rights, we shy away from following simple majority decisions with respect to public programs. We like to stress that our system is based upon representation, but concepts of representation have also come up for re-examination. The basic problem is how to mirror public desires and wishes effectively in the decisional process; or in somewhat less grandiose terms, how can government be effectively related to the public. But this statement merely shifts the problem, for we have to deal with the issue of what we mean by "The Public," and we must confront the difficult problem of "apathy" and non-participation. These issues have many facets, on that is often overlooked being the *time dimension,* i.e., the public today, the public tomorrow, or twenty years from now.

One of the really important contributions which professionals can make involves the introduction of longer range time perspectives into public decision processes. And this comment serves to identify the fact that an important structuring factor, affecting motivations, and determining the data we collect as well as setting the framework for decisions, may be our professional commitments as biologists, engineers, planners, economists, and lawyers. Such questions as where and how we get our values and what determines our outlook on the world, including our expectations and images of the good life are not irrelevant.

We can agree that man cannot live by bread alone, but unfortunately we do not have much research which seeks to identify the positive and negative behavioral consequences of environmental quality. We like to think that living in a pleasant community contributes to a positive mental outlook, but we do not know that this is the case. It seems plausible that physical environment is a factor in socialization, but we really do not know that it is. In any case, one of the real challenges in dealing with the problems of the core cities lies in learning more about how core city residents get their values and exploring how these factors may be influenced constructively.

The immigrant groups of an earlier period, who came primarily from Europe, brought with them well-developed value systems, including attitudes toward family, toward work and often toward resources. For example, in both Tennessee and northern Wisconsin small Polish settlements followed soil conservation and land use practices that put to shame those of so-called "native American farmers." As peasants, these immigrants had learned to conserve resources and to work hard. As a result, they were often successful, where others were not. The values these people brought with them significantly affected their behavior. By analogy, there is evidence that poverty stricken residents in our large cities, many of whom have been migrants from the rural South, have not brought with them values that make the adjustment to urban living easy.

Environmental quality tends at present to be a concern of the middle and upper classes, and environmental programs (e.g. Wilderness Preservation) tend too often to serve the interests of the well-to-do. I would argue, however, that environmental protection can be important to the poor as well as to the rich. But unless we find some way of arousing concern for environmental quality among large numbers of lower income groups, we may not be able to solve some of our most crucial problems in this policy area. Part of building a viable society involves developing a pride in the community (i.e., not being alienated). To illustrate—a critical problem in most large cities is trash removal, but in many cases trash removal policies are not effectively related to goals of environmental quality, but rather reflect managerial and administrative considerations.

The problems of goals in American politics is indeed a difficult one. We lack institutions charged with responsibilities for formulating and crystallizing public goals or articulating them, behaving responsively and responsibly with respect to their implementation. Hence in our concern for the environment we must recognize that our goal-choosing machinery is primitive. Together with many political scientists, I am led to believe that the political parties in England, which are programmatic and issue oriented, provide a much more effective focus for articulation of public programs and goals.

But it is idle to wish that we had a more programmatic party system. We do, however, need to recognize at least two consequences which flow from our situation in this regard. The *first* is that building majority support (or simply acceptance) for a particular course of action is very difficult. Where authoritative decisions seem called for, we tend to get pluralistic pseudo-decisions. Where forthright policy statements are required, we often get deliberate obfuscation and rationalization. Where positive social goals and purposes need to be expressed, we often resort to the rhetoric of fear and the polemic of doom! Sad to say, conservationists, environmentalists, and ecologists have often been loudest in shouting doom and in exploiting fear. What the consequences for the system and for democratic policy processes may be remains to be seen. But one wonders whether such tactics may not in their social consequences be similar to those experienced because those applying technology have not explored implications and consequences of their actions deeply enough. Not only nature, but society and the political system are fragile structures, and being consequent may require more attention to how societal goals are to be achieved.

The *second* consequence of our weak policy and goal setting institutions is the fact that planners and other bureaucrats are thrust into positions of playing substantial roles in program development and policy formation, and in making choices as to what is good for society. Yet, it is undeniable that in many respects the bureaucracy may be unresponsive and irresponsible. The bureaucracy, of course, is not a single, unified entity. It mirrors our pluralistic society; it represents a complex web of professional, clientele, and interest group relationships. And we have enough evidence to give credence to the belief that self-preservation is among the strongest bureaucratic motivations. As a result, building support and securing legitimization are often prime strategic considerations, rather than detached realization of public policies.

For many reasons, most program authorizing statutes give agencies no clear and unequivocal mandates, and their very general provisions tend to preclude criticism. At the same time, as program substance develops through a host of informal means, including practice and experiment, many citizen group demands and concern for the public interest are slighted.

The role of bureaucracy in the development of governmental goals is more important in this country than in many other democratic countries. It is unique because in one sense it is separate from the political process and in another sense it is deeply involved in guiding political choices because it is the only source of information for political decision-makers. And here organizational, professional, and individual values may be significant. For example, the industrial engineer, an economist, a sanitarian, a recreationist, a fisherman would probably give different answers to questions seeking to define environmental standards applicable to particular streams. Viewpoints and values may differ because of one's technological training, because of one's organizational responsibility or role, because of friendships and associations.

We must concede that until we can secure some agreement, or perhaps better, some decisions, as to what is a productive, pleasant, beautiful environment, and policies and programs formulated in such terms, action to protect the environment will often encounter great difficulties. Present popularity of the concern may be misleading. To paraphrase Madison, until angels govern men, the task of politics will continue to be choosing from among alternate goals, and varied programs. But it is the failure or inability of our system to choose deliberately, that would seem to be its greatest vulnerability. We must somehow seek to develop institutions which can more effectively make hard choices, as well as identify program alternatives. Even though we cannot often be sure that particular choices are right in any absolute sense and even though we recognize the many independent variables or those which we have excluded or ignored may upset our predictions, we must somehow move towards a system which more clearly identifies social value premises, and is willing to utilize social controls as devices to achieve defined societal goals. But clearly such courses of action must be researched just as thoroughly as the ecological and environmental factors. Unfortunately, the complexities of modern life cannot be dealt with by simple formulas, or desperate nostrums. Even less will glib preachments, including this one, preserve the environment or improve the quality of life, unless accompanied by careful research, and analysis, as a basis for action.

ENVIRONMENTAL POLICY AND POLITICS: VALUE AND POWER CONTEXT

DANIEL H. HENNING†

Values encompass ends, goals, interests, beliefs, ethics, biases, attitudes, traditions, morals, and objectives which have a significant input into the power sphere. In this sense, the "values" of money or power should be included along with those of quality or other intangibles. The definition also encompasses value systems of the individual and of the collective compact of the individual, including the group, agency, or organization, recognizing organizational values may be somewhat different from the individual in that the organization has a life and value system of its own. Adjustments and interactions, however, of individuals and organizations will result in interrelated value systems.

A central characteristic of our age is the ambiguity and confusion of values. America appears to have difficulty with values or goals while attaining near perfection in means through science and technology. Values, moreover, are constantly changing. Abelson notes that social goals become moving targets for science and technology. With the targets coming and going in short periods, an impossible mismatch relative to research and application occurs.[1] Priorities of individual and collective values may also vary over time, particularly as they are affected by power conflicts. By their very nature, values are difficult, if not impossible, to describe and analyze in realistic and concrete terms relative to power and policy.

Gordon Allport, a social psychologist and noted authority on values, considers values to be unattainable goals, projected criteria, social consciences, and or internalized images which exert a dynamic effect or creative pressure when applicable.[2] Numerous educators agree that values, in many instances, cannot be taught, but that they must be learned by the individual through experience or inspiration. Philosophers note that some values may not consciously emerge until one becomes angry at a particular decision or action of a negative nature.[3] It is probably safe to say that values pertain to something of worth on an individual or collective basis. This worth would have to be of sufficient degree to influence direct or indirect activity by the

---

† The author is visiting associate professor, Program for Advanced Study in Public Science Policy and Administration, The University of New Mexico.

1. Abelson, *Science and Immediate Social Goals,* 169 Science 721 (1970).

2. G. Allport, Personality and Social Encounters: Selected Essays 1-386 (1960).

3. Seminar presented by James Leland to the Public Science Policy and Administration Program, University of New Mexico (Feb. 15, 1971).

individual or organization in the power struggle for a given policy decision.

Environmental policy also encompasses added dimensions of unique values pertaining to ecology, future generations, other forms of life. Some of them are eloquently described in "The Land Ethic" as quoted from *A Sand County Almanac* by Aldo Leopold:

The Ethical Sequence

This extension of ethics, so far studied only by philosophers, is actually a process in ecological evolution. Its sequences may be described in ecological as well as in philosophical terms.

An ethic, ecologically, is a limitation on freedom of action in the struggle for existence. An ethic, philosophically, is a differentiation of social from anti-social conduct. These are two definitions of one thing. The thing has its origin in the tendency of interdependent individuals or groups to evolve modes of cooperation. The ecologist calls these symbioses. Politics and economics are advanced symbioses in which the original free-for-all competition has been replaced, in part, by cooperative mechanisms with an ethical content.

* * *

The first ethics dealt with the relation between individuals; the Mosaic Decalogue is an example. Later accretions dealt with the relation between the individual and society. The Golden Rule tries to integrate the individual to society; democracy to integrate social organization to the individual.

There is as yet no ethic dealing with man's relation to land and to the animals and plants which grow upon it. . . . The land-relation is still strictly economic, entailing privileges but not obligations.

* * *

An ethic may be regarded as a mode of guidance for meeting ecological situations so new or intricate, or involving such deferred reactions, that the path of social expediency is not discernible to the average individual. Animal instincts are modes of guidance for the individual in meeting such situations. Ethics are possibly a kind of community instinct in-the-making.

The Community Concept

All ethics so far evolved rest upon a single premise: that the individual is a member of a community of interdependent parts. His instincts prompt him to compete for his place in that community, but his ethics prompt him also to cooperate (perhaps in order that there may be a place to compete for).

The land ethic simply enlarges the boundaries of the community to include soils, waters, plants, and animals, or collectively, the land.

* * *

In short, a land ethic changes the role of *Homo sapiens* from conqueror of the land-community to plain member and citizen of it. It implies respect for his fellow-members, and also respect for the community as such.[4]

Given the above general environmental value toward harmony between man and nature, it is appropriate to recognize the complexities of environmental policy. On the assumption that there is not a transcendental type of environmental value, specific situations may dictate combinations of value interpretations on a collective basis. In fact, with the intense "popularity" of the environmental "game" in the public sphere, sound ecological and environmental values may become tools, supporting nonrelated values. With over 80 federal agencies involved in the environmental issue and with environment as a risk-free political issue, value appeals may not be value actualities in power struggles.

In the political and administrative process of environmental policy, it is appropriate to recognize that environmental values may be only limited or partial input in the power struggle for decision-making. Realistically, factors such as agency survival and expansion are a definite part of the process. In this sense, power itself can become a value or goal. Given a particular value orientation or system, it is automatic to categorize the "good guys" and the "bad guys" in a given power struggle. With the environmental movement, this categorization process becomes increasingly complex and difficult. Under the environmental umbrella however, and from a broad perspective, a multitude of values compete for limited power.

Logical positivists and "scientific" individuals argue for the application of empirical and behavioral "science" and reason in policy rather than consideration of values. David Hume, an 18th Century Scottish empiricist, noted that the use of reason is definitely limited. Although reason can be used to show logical relationships, it cannot determine values which are the products of passion or feeling. Thus reason, according to Hume, is helpful in directing action toward the attainment of values, but it is only an instrument, and cannot by itself discover values. As Hume states, reason is the "slave of passions."[5] Simon, Smithburg, and Thompson note:

Close examination of the premises that underlie any administrative choice will show that they involve two distinct kinds of elements: value elements and factual elements. Speaking very, very roughly, the distinction between value elements and factual elements corresponds to the distinction between ends and means, respectively. Before an individual can rationally choose between several courses of

4. A. Leopold, A Sand County Almanac 217-20 (1966).
5. M. J. Harmon, Political Thought: From Plato to Present 319 (1964).

action, he must ask himself: (1) what is my objective—my goal (value)? and (2) which of these courses of action is best suited to that goal?[6]

* * *

Almost every value premise has some factual element in it—an element that cannot be completely removed—because most ends or goals (values) are at least partly means to more final ends than ends in themselves.[7]

In order to affect or influence a policy decision, a particular value must have power over other values and this political process occurs through human interaction. Politics is recognized as an arena where powerful economic, social and ideological interests and values compete to attain their objective through government. Lasswell in Politics, Who Gets What, When, and How considers politics to be the study of the influenced and the influential. The latter are those who get the most of what there is to get and are referred to as the elite who make the governmental decisions.[8] Lasswell also notes that political life is a life of conflict and competition for scarce power resources.[9]

In the Federalist Paper No. 10., Madison notes:

The latent cause of factions are thus sown in the nature of man; and we see them everywhere brought into different degrees of activity, according to the different circumstances of civil society.

* * *

The regulation of these various and interfering interests forms the principal task of modern legislation and involves the spirit of party and faction in the necessary and ordinary operation of government.[10]

Madison thought that factions of interest were bound to emerge in government problems causing conflict and that many of these factions were based on property. In a pluralistic society, the group basis of politics is stressed. Various groups (including governmental agencies) representing numerous values are constantly competing for power and decisions which are favorable for their particular vested interests.

Some of the major reasons for the political concern of environmental policy are: (a) when segments of the public are affected in a negative or positive manner, (b) when a particular environmental

---

6. H. Simon, D. Smithburg & U. Thompson, Public Administration 38 (1962).

7. *Id.* at 182.

8. H. Lasswell, Politics: Who Gets What, When, and How 1 (1963).

9. *Id.* at 182.

10. The Federalist No. 10, at 79 (New York: Mentor Book, New American Library, 1964) (J. Madison).

segment or natural resource has present or future possibilities for utilization with automatic alternatives and alignments created (including and excluding public lands), (c) when economic, social, and ideological impacts are present or possible.

According to Wengert although many policy decisions for the environment and natural resources are made by private, nongovernmental means, public concerns and hence governments are increasingly involved, particularly with the environmental movement.[11] With the involvement of government, politics becomes the dominant way of decision-making.

A major aspect of politics in all government, including environmental policy, is the exercise of power through informal means. Livingston and Thompson note that bureaucracies frequently rely on brokerage politics to solve problems. This process involves informal bargaining, compromising, and dealing with involved interests and groups in value conflicts.[12] Griffith describes this brokerage process with his whirlpool theory, which involves informal and formal associations and conferences between various types of people (including governmental officials) who are interested in common objectives or problems. These individuals are often on a first-name basis with representatives of other interests. People are whirlpooled or drawn into the decision-making process by bargaining or compromising. According to Griffith, much of governmental policy is matured in this process.[13]

Policy, in general, is a reflection of the culture where it operates. In the American culture, pragmatic and pluralistic characteristics are dominant in general policy areas. Wengert notes that this orientation results in an absence of an overall, comprehensive and ideological policy for the environment and natural resources. He recognizes only one clearcut and common ideological basis for all environmental policies and programs; this is the use and involvement of government with the recognition of the social goals and problems in environment and natural resources.[14] Without a general value or ideological base, numerous values and interests are reflected in the fragmented, diverse, and short-range policies throughout the spectrum of environmental policy.

Modern public administration appears to operate on a crisis basis with an immediate problem-solving orientation. At present the political climate and changing conditions do not appear to give much

11. N. Wengert, Natural Resources and Political Struggle 6-9 (1955).
12. J. Livingston & R. Thompson, The Consent of the Governed 238-41 (1966).
13. E.S. Griffith, Congress: Its Contemporary Role 127 (1956).
14. Wengert, *The Ideological Basis of Conservation and Natural Resources Policies and Programs,* 344 Annals of the Am. Acad. of Pol. and Soc. Sci. 65 (1962).

stability and authority to policy in general. Given the thousands of legislative acts pertaining to the environment, macro and micro policies have a tendency toward pragmatism. Regarding this approach, Wengert notes:

> A critic once wrote that a major characteristic of pragmatic philosophy was that it was no philosophy. Although this judgment is perhaps unduly harsh, it points to a lack of interest in the formulation of general principles or ideological systems among those pragmatically oriented. Pragmatism is pluralistic and eclectic, focusing on problems and performance rather than principles, upon action rather than upon ideas. The pragmatic test of 'will it work' or 'how does it work' deemphasizes ideology in the sense of a developed synthetic system of beliefs and values to govern action.[15]

With the pragmatic and pluralistic (group) orientation of environmental policies, the one unifying, ideological aspect is that of ecological and environmental force. Although this concept has been present in varying forms and degrees from the early conservation days, it has only recently attained stature in legislative and policy decisions. During the last several years, legislation and agency policies have greatly expounded this ideology of ecology. A central piece of legislation typifying this concept was the National Environmental Policy Act of 1969; the purposes of the Act are:

> To declare a national policy which will encourage productive and enjoyable harmony between man and his environment; to promote efforts which will prevent or eliminate damage to the environment and biosphere and stimulate the health and welfare of man; to enrich the understanding of the ecological systems and natural resources important to the Nation; and to establish a Council on Environmental Quality.[16]

The Environmental Quality Act stipulates that a systematic, interdisciplinary approach for environmental quality be followed by the 80 agencies concerned;[17] this and other environmental requirements are considered as supplemental to the original agency's legislation and policy. The agencies are also to report any inconsistencies and deficiencies of legislation, policies, or procedures which interfere with compliance with the purposes and provisions of the Act.[18] It is obvious that the majority of the agencies are mission and policy organizations with vested and dominant interests. Under broad Congressional legislation over the years, they have evolved policies, pro-

---

15. *Id.* at 69.
16. *Id.*
17. White, *How Do We Get From Here To There?*, Life, June 26, 1970, at 36, 39.
18. Environment Quality Council, First Annual Report 243-53 (1970).

cedures, programs, philosophies and clientele which limit their responsiveness to a broad, environmental policy. In a sense, the limitations and definitions of policy responsibility and evolution have served to comfort and protect agencies from complexities and demands. Through politics and legislation, the agencies are forced into a position of policy change and into neglected problem areas and considerations of the total environment. Although outward conformance and change to environmental quality policy is required, this does not necessarily mean past policies will not still play a key role in the actual direction of the agency.

At the same time, under the constant crisis situation of modern public administration, executives are increasingly making macro and micro policy on a common basis as well as drafting the majority policy legislation. Thus the American Society for Public Administration Task Force on Society Goals notes:

> The jamming together of policy and administration raised an eyebrow a generation and a half ago; now it is so much the case that the administrators make up a very high proportion of the policy makers. Today's crisis exceeds all historical crises in public administration. Due to the complexity of government, the intricate interrelationships between policy and administration, the public executive of today and tomorrow has a newly recognized role and responsibility, whether he or she is on a public or private payroll. Public executives, taken as a group, have not yet awakened to the fact that they are in charge. They are responsible for the operation of our society; they cannot wait around for somebody to tell them what to do. If they don't know the answers, we're lost.[19]

Under the above orientation, there are definite indications that much of macro and micro environmental policies will be formulated and implemented by public executives. Hence their value systems are indeed a crucial factor for environmental policy.

In essence, policy itself is a statement of principles and objectives which serves as a guide or framework for operation of an agency or an area of responsibility. Policy is based upon legislation, but the latter usually provides broad, idealistic guidelines which are subject to interpretations of legislative intent. Ambiguity naturally enters the picture, particularly with the lapse of time. This is especially true with the crisis type of administrative policy-making of today in which policy appears to be losing its sense of stability and permanence.

Given the value emphasis of policy, Lindblom notes that values are

---

19. American Society for Public Administration Task Force on Society Goals, *The Future of ASPA—A Super Everest or a Higher Hill?* News and Views, Oct. 1970, at 5-6.

always a problem of adjustments at a margin and that there is no practial way to state marginal objectives or values without reference in terms of particular situations.[20] Relative to the individual administrator's value system, he notes that shifts in values occur according to the situations and hence it is impossible to establish a rank order of values which would apply to different situations. Thus Lindblom states that: (a) ". . .one chooses among values and among policies at one and the same time," and (b) ". . . the administrator focuses his attention on marginal or incremental values."[21] Lindblom considers policy making to be of an incremental nature (rather than major or large changes) based on adding to past precedents on a relevancy and simplicity basis. He also notes that policy is formulated and decided through a group process by acceptance or by sounding good, but that the administrators cannot explain the "whys," theory, or values behind policy decisions. Regardless of the complexity or ambiguity of value identification and alliances for only realistic to recognize that values are the basis for power conflict and alliances for environmental policy. The problems and complexity of these values with the resulting policy can produce the destruction or conservation of survival and quality of the environment for man and other forms of life.

---

20. Lindblom, *The Science of Muddling Through,* 20 Pub. Ad. Rev. 79-88 (1959).
21. *Id.*

THE COORDINATION OF LEGISLATIVE POLICY AND THE REGULATION OF PRIVATE INTERESTS: SOME SUGGESTED PRAGMATIC PRINCIPLES FOR ENVIRONMENTAL POLICY

WOLFGANG E. BURHENNE† and
WILLIAM A. IRWIN††

Man must conserve the world's natural resources, not only for their sake, but for his own. Conserving our environment requires rethinking the relationship between private interests and public needs. Adjusting the balance between them to correct the excesses and remedy the shortcomings will demand changes and sacrifices. Education is slow to persuade the majority of people that they must modify their traditional behavior and beliefs. Meanwhile, responsible governments must plan and execute policies which will prevent environmental crises. The appropriate philosophical basis for these policies is pragmatism, the circumspect employing of principles to produce desired consequences which will be compatible with other policies.

This article suggests a series of such principles, to be kept in mind in formulating environmental policies, divided roughly into a) the regulation of private interests; b) the coordination of legislative policy; and c) the participation of the public.

REGULATION OF PRIVATE INTERESTS

A. Objectively Reviewing Governmental and Commercial Projects, Processes and Products for Environmental Effects

Considering the expense and occasional impossibility of remedying environmental damage, an ounce of prevention may today require several pounds of "cure."

Prevention of environmental crises is the goal of the National Environmental Policy Act of 1969.[1] Broadly, this statute requires federal agencies to make a comprehensive study of environmental effects before action is taken on proposed legislation or programs. Whether or not the statute is effective is another and important issue. But the practices of consulting with others, comparing alternatives and considering potential environmental impacts should be more fully

† Secretary-General, Interparlamentarische Arbeitsgemeinschaft (Interparliamentary Working Center), Bonn, Germany; Chairman, Committee on Environmental Law, International Union for the Conservation of Nature and Natural Resources.
†† A.B., 1965, J.D., 1970, University of Michigan.
1. 42 U.S.C. § § 4321-43 (Supp. V, 1970).

adopted by *all* governmental units. They are simply rational means of making decisions with sufficient information and perspective.

Currently private enterprise in introducing new products and processes is under public pressure to conform to standards which will conserve the world's natural resources and leave the earth a pleasant place. Just as drug and foodstuff producers must now test products carefully before marketing them,[2] all commercial enterprises should be required both to test new products and processes of production before introducing them and to consider environmental effects in plant location. Obviously, most manufacturers do some testing now. The need is to broaden the scope of questions asked beyond effectiveness and predicted profits to such matters as long-run environmental and health effects, alternatives, and possibilities for recycling. This testing should be followed by an objective check, either by an improved licensing procedure for trade products and processes, or by judicial examination of potential adverse environmental effects, as is possible in Michigan under Public Act 127 of 1970.[3]

B. Require Compulsory Insurance for Unusually Dangerous Enterprises

Compulsory insurance should be required for enterprises which currently engage in activities unusually dangerous to the environment, such as drilling and transportation of oil. Up to a certain limit, the insurance would cover the damage these enterprises might cause. Whether liability should be based on negligence,[4] or whether the enterprises should be liable up to the established limit without fault, might be determined according to the nature of the activity and its potential for damage. Strict liability is not a radical proposal; in 1970 the members of both the U.S. Congress and the Intergovernmental Maritime Consultative Organization adopted such an approach for damages caused by oil spills at sea.[5] Nor is the problem of measuring environmental damages any longer insuperable.

Above the limit of liability, the government might assume responsibility for sharing the burden of costs and losses.[6] If it is unwilling to undertake this risk, it should refuse to license the enterprise.

2. 21 U.S.C. § 355(b) (1964).

3. Mich. Compiled Laws § § 691.1201–691.1207 (Supp. 1970).

4. Or its variant, *res ipsa loquitur,* which creates a rebuttable presumption of defendant's negligence if he is in exclusive control of the instrumentality of damage and the event would not normally occur in the absence of negligence.

5. 33 U.S.C. § 1161(f) (Supp. 1970-71); *Int'l Convention on Civil Liability For Oil Pollution Damage,* Art. III, 2, 1 I.E.L.R. 40307 (1971). There are exceptions to liability, so that it is not absolutely strict, but they are quite narrow. *See* Goldie, *Int'l Principles of Responsibility for Pollution,* 9 Colum. J. Transnat'l L. 283 (1970).

6. *Cf.* 42 U.S.C. § 2210(c) (1964).

Holding the government jointly liable might have the beneficial side effect of improving the care and integrity of its licensing procedures.[7]

Compulsory insurance can serve as an effective device to promote self-enforcement of safety standards. Instead of relying on (and paying for) maritime officials to enforce safety standards for oil tankers, for example—which allows all sorts of possibilities for abuse—requiring insurance would impel ship-owners to provide the necessary precautions in order to pass the insurance companies' inspection, and procure the lowest possible premium. This approach would require government regulation of insurance companies but such is already common practice.

C. Implementing the Principle That He Who Generates Wastes Should Pay For Disposing of Them

Instead of employing already insufficient public revenues to pay for the disposal of abandoned waste, e.g., beer cans, old tires, used oil, dead cars—all too often simply deposited at the first convenient spot—the principle should be that he who is responsible for creating wastes should pay the costs of their disposal or delivery for recycling.

Germany has put this concept of charging the originator of the waste into practice in a unique system for the disposal of used lubricating oils.[8] Prior to the new law, the government tried making subsidy payments to refineries which collected and reprocessed waste oil into lubricating oils, but this proved ineffective, since the refineries collected only from profitable areas and accepted only those waste oils which could be easily regenerated. As of 1969, all producers and importers of oil were required to pay the government a fee for every ton of fresh oil.[9] They pass along this extra expense in the form of higher prices (about 1½ cents per quart) to their customers. The government uses the collected fees to fund payments to contractors obligated to pick up any waste oil free of charge from anyone in Germany. These payments are to cover the contractors' costs of collection and harmless disposal. The contractors may either reprocess the waste oils (and sell their end products) or burn them. The Waste Oil Law establishing this system provides several means

7. *Cf.* Cavers, *Improving Financial Protection of the Public Against the Hazards of Nuclear Power,* 77 Harv. L. Rev. 644 (1964); Katz, *The Function of Tort Liability in Technology Assessment,* 38 U. Cin. L. Rev. 587, 653-55 (1969).

8. Gesetz Über Massnahmen Zur Sicherung der Altoelbeseitigung (Law Concerning Measures To Assure The Disposal Of Waste Oil), I Bundesgesetzblatt (BGBl.) 1419 (1968).

9. *Id.,* § 4(2). The fee is approximately $20/ton.

for close checking to assure that disposal does not contribute to air, water, or soil pollution.[10]

How the system of making the originator of an environmental problem bear the cost of its solution is set up depends largely on the government's administrative organization. Ideally, the system should be self-supporting and offer comprehensive collection, assured safe disposal or recycling, and careful supervision. New York City, for example, where an average of 200 cars are abandoned every day and 50,000 summonses were issued last year as a result, has requested the legislature to enact a bill requiring the purchaser of any new car to deposit one hundred dollars with the state.[11] If the car is resold during its lifetime, the certificate of deposit would figure in the price and pass to the new owner. The final owner would be refunded the sum upon providing he had disposed of the car "in an environmentally acceptable manner." One acceptable manner might be delivery to a scrap metal dealer. In Maryland these dealers are paid ten dollars per disposed car and are fined for every one they keep over 18 months. This program is funded by a one dollar fee imposed on every car title transaction in the state.

D. *Redefine the Scope of Private Land Ownership Rights*

The inviolability of all privately owned land on our crowded planet is no longer either realistic or consonant with this century's democratic social values. No man is an island in our society, and neither should his property be. We are beyond the time when the principle of *sic utero tuo ut alienum non laedus*—use your property only thus as will not harm another's—is alone an adequate basis for public policy. Environmental planning and policy administration responsive to evolving needs are only possible where the definitions of private property are flexible and permit the implementation of different policies suitable to the special requirements of particular areas. We pay the price of our unwillingness to limit our continually expanding populations and economies in many ways. Perhaps tol-

10. *See* Irwin and Burhenne, *A Model Waste Oil Disposal Program in the Federal Republic of Germany*, forthcoming in 1 Ecology L.Q.

11. London Daily Telegraph, Jan. 21, 1971, at 1, col. 6. The Council on Environmental Quality has concluded that such a "bounty system . . . is not practicable." Its arguments are listed in *Environmental Quality*, First Annual Rep. of the Council on Environmental Quality 116 (1970). They include: "The resulting fund of payments would divert billions of dollars from other investments in the private economy. Administration and enforcement of the system would require excessive increases in government personnel and expenditures." Such arguments might be made against almost every proposal to do something on behalf of the environment. Perhaps judgment might be withheld until after some state had given such a system a fair trial.

erating increased public regulation of land use is preferable to suffering increased trespass, vandalism, or worse.

Redefining the scope of private ownership rights to reflect the increasing needs of society must be accomplished with the utmost circumspection. Regulating what the owner must endure and what the public may do should be based on a thorough and continual assessment of the interests and requirements peculiar to defined areas of settlement. In return for his sacrifices, the owner must be assured that public access to his forest land, for example, will be adequately controlled so that his land will not be overrun or its value to him destroyed. There must be specific and enforceable minimum standards to protect his personal property.

Eighty percent of the land in West German nature preserves established by public authority is under private ownership. An owner whose property is taken into a preserve may not be prevented, without compensation, from continuing his previous use of the land, but he is prohibited from changing or expanding its existing use without special permission.[12] Being deprived of the chance to take advantage of increases in the land's speculative value is not a compensable taking of private property—it is a sacrifice the owner must make as a member of society.

If society must expropriate private property to serve public needs, the owner should not be allowed unlimited compensation. It is unfair for one who happens to be located where a waste water treatment plant is required to get rich on public tax revenues. This can be remedied by placing a legal limit on the percentage increase over the land's previous value which one may collect. If the limit were exceeded, the excess could be taxed as the luxury it is. Similarly, if the value of land of those living near a new public highway or recreation project increases by more than a certain percentage, the excess could be collected and redistributed to those whose land was taken.

The legislature of the densely populated industrial state of North Rhine-Westphalia in Germany recently enacted an unusual approach to balancing public and private land use. To provide sorely needed additional recreational opportunities, privately owned forest lands were opened to use by the public, which enters at its own risk, without compensation to the owners.[13] The results of this law are still uncertain. Some forests near large cities are so heavily used by walkers and picnickers as to constitute an arguable partial ex-

---

12. Reichsnaturschutzgesetz § 16(2), of June 26, 1935, Reichsgesetzblatt I 821.

13. Forstgesetz fur das Land NordrheinWestfalen (Forest Law of the State of North Rhine-Westphalia) of July 29, 1969, GVB1.588, *as amended* Dec. 16, 1969, [1970] GVB1.

propriation. In other areas where owners' fire insurance premiums or refuse collection costs have increased significantly as a result of the law, the State may need to help defray these expenses.

COORDINATION OF LEGISLATIVE POLICY

A. Use Both Sugarbread and the Whip

Many countries have learned that prohibitions alone are not enough to effectuate environmental conservation policies. The problem is that the prohibitions cannot be adequately enforced. What is needed is the coordinated use of both prohibitions and incentives. Begin by setting air pollution emission limits, for example, necessitating the purchase of control equipment. In conjunction, offer reduced property or sales tax on the equipment, accelerated depreciation for tax write-offs of its purchase price, or less expensive government-supported loans to finance the investment. These are rational, if not always stunningly successful, economic incentives.

Outright grants to private enterprise, on the other hand, are rarely, if ever, justified. They conflict with the principle, discussed above, that those who cause environmental hazards should pay for disposing of them. And—if supported from tax revenues—they unfairly subsidize, at the public's expense, marginal or inefficient enterprises which probably should be reorganized, absorbed, or dismantled.

The critical element in an effective tax incentive policy is thorough and ready enforcement of the legal standards. Since the amount of incentive given (unless it is an outright grant) will always be less than the expense of control, a person or enterprise will always be tempted to keep expenses down by doing as little as possible. Penalties if one is caught violating the standards must be severe enough, and the publicity given the infraction by the media unpleasant enough, that it is less expensive to take advantage of the incentive and carry out the necessary measures.

B. Avoid Public Finance Policies With Negative Environmental Side-Effects

Incentives offered via tax or fee provisions are conscious legislative decisions. Unfortunately, not all taxes and fees are free from inadvertent negative consequences for the environment. In Germany, for example, where yearly automobile license fees are based on the volume of the car's cylinders (the larger the volume, the higher the fee), auto manufacturers have, as a result, developed and are producing cars with very small cylinders but remarkably high power. To achieve this power the engine must work much faster, causing less efficient combustion proportionally than in larger cylinders—hence more air pollutants, and incidentally, more noise.

In many countries, the community where an industry locates receives both property and business taxes from it. Understandably, to increase their tax base and job opportunities for their citizens, many communities strive to attract industries. Sometimes they offer them a special concession which disadvantages the environment—zoning variances, or *sotto voce* assurances that pollution control standards will not be "unreasonably" enforced. To alleviate this problem, and to equalize the distribution of revenues, Germany recently revised its tax laws so that communities can receive only a certain percentage of all taxes paid by local businesses. The remaining revenues are passed to the individual states for redistribution among their communities on a per capita basis.

Another common problem is unrealistically low municipal charges for supplying residents or commercial establishments with water, or accepting their wastewaters or garbage, reflecting political expediency rather than actual costs. As a result, supply systems are often poorly maintained and treatment plants are insufficient and inadequate. Countless cities the world over simply unload raw sewage and industrial effluents directly into already polluted rivers. The answer is not to look to the nation's capital for more and more central support, for however much aid is promised it invariably falls short of the needs. Rather the answer is to form more regional waste disposal districts and to pay the actual cost of operating them. The former requires overcoming local pride to gain the economic efficiencies of regionalization; the latter requires having the political courage to vote for new garbage and sewage treatment plants rather than new stadiums and swimming pools.

C. Set Flexible Legal Standards to be Administered According to the State of the Art

In a young and swiftly moving field such as environmental control and technology, laws need to be written so that they can be administered according to the latest knowledge. Legal definitions are rarely flexible enough to cover the many new developments and discoveries in this field, and, as a result, many serious problems are inadequately handled because they do not fit the scope of the legislature's previous formulations. Likewise, if specific technical details are written into a law it is often necessary to change them to reflect continuing advances.

One way of dealing with this problem is to provide the maximum and minimum standards acceptable to the legislature in the law and to include a provision that the law be administered within these limits according to the current state of the art. If this is done there must be ways to insure that administrators do not abuse their discretion, and to incorporate recent advances in scientific or technological understanding into the daily execution of the law.

In Germany, the minister responsible for supervising the administration of a law according to the state of technology publishes directives which bind administrators to exercise their discretion within the limits set by the minister, which in turn must be within those established by the law. If an administrator exceeds these guidelines by granting permission to a factory to discharge over the maximum allowed in the limits, for example, he may be relieved of his post or subject to lesser disciplines provided by the laws governing the civil service.

It is largely left to private enterprise, research centers, and individuals to provide the input which causes the minister to modify the administration of the law according to current knowledge. Suppose permissible automobile exhaust emissions were so regulated. If a Mr. Acme developed a device in his basement which if built into all cars would reduce their emissions by 95%, he could present it to the supervising ministry for complete testing in state laboratories. On the basis of the tests, the minister would decide whether it was technically feasible and economically reasonable to require the device. If so, he would promulgate regulations requiring all future manufactured cars to have it. If not, Mr. Acme would be so informed. Either decision by the minister would constitute an administrative act in German law, subject to administrative court review.

Legislative deadlines for achieving such standards as a 95% reduction in auto emissions may be a necessary spur, if they are realistic. The U.S. Congress has set 1975 for this goal, with the possibility of a one-year extension if absolutely necessary.[14] In 1961 the German parliament similarly required detergents to be manufactured with less permanent sudsing agents within three years.[15] But care should be taken not to simply build castles in the air in setting such deadlines. Then they merely serve to arouse public expectations which in turn tend politically to lock legislators into what may have been a mis-

---

14. Pub. L. No. 91-604, § 6(a), 84 Stat. 1690, *amending* 42 U.S.C. § 1857(f) (1963).

15. Gesetz Über Detergentien In Wasch- und Reinigungsmitteln (Law Concerning Detergents in Washing and Cleaning Agents) of Sep. 5, 1961, [1961] BGBl. I 1653, *as amended* May 24, 1968, BGBl. I 503. The applicable regulations are contained in the Verordnung Über Die Abbaubarkeit von Detergentien In Wasch- und Reinigungsmitteln (Regulations Concerning the Degradability of Detergents in Washing and Cleaning Agents) of Dec. 1, 1962, BGBl. I 698.

take. This could result either in the law not being enforced when the deadline comes or in unnecessary hardships if violations are in fact prosecuted. Even if such deadlines are included, provisions should be made for adopting technical advancements as they develop, so that attainable progress is not unnecessarily postponed.

D. Work Toward the Equalization of Burdens on Industry in All Countries

The burdens placed on business and industry by environmental policies need to be coordinated, both intra- and internationally, to avoid giving unwarranted economic advantages to any particular area or country. The Treaty of Rome creating the European Economic Community provides that no member country's government may offer industry special advantages which undermine the common commercial basis within the community.[16]

A similar principle needs to be extended to world commercial activity, so that no country can gain a larger share of the markets simply by allowing its enterprises to cut costs and keep their prices lower by abusing the environment. Some state governments in the United States are familiar with industry's threats to move to or locate in other states with less stringent standards for environmental protection. The result has often been reluctance to move ahead of the lowest common denominator. In Europe some industries, notably steel and chemicals, have either located new plants in or moved to permissive countries with long coastlines in order to avoid internalizing their externalities. Elsewhere in the world, some nations have benefited economically at nature's expense by condoning the dumping of millions of tons of waste and poison into the ocean.

This situation is both economically unfair and environmentally unwise. The world's natural resources can be conserved only if the major export-producing countries, both developed and developing, agree to enforce policies which prohibit gaining competitive advantage by ignoring external costs. Just as such inequities are avoided within a country by adopting national standards, joint economic action on a worldwide basis is necessary so that no country's commerce is unfairly disadvantaged. Perhaps a framework treaty, with standards regulated in detail by more limited agreements under it, would be an appropriate vehicle to achieve this needed equalization.

16. *See* Treaty of the Inter-governmental Conference on The Common Market and Euratom, Mar. 25, 1957, arts. 92 and 95, [1957] Europaeische Gemeinschaften 2(G), 296 U.N.T.S. 2.

PARTICIPATION OF THE PUBLIC

A. Expand the Citizens' Role in Public Planning, But Provide a Cut-Off

Proposed public projects in many countries are subject to scrutiny both from within the government and without. A German water association's draft plans for building a large sewage treatment plant must be approved by a state minister with authority over water, agriculture, and natural resources.[17] Before he gives his approval, his professional staff, as well as the staffs of other interested ministers (i.e., public health, transportation) discuss the plan, considering how the proposed plant will fit into their own overall plans. The minister thereby assures that developments in his field will be internally co-ordinated, and harmonized with those in other fields. This is essential to environmental planning policy and execution.

Many governments also provide an opportunity for their citizens to register their opinions. However, often there is no apparent possibility that objections or suggestions will be seriously considered. On the other hand, sometimes there seems to be no way to put an end to considerations and to proceed with executing a plan. Consolidated Edison's efforts to provide for increasing electricity demands in New York City are an illustration of the delays which can result if no cut-off date for registering objections exists. Because no opportunity for public input into the development of plans was ever given, endless litigation has resulted from each successive announcement of intentions.

To solve this dilemma, German administrative law provides a system which has proved fair and effective. After the minister gives his general approval—often conditional—he forwards the plan to the state's chief regional administrator for the area where the project is to be carried out. This administrator holds a Plan Determination Proceeding, which may take several years. It is not unlike many similar procedures in the U.S.: notice is given the public in newspapers, the plan is displayed in public before an open hearing, written objections and oral testimony are accepted, conferences between the administrator and all concerned parties take place, expert opinions are sometimes sought, etc. Quite frequently, the plan is modified in response to legitimate individual objections. Ultimately it is promulgated by the administrator, an act which may be challenged in an administrative court by anyone burdened by it. The

---

17. Kneese & Bower, *Managing Water Quality*, Economics, Technology, Institutions 262, n.4 (1968). *E.g.*, Ruhrreinhaltungsgesetz § 2(3) of June 5, 1913, PrGSNW 210.

court may not simply replace the administrator's exercise of discretion with its own opinion.

A citizen, or a group representing citizen interests, has a complementary obligation of prompt participation. If objections are not raised within the period allowed by the Plan Determination Proceeding—usually within two weeks after public display and discussion—they are foreclosed from being entered. This prevents playing dog in the manger and continually delaying a plan's execution. Once the approved plan has been adjusted and promulgated by the administrator in its final form, it is fixed. If an affected party files a complaint with the administrative court the plan's implementation is delayed, unless special permission to proceed is sought and gained from the court because of an overriding public interest. He who proceeds does so at the risk of having to modify what he has done according to the court decision. Only unforeseen eventualities, e.g., odors from a sewage treatment plant due to unexpected wastes it must process, arising from the plan may be challenged after it has been undertaken. Both meaningful public participation with opportunity for appeal to the courts and a firm cut-off are necessary to efficient planning to meet the expanding demands on our environment.

B. Exert Public Pressure for Adequate Funding and Enforcement

Too often, public response to the discovery of another environmental crisis is a demand for new legislation. Sometimes, if the problem is novel, there may be no applicable legal provisions, and if this is the case, a law should then be drafted carefully and with the minimum of procedural hurdles impeding the realization of its purposes. But this need exists in only a few areas of the world. The real needs now increasingly recognized are adapting existing laws to current conditions, amending them for easier administration and enforcement, and assuring that adequate means are provided for their conscientious execution by qualified and dedicated personnel.

A law is only as effective as public consciousness allows it to be and a sufficient number of concerned people insists that it be. Politicians must be pressured to allocate and appropriate much more money for comprehensive environmental programs—research, planning, enforcement, and reform. Public speeches about rearranging priorities are not enough. Our representatives must be shown that if they do not represent us, they will lose their seats. Once the money is voted, the administrative programs it supports must be carefully monitored. Bureaucrats respond to complaints and reminders from the public, and if they do not, they can be prodded to do so by politicians.

In the environmental field, at least, the democratic political system seems to be responsive to the people it was designed to serve. But environmentally oriented constituencies must work for the results they want. It is a proven proposition that they will succeed in direct proportion to the extent that they are organized, informed, reasonable, persuasive, and persistent. Maintaining a healthy balance between public needs and private interests can be frustrating, time-consuming, even exhausting; but settling for less is an abdication of responsibility to ourselves and our heirs.

THE ROLE OF LITIGATION IN ENVIRONMENTAL POLICY: THE POWER PLANT SITING PROBLEM†

DAVID SIVE††

THE *WHETHER* QUESTION

It is unfortunate that in virtually all of the literature and discussion of problems of power plant siting and the environment, the very denomination of the problem entraps the environmentalist. To escape from that trap, the very statement of the problem must first be broadened to pose what I call the *whether* question, as well as the where and how questions. By this I mean that in connection with any particular proposed plant—atomic, fossil fuel or pumped storage —the alternatives we want considered include that of not building the plant at all and not supplying at all the particular power.

I hasten to add that this does not mean that I take the position that no additional power is needed. In most areas, if only because of population increases, *some* additional power is needed. But if that additional amount is represented as "X," and the portion of it to be supplied by any proposed plant by "Y," the alternative I want considered is simply that the total additional amount that is to be supplied be "X" minus "Y," or that the "Y" portion be postponed.

Asking the *whether* question, considering the no-plant alternative, is not simply an environmentalist's plea. It is a sound, currently applicable rule of law. In the leading Supreme Court case of *Udall v Federal Power Commission,* generally referred to as the "High Mountain Sheep" case,[1] the Supreme Court found that the question of "whether *any* dam should be constructed" as distinguished from the question of whether a private or federal agency should construct the High Mountain Sheep Dam, was unexplored in the record.[2] The Court held that the public interest required a consideration of the more basic issue.

The Court observed that:

> The issues of whether deferral of construction would be more in the public interest than immediate construction and whether preservation of the reaches of the river affected would be more desirable and in the public interest than the proposed development are largely unexplored in this record.

---

†Portions of this article were presented to the National Academy of Engineering the "Committee on Power Plant Siting."

††Member of the firm of Winer, Neuburger & Sive, New York City; LL.B. 1948, Columbia University.

1. 387 U.S. 428 (1967).

2. *Id.* at 436.

* * *

A license under the [Federal Power] Act empowers the licensee to construct, for its own use and benefit, hydroelectric projects utilizing the flow of navigable waters and thus, in effect, to appropriate water resources from the public domain. The grant of authority to the Commission to alienate federal water resources does not, of course, turn simply on whether the project will be beneficial to the licensee. Nor is the test solely whether the region will be able to use the additional power. The test is whether the project will be in the public interest. And that determination can be made only after an exploration of all issues relevant to the "public interest," including future power demand and supply, alternate sources of power, and public interest in preserving reaches of wild rivers and wilderness areas, the preservation of anadromous fish for commercial and recreational purposes, and the protection of wildlife.[3]

Another recent judicial recognition of the *whether* question is set forth in the case of *Department of Water and Power v. Hearing Board of the Air Pollution Control District of the County of Los Angeles.*[4] The court, recognizing the need in the city of Los Angeles for additional electricity, stated:

It is reasonable to hold, therefore, that the public interest in preventing any increase in the levels of air pollution and in seeking a diminution in the current levels of air pollution in the Los Angeles Basin, is an overriding public interest which must stand paramount and supreme when contrasted with the public interest of the residents of Los Angeles in obtaining all the electrical power they may desire. No substantial evidence has been presented to prove that the residents of Los Angeles are in any real danger in the foreseeable future of having an insufficient amount of electric power to supply their *basic* needs. They may not have sufficient electrical power to supply all of their peripheral needs or demands created by good and effective advertising copy put out by the Department of Water and Power. But if the residents of the Los Angeles Basin are ever to live in an atmosphere having air of a satisfactory quality, it may be essential that they be willing to make some sacrifice in the amount of electricity they use and enjoy over the next few years.[5]

The refashioning of national priorities which poses the whether question, as a matter of law in important resources disposition cases, is also manifested in the National Environmental Policy Act of 1969,[6] Title I of which sets forth a "Declaration of National En-

---

3. *Id.* at 449.
4. No. 971, 991 (Cal. Super. Ct., Los Angeles County, Jul. 9, 1970), 1 Environment Reporter 1580 (1970).
5. *Id.* at 1624-5.
6. 42 U.S.C.A. 4321 (Supp. 1971).

vironmental Policy" and a mandate that federal agencies effect that policy, and Title II, creating the "Council on Environmental Quality" ("CEQ"). The declared purpose is broad:

> To declare a national policy which will encourage productive and enjoyable harmony between man and his environment; to promote efforts which will prevent or eliminate damage to the environment and biosphere and stimulate the health and welfare of man; to enrich the understanding of the ecological systems and natural resources important to the Nation; and to establish a Council on Environmental Quality.[7]

The Act further directs that "the Congress authorizes and directs that, to the fullest extent possible (1) the policies, regulations and public laws of the United States shall be interpreted and administered in accordance with the policies set forth in this Act."

My last citation with respect to the whether question is perhaps more authoritative than the strictly legal sources. The August, 1970 Report of the Energy Policy Staff, Office of Science and Technology,[8] in its basic conclusions and recommendations, sets forth as the last of its "Conclusions and Recommendations" the following comments on "The Role of Growth in Demand":

> 1. The rapid growth in demand for electricity and energy and materials generally will continue to exacerbate the environmental problems even though part of the growth will be needed to utilize electricity for uses such as sewage treatment plants, rapid transit systems, and recycling wastes which effect major improvements in the quality of the environment. The issue is often raised: "Is this plant really needed?" But the basic question of whether electricity use is growing too rapidly cannot be answered on an individual plant basis. It is but part of the much larger and fundamental question of the pattern of growth for the nation's future. An answer requires a broad examination of the significance of all forms of energy to the economy and the public welfare, including analysis of the form and amount of energy that would be used if the projected increases in electricity consumption were materially curtailed. It would also involve an examination of pricing policies, rate structures, advertising programs, tax policies, and other factors in the economy affecting growth.
>
> 2. The relative costs and benefits of present policies as contrasted

---

7. The Act declares a number of other policies and objectives in great detail. Its first two subsections (a) and (b), are replete with references to the need for harmonizing Man and Nature. Subsection (c) sets forth a congressional declaration, "that each person should enjoy a healthful environment and that each person has a responsibility to contribute to the preservation and enhancement of the environment. *Id.*

8. *U.S. Office of Science and Technology, Electric Power and the Environment* (1970) [hereinafter cited as O.S.T. Report].

with a policy of discouraging growth in energy use should be carefully evaluated. *It may well be timely to re-examine all of the basic factors that shape the present rapid rate of energy growth in the light of our resource base and the impact of growth on the environment.* We raise the issue here for further study and discussion.[9] (emphasis supplied)

The foregoing is proof that the *whether* question is a legitimate one. Perhaps the single most important aspect to environmentalists of any proposed resolution of the problems which are the subject of your Committee's study is the capacity to litigate fairly that whether question. What is meant by "litigate" and why that procedural aspect of our complex of problems is so important leads me to a short discussion of adversary proceedings and their place in the resolution of those problems.

THE PLACE OF ADVERSARY PROCEEDINGS

The historical place of adversary proceedings in the development of the problems and controversies to which we now apply ourselves need not be documented at length. That such private litigation, meaning litigation by responsible organizations of what constitutes the public interest in important environmental cases, is an important environmental enforcement technique, was officially determined by the Internal Revenue Service in its resolution of the question it itself raised approximately six months ago with respect to the proposed denial of the right to deduct as charitable contributions grants by foundations and other grantors to public interest law firms. IRS officially sustained the place of public interest law firms (which include the legal arms of the principal national conservation organizations) as long as they follow certain guidelines fashioned primarily to prevent the representation of the "public interest" from becoming a device for private profit.

Why do environmentalists regard the adversary process and the role of the courts so highly? The first reason is the adversary proceeding has been most successful, particularly in the early years when the environmentalist cause was more wilderness oriented, more provincial, than today. The second and more important reason involves both a philosophical proposition and a basic look at techniques for arriving at truth and wisdom in cases where both unreasonable and reasonable minds may differ.

The philosophical proposition is, at the heart of the democracy versus plutocracy argument. How often have all of us heard the

---

9. *Id.* at 5.

suggestion that we could solve our difficult environmental problems —power versus natural beauty, downhill skiing versus wilderness, and others—if only we would get the right people around a quiet table, to talk it over in cocktail-softened tones, and compromise? The answer given is that (1) the problems are too complex, (2) they need the clarification of a clash, and (3) nobody can really tell by whom and how it is to be determined who are the "right people."

There is no set of "right people" to make important environmental decisions. Those basic and general enough to call for legislative or other political resolution require the melting pot of our traditional political processes. Not wanted is an environmental aristocracy of Weyerhausers, Udalls, or Charles Reich's, any more than one wants a foreign policy dictated solely by a few generals or Yale or Harvard professors. Important environmental controversies not basic or general enough to be susceptible of express legislative determination should be aired and enlightened by a litigating process. That process has as its principal features examination and cross-examination and reasoned exclusion of what is irrelevant from the bases of determination.

Part of the environmentalist's philosophy of faith in adversary proceedings is the rejection of the expertise of administrative agencies in the resolution of important environmental disputes. Succinctly stated, it is believed that in any environmental controversy involving the weighing of conflicting values, the weigher should be a court, a generalist, rather than an administrative agency whose outlook is organically developmental and provincial. It is beyond the scope of this article to state with any more particularity why environmentalists do not want a single purpose administrative agency to weigh the conflicting values.[10]

The litigation process should not alarm us. It need not, and conducted by responsible attorneys and principals generally is not, hostile or bitter. The capacity of groups representing different interests to present their views forcefully and even passionately, but with tolerance and appreciation of opposing views, is, fundamental to the very survival of our political and judicial processes. Much of the explosive force of the environmental movement results from the at first small and now growing number of important litigations. Litigation has inherent drama. Claims and counterclaims somehow achieve legitimacy and importance when made within the bounds of

---

10. The best statement of this is in the detailed eloquence of Professor Sax. J. Sax, Defending the Environment (1971). *See also* William O. Douglas, Points of Rebellion (1969). My own analysis of the subject is in Sive, *Some Thoughts of an Environmental Lawer in the Wilderness of Administrative Law,* 70 Colum. L. Rev. 612-15 (1970).

a legal proceeding. Whatever the explanation, an environmental lawsuit can be and has frequently been an effective political instrument. The conservationist may lose the case and win the war. The examples are legion. I cite only the one that was my first court involvement for the Sierra Club or a similar group. Three years of legal effort resulted in the defeat in court of individuals and corporations seeking to enjoin the construction of a cafe in the southeastern corner of Central Park, New York, which was to be financed by a gift of Huntington Hartford, Jr., by which, I have always assumed, he sought to set out the intimations of his own immortality. By the time of the final turndown of the opponents of the cafe by the highest Court of Appeals of New York State, however, Lindsay became Mayor, and the son of one of the plaintiffs, Thomas Hoving, Jr., became Park Commissioner. Mr. Hartford's fame rests primarily on a museum a few blocks west and out of the Park.

The possibilities of litigation as a political instrument in our environmental cause pose some dangers. Courts should not be used as political ploys, for reasons which go much beyond the breach of lawyers' professional ethics which may be involved. Their functions are far too important and their difficulties far too great to subject them to being turned into such instrumentalities. On the other hand the fact that there may be a political means of resolving a legal issue, particularly one involving important public environmental claims, should not forbid resort to the litigating process. The use of litigation as a part and parcel of corporate proxy fights has always seemed to me to raise similar questions. Perhaps environmentalists should have the same rights as corporate empire builders.

My upholding of the litigating process does not mean that I am satisfied with present procedures. I think most environmentalists are as dissatisfied as power proponents with the length and complexity of present procedures, particularly those before the regulatory commissions. While delay in one sense serves the purposes of those who oppose any building projects, it should be clear that the resources of the environmentalist opponents are a tiny fraction of those of the proponents, and that the opponents do not have the ready vehicle of rate charges by which they pass their costs on to consumers.

SOME SUBSTANTIVE AND PROCEDURAL CHANGES

There is widespread demand, perhaps stronger among power proponents than opponents, for reform of power plant siting proceedings, to simplify and shorten the processes. One of the longest and most complex, and one which is in many respects the very womb of our power plant siting problems and environmental law as a separate field of law, is, of course, the *Storm King Mountain* case. Seven years is, of course, too long to resolve most power plant controversies. It is not too long, in my opinion, for a landmark case, if we can assume that there are not more than a few of such character.

Perhaps the principal plea of power proponents and many of the public regulatory bodies is to simplify and speed up the permit process. One of the suggested ways of doing so is to have a "one-stop" proceeding, meaning, one proceeding in which all of the aspects of a particular project, including the environmental aspects, can be heard and determined. The clearest and sincerest plea for this reform is that made by Charles Luce, President of Consolidated Edison, summarized in the Interim Report of the New York Temporary State Commission on the Environmental Impact of Major Public Utility Facilities:

> After reviewing the many questions involved, that executive suggested "better mechanisms were needed to resolve the conflict between these two incompatible goals." He further concluded: "the shortcoming, I believe, is that there is no coordinated, systematic review by a single regulatory agency in which all of the factors necessary to a wise decision can be considered: the need for the new power supply, the reliability of the proposed project, the relationship of the project to other new power projects to be constructed in the region, the cost of the project, its impact on the environment and the available alternatives."[11]

The coordinated, systematic review by a single regulatory agency is the one-stop process. The one-stop process is suggested to avoid a horizontal profusion of administrative agencies and the vertical profusion of state, local and regional authorities.

Most responsible environmentalists would agree that there should be a one-stop process, with the following provisos: (1) that the determination by the "single regulatory agency" is subject to adequate judicial review, assuming that the single regulatory agency is an administrative agency of the traditional public utility commission type; and (2) that there is also, both at the administrative, regulatory agency level, and on the judicial review level, private representation of the public environmental interest, of the type and in the manner that such representation has developed in recent years.

There is a certain skepticism concerning the sincerity of some of the advocates, not including Mr. Luce, of the single regulatory

---

11. Interim Report of the New York Temporary State Commission on the Environmental Impact of Major Public Utility Facilities, Dec. 15, 1970 [hereinafter cited as McGowan Commission].

agency suggestion and the underlying plea for some speed-up of the procedures. It is not uncharitable to express the view that some of the cries for such simplification result from the difficulties of the present system. Use of long drawn out legal proceedings by corporate enterprises, including public utilities, to serve their own purposes, is not a new idea of mine. The merits of the plea for a single regulatory agency and speed up of the procedures cannot and should not, however, be determined by speculation as to the motivation of some of the pleaders.

Support of a one-stop process, eliminating the power of small municipalities to prevent the construction of important power plants or transmission lines by the exercise of their zoning powers, is stated with full knowledge that in several cases presently pending, zoning power has been exercised by municipalities with the fervent support of environmental groups to prevent such construction. It is my sincere conviction that environmentalists cannot call for regional planning to prevent the authorization by municipalities of garbage dumps in the center of lovely rural areas, and at the same time be against regional planning with respect to power plants and transmission facilities.

Environmentalists also support simplification and speed-up of the actual proceedings. Any discussion of the means by which this can be done is beyond the scope of this article.

Any speed-up of procedures should not, however, be at the expense of the full and fair presentation of their positions by all responsible parties and agencies. That full and fair presentation requires, in my opinion, a basic addition to the quasi-judicial process of determination of power plant applications and controversies— provision for adequate discovery of all of the relevant information, in substantially the same manner provided by most codes of civil procedure, the best example of which is the Federal Rules of Civil Procedure for discovery in all plenary suits.

There is little use to an environmentalist group or any other person or group with the right to intervene to have simply 30, 60 or 90 days' notice of the hearing at which the issues will be tried. If one side to the controversy, the applicant-company side, is permitted to take as many months as necessary in the preparation of the application and case, with all of the information in thier possession only, the other side can not be expected to make any effective presentation of their case on such notice. Far longer notice is necessary, together with the right to examine all of the underlying documents and data and to question the proponents of the project by written interrogatories or oral depositions, substantially in the same manner as that which is deemed indispensable in the trial of most civil actions.

The grant of such discovery rights is not inconsistent with speeding up the entire process. What is necessary is a far earlier disclosure by the applicant utility company of its long-range plans and of its specific plan for any particular project. Such disclosure should not be resisted. The information, as well as every other asset of the utility company, belongs to the public who are its subscribers and consumers. There should be no place for what lawyers call the "supporting theory of justice" in power plant proceedings.

A second reform environmentalists seek is substantive. It goes to the heart of the *whether* question and our national priorities. The basic criteria by which the to-build-or-not-to-build question is determined must be stated so as to avoid a presumption that what an applicant seeks to build should be built. The environmental effects should be given at least equal weight with the desire for more power in the determination of whether to build or not to build. The clearest statement of the problem of the basic criteria and priorities is detailed in *Comments on Legislation to be Proposed Regarding Procedures to Regulate Siting of Major Public Utility Facilities.*[12] Drafted initially by Albert Butzel, Esq., it describes "three different policy determinations that might be made in connection with siting legislation for major public utility facilities," to wit:

> A. *The importance of meeting the demands for more electricity may be regarded as paramount.* In this event, the demand for electricity would be the controlling factor, requiring the construction of new facilities even if the environmental impact were serious and substantial. Environmental factors would still be relevant insofar as it was possible to minimize the adverse impact, and, in this connection, the availability of alternatives, together with their relative costs, would be an important consideration. But given a choice between unmet demand and substantial damage to the environment, the demand factor would control.
>
> B. *The importance of preserving the environment from substantial damage may be regarded as paramount.* In this event, preservation of the environment from serious and substantial damage would be regarded as the controlling factor, requiring that no facility be built if such were the impact even though this resulted (or might result) in compulsory restrictions on power consumption.
>
> C. *The importance of meeting power demands and protecting the environment may each be regarded as basic concerns, with neither*

---

12. Committees on Administrative Law, on Atomic Energy, on Environmental Law and on Science and Law of the Bar Association of the City of New York, submitted to the McGowan Commission.

given priority over the other. In this event, no single consideration would be regarded as controlling as a general policy. The demand for electricity, the relative economics of meeting this demand, the adverse effect on the environment and other relevant social costs and benefits would be considered on a case-by-case basis, with authority in the certifying agency to balance all the pertinent factors and, in effect, to establish priorities in the light of all the circumstances, including the quality of the environmental resource involved and the adverse impact of construction upon such resource. A determination of policy along these lines should make it clear that, depending upon the particular circumstances, power demands might be regarded as controlling in one instance even though the adverse environmental impact were substantial, whereas in another case the protection of the environment might be given priority even though this might result in compulsory restrictions on power consumption.[13]

Most of the organic statutes creating and describing the powers and jurisdiction of utilities commissions adopt the first of the policy determinations described above. The power demands are regarded as paramount; the environmental considerations are secondary and often limited to dressing up the affected terrain by the planting of vines, painting concrete green, and other deceptions. Federal law now places environmental considerations on or close to a parity. The parity, however, should be clearly and expressly stated in the organic statute, and not left to deduction.

The McGowan Commission has prejudged this issue. A quote from its Interim Report of December 15, 1970, demonstrates this, expressing not only such pre-judgment but some barbs at environmentalists not becoming a supposedly quasi-judicial body at all cognizant of the crisis that brings us together in a search for environmental wisdom:

> Electric energy requirements are known to be growing rapidly. New York State generating companies and agencies had capability for supplying electric energy at a rate of 11.6 million kilowatts in 1960. This capability had increased about 100% to 23 million kilowatts by mid-1970. It is estimated that this capability *must be* 41 million kilowatts by 1980, *55 to 65 million kilowatts by 1990* and substantially more than that by the turn of the century, although quantitative projections beyond 1990 are considered to be nebulous at best. The utility facilities required to supply these needs are recognized to have important, in some cases dramatic effects on the environment in the localities where they are built and operated. That is particularly so in cases of large generating stations.
>
> Air, water and land pollution and aesthetic factors are significant in this regard. Some, perhaps including a few who most desire the

---

13. *Id.*

convenience of electric service, decry and would even seek to forbid creation of the necessary facilities because of these factors. Within the framework of existing statutory, administrative and judicial procedures means have been found whereby major utility plant construction projects have been delayed, some for many years, beyond initial planned operating dates and some have been cancelled notwithstanding demonstrable requirements for added capability.

As is indicated in further detail below, this is in part due to the existence of an overlay of regulatory jurisdiction affording, in some cases, as many as thirty agencies of government an opportunity to refuse to approve or to delay a proposed project. Some have been delayed at the federal level; at least one, in New York State, at the municipal level. Companies affected are concerned over their future ability to provide service unless there is created a new governmental mechanism qualified to recognize the needs of a community for additional electricity, and authorized to provide for that need, notwithstanding contrary views from many persuasive elements of society. Others, perhaps no less concerned, suggest an agency so authorized could infuriate such elements of society and make matters more difficult.[14]

The McGowan Commission should have read the O.S.T. Report.

A final comment on statutory reform relates to the definition of the scope of review by courts of the regulatory agency's power plant determinations. I strongly support review somewhat broader and deeper than that under the traditional arbitrary and capricious rule.[15] How much broader and how much deeper I do not know. Nor do I have the expertise to attempt to draft a different rule, or to determine whether the common law can work out refinements necessary in this environmental age. I leave that to the law and public administration scholars such as Professors Louis Jaffe, Walter Gellhorn, Kenneth Culp Davis, and Joseph Sax.

---

14. *Id.*
15. *See* Citizens to Preserve Overton Park, Inc. v. Volpe, 401 U.S. 402 (1971). *See generally* Administrative Procedure Act, 5 U.S.C. § 551 *et seq.* and L. Jaffe, Judicial Control of Administrative Action (1965).

THE BUREAUCRATIC RESPONSE TO ENVIRONMENTAL POLITICS

GEOFFREY WANDESFORDE-SMITH†

As a result of developments in environmental politics in the United States within the last five years, most existing resource management agencies realize that they are in deep trouble. The trouble is not primarily economic in nature, although a questioning of well-established economic tools for the management of natural resources is an important part of the total problem.[1] Rather, the difficulties are essentially political. Resource management agencies at all levels of government appear to have reached, or to be rapidly approaching, a point at which their behavior and performance are unacceptable to a substantial, vocal, and growing segment of the American public.

Many state water agencies, for example, must be wondering whether they will suffer the same fate as the Department of Water Resources in the State of Washington. The department was recently absorbed, along with several other agencies, into a new Department of Ecology. And at the federal level there exists the possibility that persistent public expression of dissatisfaction will lead Congress to reduce, or refuse to increase substantially, appropriations for programs with major environmental impacts.

Since few bureaucracies readily accept a reduction of their budget or a drastic reorganization of their programs, it is not surprising that existing agencies are looking for ways to ensure their survival, and perhaps even to improve their position by putting essentially unchanged programs in a new linguistic wrapping.[2] Nor is there anything reprehensible about this. Much of what is known about bureaucratic behavior suggests that this kind of response is to be expected, and therefore guarded against by those seeking fundamental change. The majority of agency personnel are sincere and dedicated public servants, giving administrative expression to the public interest as they see it. It is to some extent natural that they are inclined to be

---

†Assistant Professor of Political Science and Environmental Studies, University of California, Davis.

1. *See, e.g.,* Dales, Pollution, Property, and Prices (1968); Jarrett, Environmental Quality in a Growing Economy (Jarrett ed. 1966); Krutilla, *Conservation Reconsidered,* 57 Am. Econ. Rev. 777-86 (1967).

2. In this connection, Secretary of Agriculture Clifford M. Hardin made the following interesting statement to a Department of Agriculture seminar on environmental problems in January, 1971: "I think we're operating in an environment in which the public wants more attention to these [environmental quality] items and we're going to try to take advantage of this and provide it, building on the good work of the past." Sacramento Bee, Jan. 15, 1971, at CL2, col. 1.

defensive in the face of the uncertainties that budget reductions and agency reorganizations generate. They do not particularly like being told that they have done a less than adequate job in the past. And this kind of criticism is especially unpalatable when it comes from groups, such as the Sierra Club, that make claims on the public's attention in the name of conservation. After all, it was the men who first provided political and administrative leadership to resource management as a public function who also first popularized the term conservation in the United States.[3]

One of the important questions a symposium such as this must come to grips with is the extent to which defensive and essentially short run responses by existing agencies are likely to get them out of their present difficulties. Or, to put it another way, to what extent can resource management agencies ride out the storm by promoting one form or another of administrative gadgetry? If their present difficulties are simply the product of unusual and temporary political circumstances, the agencies may eventually be able to continue with business as usual, having made at most some minor and insubstantial changes in their management and policy planning procedures. In this case a theory of environmental administration would not require assumptions about the nature of contemporary American politics and administration that are radically different from those that have been entertained in the past.

If, on the other hand, the politics of the environment are fundamentally different in kind from the politics of natural resources management, and if this difference is reflected in American political life generally, then a theory of environmental administration will be required that both reinterprets present experience and provides the basis for some drastic, long-run alterations in administrative practices.

While it would be inappropriate in an article of this length to attempt to present a thoroughly convincing case for the second of the two possibilities just described, or to pretend to have developed a suitable theory of environmental administration, I should like to discuss in the next few pages some ideas that may begin to make the second possibility appear worthy of further thought and research.

One index of the extent to which resource managers and their agencies are in trouble is to be found in the fact that they frequently have a hard time understanding the nature of the modern conserva-

---

3. This is not to say, however, that the first conservation movement ever became a movement with a strong popular base. *See* McConnell, *Environment and the Quality of Political Life,* in Congress and the Environment 8-9 (Cooley and Wandesforde-Smith ed. 1970).

tion movement. Their attitude is often that the Sierra Club, the Friends of the Earth, the California Planning and Conservation League, the local chapters of Ecology Action, and other groups are merely new interest groups, joining those that have traditionally fought over the material benefits to be derived from the productive use of resources.[4] Some also argue that, as the direct descendants of the movement founded by Gifford Pinchot and the first President Roosevelt, they have always sought the ends the environmentalists now seek. What they overlook in their efforts to reconcile the modern conservation movement with those of the past, and with their own experience, is the environmentalist's primary concern with non-economic values.

When the Forest Service, for example, offers environmentalists three-quarters of a wilderness area, in return for the development of a ski resort and the continuation of grazing and a little mining on the remaining quarter, the offer is often refused. Treating the environmentalists like any other interest group does not seem to work. It seems often to be impossible to satisfy them as well as the week-end campers, the cattlemen, the miners, the subdivision developers, and the resort owners. The environmentalists appear intransigent, extremely difficult to bargain with, and unwilling to accept a compromise. The reason is that in their terms three-quarters of a wilderness area is not good enough. To them it is an all or nothing proposition because wilderness values are irreplaceable and priceless; not the kind of values that can be traded-off under the rubric of multiple use or according to the principles of professional forestry. The environmentalists even go so far as to question the rights of professional resource managers to make binding determinations about the most appropriate uses of the resources of the nation's lands.

This last position is based on the assertion that in terms of the values and long-range social goals being sought the views of the professional resource manager are not all that much more valuable than anyone else's. Indeed, they may be less valuable despite the manager's professional training, because the record shows that by training and experience resource managers tend to regard the productive use of resources as paramount. Using again the example of the Forest Service, this point was made by a university group investigating the management of the Bitterroot National Forest in western Montana.[5] The group noted in its recent report that the position adopted by the

4. This point is discussed in L.K. Caldwell, *Politics and the Public Lands,* Paper presented to a Conference on the Public Land Law Review Comm. Rep., San Francisco, Cal., Dec. 8, 1970, at 19-20.

5. A University View of the Forest Service, S. Doc. No. 115, 91st Cong., 2d Sess. (1970).

environmentalists strikes at the root of professional forestry education.[6] And toward the end of their report they comment on the resulting political situation that resource managers find it terribly frustrating to deal with:

> We doubt that the most carefully developed arguments will ever convince opponents of the appropriateness of some of the now practiced land management practices, . . . Regardless of any developed fund of knowledge, research results, or even conditions of pure and simple fact, some of the groups involved in the Bitterroot National Forest are opposed to these land management practices under any and all circumstances; and nothing that can be said is likely to change their views, their positions or their unconditional opposition. At this point we must note that the crucial issue then becomes one of examining the process through which unpopular decisions involving public policy must be made.[7]

The modern conservation movement will not accept the claim of resource managers to determine future resource uses almost exclusively on professional grounds. Even if resource managers appeared converted to the point of pressing for the management of environments or ecosystems, rather than discrete resources, this position probably would not change. In addition to being, in their view, irreplaceable, priceless, and based on sound ecological principles, the values of the environmentalists are values that have adherents, both actual and potential, drawn from a broad constituency. Because of this the environmentalists are arguing that decisions about resources must be made by a larger public than is represented by interests likely to gain from the economic or productive use of those resources. The reluctance of resource management agencies to recognize the legitimacy of this claim is a principal reason why the politics of the environment is marked by some tough and protracted political struggles and an increasing amount of litigation.

It will not be easy for existing agencies to grant this recognition because it amounts to an admission that environmental management, and even the older form of resource management, is a much more political process than most professional resource managers are willing to concede. With it goes a reduction of the role of the professional manager to that of consultant rather than policy maker. Although this is a change that will not occur overnight, nor be perhaps as complete as the preceding sentence might suggest, it is inevitable if the general public is to reclaim in a direct and meaningful way the

6. *Id.* at 22.
7. *Id.* at 25.

control over environmental management it has heretofore placed in the professional manager's hands.

In the context of contemporary environmental politics, it is not going to be enough for resource management agencies to appoint environmental advisory boards[8] or to broaden the educational experience of their personnel,[9] though these are both welcome developments. Nor will it be sufficient for these agencies to argue that they are earnestly seeking new organizational concepts and arrangements because they are persuaded that environmental management demands a broader interdisciplinary approach to problem solving and a total systems approach to decision-making.[10] To the environmentalist seeking a grossly observable change in the impact of administrative decisions on the quality of his environment, talk of total systems management and interdisciplinary problem solving can be just as obfuscatory as earlier slogans such as multiple use and conservation. He is more likely to be interested in bureaucratic responses that result in a more overt and participatory redistribution of influence and the power to decide.

The preceding comments relate primarily to bureaucratic responses which effect the way resource management agencies and resource managers think about themselves and their role vis-a-vis the public they serve. However, in a larger sense these actual and potential changes can be related to political developments that have affected a wide variety of institutions in the American political system. Many, but not all, political scientists would argue that in the last five years or so there has emerged a new perspective on the nature of this system. Professor William Connolly, for example, has attributed this new perspective to a critical temper among political scientists that stems in large part from dissatisfaction with the pluralist theory of American politics.[11] Professor Grant McConnell has explored some of the consequences of this re-evaluation of pluralist thought for environmental politics and administration,[12]

8. This is a mechanism recently adopted by the U.S. Army Corps of Engineers. Conservation Foundation Letter, Jan. 1971, at 2-3.

9. Recommendations along these lines are made by Henning, *Natural Resources Administration and the Public Interest,* 30 Pub. Ad. Rev. 134, 137 (1970).

10. These are frequent recommendations for improving environmental policy-making. *See, e.g.,* Lieber, *Public Administration and Environmental Quality,* 30 Pub. Ad. Rev. 277, 284 (1970); Henning, *Comments on an Interdisciplinary Social Science Approach for Conservation Administration,* BioScience II (Jan. 1, 1970); Senate Comm. on Interior and Insular Affairs, Definition of the Scope of Environmental Management, Comm. Print, 91st Cong., 2d Sess. (1970).

11. W. Connolly, The Bias of Pluralism 19 (Connolly ed. 1969).

12. G. McConnell, The Political Context of the Environmental Movement, Paper presented to the Forum for a Future Conference, Aspen, Colorado, June 13-14, 1970.

and some of his tentative conclusions should be noted and elaborated in the context of the present discussion.

McConnell observes that from the findings of political science research there emerges a portrait of the political process in America that has several salient characteristics:

> We have an open society, one accessible in all its aspects to all citizens. We have a set of guarantees of individual freedoms and assurances that each man has at least the opportunity to make his voice heard as common decisions are made. As a consequence, large decisions are few and even these tend to be cumulative in nature. The basic allocation of values at the heart of the process itself is aggregative, that is, it is the outcome of a multitude of individual and group choices mingled together in ways of almost infinite complexity. We are firmly convinced that the process itself is neutral as to values and that the openness of the system extends not only to all members but to all their desires and aspirations as well. If some of these are disappointed at a given moment, opportunity for a renewal of claims will come again, and the test will remain what it has always been, the construction of a majority.[13]

From among these characteristics of the political process that can be deduced from the conventional wisdom about American politics McConnell selects two for special attention. He remarks on the experience of the blacks and Chicanos, noting that this appears to deny the assumption that all individuals and groups in society have the same access as other groups.[14] He comments also on the assumption of neutrality with respect to values and concludes tentatively that much of American political experience calls it into question.[15] He advances the notion that American politics has revolved for the most part around questions about "the distribution of material benefits and costs, and the control of wealth and productive facilities."[16] Even issues such as race and religion, treated in other political systems as non-economic issues, have been dealt with as though they were economic in nature. The American system of economic politics has served the nation remarkably well as a device for securing social peace. It has been highly pragmatic, characterized by bargaining in terms of common units of value that could be distributed in a way that would leave each side in a dispute better off in a material sense than they were originally. However, McConnell also points out that the conditions needed to sustain a system of economic politics have

13. *Id.* at 4.
14. *Id.* at 5.
15. *Id.* at 9-10.
16. *Id.* at 6.

been subject in recent years to erosion.[17] In particular, a decline in the value that more and more Americans place upon material goods and a substantial reduction in the fear of major economic depression have contributed to an increasing concern with issues involving values ultimately more important than the accretion of wealth, including the preservation of natural beauty and wilderness. With respect to these kinds of issues it may be impossible "to buy acquiescence. . . by a simple substitution of some economic gain for other demanded benefits."[18]

McConnell underscores the possibility that, as non-economic values become more important in American politics, governmental responses typical of the past will prove grossly inadequate. He cites the example of anti-pollution programs, which typically propose the spending of more and more money for more and better ameliorative technology. Such programs do little or nothing to challenge and redefine the long term goals of society, something many environmentalists are interested in doing. They tend, on the contrary, to accept established goals and their accompanying life styles as givens. However, in addition to being applicable to the substance of governmental response, McConnell's argument has relevance for the form of the response. Many Americans are concerned not only with the quality of their physical environment, and with the extent to which its deterioration affects the quality of life, but also with the quality of their politico-administrative environment. And the re-evaluation of accessibility and value preferences within the American political process has important consequences for the means by which goals are defined and attained, as well as for the nature of the goals themselves.

A glance at some recent pieces of federal and state legislation indicates that questions of accessibility and the treatment of values have received attention in formulating new institutional arrangements. This is true of a variety of policy issues, including the poverty program, regional economic development, urban renewal, the rehabilitation of rural areas, and education.[19] The kinds of responses

17. *Id.* at 13.
18. *Id.* at 15. McConnell also discusses the notion of economic politics, and the consequences of its displacement, in the reference given at *supra* note 3. These recent writings build upon his earlier work, which is particularly important for its development of the concept of constituency. *See* McConnell, Private Power and American Democracy, chs. 4 and 7 (1966).
19. For a useful general introduction to the institutional arrangements associated with these issues, *see* Davis and Sundquist, Making Federalism Work (1969); Fantini, Gittell and Magat, Community Control and the Urban School (1970). On the particular questions of accessibility and value biases in the context of economic development planning, *see* Warren, *Federal-Local Development Planning: Scale Effects in Representation and Policy Making,* 30 Pub. Ad. Rev. 584 (1970).

noted earlier at the level of the individual resource agency, such as the Forest Service, and the individual resource manager, reflect a concern with accessibility and value preferences in connection with environmental policy. However, the voluntary improvement of agency devices for public participation in policy planning, or the up-dating of professional resource management education, can be uneven and uncertain tools for modifying policy outcomes. The remarkable feature of some recent environmental legislation is that it has sought to overcome these limitations by granting statutory protection for the public's right to an open decision-making process and a full consideration of all relevant values. And it has done so in a way that applies equally to all resource management agencies.

The most familiar enactment with these attributes is the National Environmental Policy Act of 1969.[20] Among other things, this law requires all federal agencies to give explicit recognition and consideration to "presently unquantified environmental amenities and values"[21] in their decision making. It also requires a statement describing the environmental impact of proposed agency actions which significantly affect the quality of the human environment, with particular attention to the justification of impacts that are irreversible.[22] An equally significant portion of the law is that requiring copies of environmental impact statements, and agency comments thereon, to be made public.[23] Although there are conflicting interpretations of this last section of the law,[24] one observer has noted that presidential Executive Order 11514 of March 5, 1970, appears to conform to both the spirit of the act and the intent of Congress.[25] The order charges federal agencies with the responsibility of ensuring the fullest practicable provision of timely information for the public with respect to federal plans and programs with environmental impacts.[26] The stated purpose of this directive is to obtain the views of and provide access for interested parties, and it seems reasonably clear that without adequate information such views may be less meaningful and be less effective from the point of view of political strategy than they might otherwise be.

A review of developments at the state level reveals several similar changes.[27] The Environmental Protection Act of 1970 in Michigan

20. 42 U.S.C. § § 4321-47 (Supp. V, 1964).
21. 42 U.S.C. § 4332(B) (Supp. V, 1964).
22. 42 U.S.C. § 4332(C) (Supp. V, 1964).
23. *Id.*
24. Fisher, *Environmental Law,* Sierra Club Bull. 27 (Jan. 1971).
25. Not Man Apart, at 1 and 21-23 (Feb. 1971).
26. 35 Fed. Reg. 4247.
27. Conservation Foundation Letter, Nov. 1970.

provides citizens with an unencumbered right to sue.[28] The law allows any citizen to institute a suit against public agencies, and others, to protect resources and the public trust therein from pollution, impairment, or destruction. And it is not necessary under the act for the plaintiff to prove he has suffered direct or special damage and has legal standing.[29] In Illinois, the 1970 Environmental Protection Act allows any citizen to file a complaint with the Pollution Control Board and to be guaranteed both an investigation by the state Environmental Protection Agency and a hearing before the Board. The Illinois act also permits any citizen to propose new pollution control regulations and have them considered publicly if they meet certain modest criteria.[30] New land use laws in Maine and Vermont have required careful consideration of the environmental impact of proposed developments, and have placed the burden of proof upon the developers rather than the public that suffers if impacts are not minimized.[31]

Additional changes along these lines can be expected at both the state and federal levels. Among the first measures introduced into the ninety-second Congress, for example, were an environmental class actions bill[32] and a bill to provide Constitutional guarantees for each person's right to a decent environment.[33] While there remains some uncertainty that the courts will promptly and fully sustain all of these legislative shifts, it is clear that in the future bureaucratic re-

---

28. Mich. Comp. Laws Ann. § § 691.1201-07 (1970). The original draft of this law was prepared by Professor Joseph Sax, School of Law, University of Michigan. It is discussed by Sax in his recent book. *See* Sax, Defending the Environment 247-248 (1970). Similar legislation for the nation as a whole was brought before Congress in 1970 [S.3575 and H.R.16436, 91st Cong., 2d Sess. (1970)] by Senators Philip Hart and George McGovern and by Representative Morris Udall. In April 1971, the Subcommittee on the Environment of the Senate Commerce Committee held hearings on the Hart-McGovern bill, reintroduced as S.1032, 92d Cong., 1st Sess. (1971). The Nixon administration, represented by the General Counsel for the Council on Environmental Quality, opposed the bill because it would assign to an already overburdened court system the task of writing environmental laws and setting pollution standards, which could better be left to Congress, the Environmental Protection Agency, and the states. However, Mr. William Butler of the Environmental Defense Fund argued that fears of a flood of litigation following enactment of the bill did not appear to be justified by early experience with the Michigan law. *See* National Wildlife Federation Conservation Rep., 128-29 (Apr. 23, 1971).

29. *Supra* note 27, at 11.

30. *Id.* at 8-9.

31. *Id.* at 2-4. For a more adequate treatment of the legal issues raised by recent legislation and court decisions, *see* Law and the Environment (Baldwin and Page ed. 1970); Beecher and Nestle, Environmental Law Handbook (1970); and Landau and Rheingold, The Environmental Law Handbook (1971).

32. H.R. 49 and H.R. 290, 92d Cong., 1st Sess. (1971).

33. S.J. Res. 14, 92d Cong., 1st Sess. (1971). An earlier version of this bill is discussed in Ottinger, *Legislation and the Environment: Individual Rights and Government Accountability,* 55 Cornell L. Rev. 666 (1970).

sponse to environmental politics will have to contend increasingly with much stronger public rights in two respects. The agencies will have to show, upon pain of litigation, that all relevant interests are afforded access to information and the decision-making procedures relevant to environmental policy issues. And secondly, they will have to establish and adhere to clearer public procedures and criteria for making value choices.

One probable consequence of these changes, at least in the short run, is a slowing down of the policy-making process. Agencies that pride themselves on their capacity to project public needs and to meet them, whether it be for power, lumber, flood control, or irrigation, are likely to protest this hinderance of their progress, partly on the grounds that they are legally constituted entities charged with these functions. Some might also protest that it is unreasonable to expect, on the basis of past experience, more extensive and informed public involvement in environmental policy-making. If the public is to realize the benefits associated with a more open system of policy-making, its response will have to differ both quantitatively and qualitatively from that of the past. All too often the environmentalists have appeared to be mere obstructionists. But the responsibility for producing better environmental policy cannot be achieved simply by forcing the agencies to make new responses of the kind analyzed here.

In the long run, therefore, we may expect to find new kinds of organizations whose purpose is to articulate the interests and values of some part of the public in environmental matters. It is difficult to say precisely what form these might take, or how they would be funded, or what provision would have to be made for those segments of the public that lack the resources to hire a spokesman.[34] A future symposium might usefully explore these questions and their significance for a theory of environmental administration.

---

34. For some interesting, if preliminary, thoughts along these lines, *see* Michael, The Unprepared Society, ch. 5 (1968).

ENVIRONMENTAL POLICY: PUBLIC PARTICIPATION AND THE OPEN INFORMATION SYSTEM

HARVEY FRAUENGLASS†

For reasons both obvious and obscure, the level of awareness of the natural environment in the United States is today higher than it has ever been. While this new public awareness must be a delight to the professional managers of our natural resources, it also presents a dilemma. Being the object of public attention brings prestige, a feeling of social accomplishment, and allocations of public funds not given to unrecognized undertakings. The prospect of praise also stimulates men to create new ways and means of improving the common wealth. Yet at the same time public awareness may broaden public scrutiny to uncomfortable dimensions. For the first time questions are raised about basic operating assumptions, long-established procedures, standard methods of cost-benefit analysis, resource management philosophy, and aesthetic value systems. Along with the questions come requests for information, detailed information on every aspect of administration.

After generations of being taken on faith, the professional manager is at first incredulous. He must be "hearing things"; surely "this too will pass." So the questions are either ignored, or answered in the manner of the doctor responding to his patient's query: "What's the matter, don't you trust me?" When significant effects must finally be acknowledged—officials are investigated by Congress, for instance, or construction projects are halted by court injunction—the public resource management agency may literally go into shock. As when local Tennessee groups got the U.S. Supreme Court to stop the Department of Transportation from violating a highly regarded Memphis park with a six-lane superhighway.[1] Or in numerous other instances where citizens have invoked political, legislative, and judicial sanctions against the environmentally damaging projects and decisions of federal agencies. Depending on the severity of the shock, the traumatized organism may need an emergency transfusion from above, and then long convalescence and extensive rehabilitation—assuming the organism survives.

In many ways the professional resource manager, whatever his age, resembles the short-haired, well-groomed father of the long-haired,

---

†President, The Environmental Reporter Foundation, Albuquerque, New Mexico.
1. Albuquerque Journal, Mar. 5, 1971, at 4, col. 1. Citizens To Preserve Overton Park, Inc., v. Volpe, 91 S. Ct. 814 (1971).

ungroomed son. At first he does not see the need to accommodate, and then when he does see the need, he does not know how. Both the posture and the problem of those administering public resources today have a certain social logic. (And within the posture and the problem lies the solution, which we shall consider shortly.) As predictability seems to be the mark of the visible universe, change is the mark of human society. In the twentieth century the mark is accelerating change in the total environment social, technological, biological, and geophysical. Where cultural institutions readily adapt to change, spectacular achievements are the rule. Where they resist, the rule is fracturing, suffering, and destruction. For "the culture that was adequate for yesterday is inadequate for today, and disasterous for tomorrow..."[2] And so in particular with communications, the manner of sharing, receiving, and withholding information which is the control for a cultural institution.

No matter how thoroughly schooled in scientific method, professionals in the natural resource area always retain some very human characteristics when it comes to communications. Their natural tendency is to hear only what they want to hear and see only what they want to see and then speak only what they feel outsiders ought to know. Yesterday that tendency in government was usually harmful only in the long run. Today, in at least some phases of public affairs, it can lead to total disaster in a very short time. The Torrey Canyon, Santa Barbara Channel, and Gulf of Mexico oil disasters of the last decade are examples. For the sake of survival, then, if for no other reason, managers find it desirable to modify traditional information policy.

THE MANAGEMENT INFORMATION SYSTEM— AN INTERMEDIATE ADAPTATION

Modern information systems developed to serve management in both public and private enterprises may employ data gathering procedures and data processing equipment of varying degrees of sophistication, but all systems have the same basic purposes. First they must collect all possible information from all possible sources: private and public, reliable and unreliable, legal and extra legal, and scientific, political, economic, and even environmental. Then they have to reduce, analyze, and evaluate the information to suit the needs of the managers. Finally they have to determine ways to use the processed information to implement policy.

Unlike the restricted intake of hear-no-evil systems, now every-

2. Bohannan, *Beyond Culture,* 80 Natural History 50 (1971).

thing possible must go up to the top—good, bad, and indifferent. But still very little can come down; it is again only what the managers deem prudent and this only in the form they deem prudent. Sociologist Norman Johnson of Carnegie-Mellon University gives these examples of how the management information system works in a typical urban power structure.[3]

1. An urban renewal agency set up by the political leaders in conjunction with the business and industrial community develops plans and then sets up citizen committees which discuss ways of getting people to carry out the plans.

2. After discovering extensive anti-social opinions among certain segments of the population, a local government body plans educational therapy to remold the thinking of these groups.

3. Neighborhood corporations are set up to extend civic power to the people. Neighborhood leaders then end up withholding information as a means of retaining their new positions.

In all three cases private citizens who would attempt to alter policy find it difficult to support their positions because information resources are completely controlled by management, which is exactly the goal of the management information system. However modern its tools, the modern management information policy is still no different in intent from the policy of early civilizations which made "writing and reckoning the prerogative of special classes—either privileged classes of priests or else slaves in the hands of kings."[4] Knowledge was power then and knowledge is power now.

The difference lies in the informational resources of the contemporary public. The most economically disadvantaged minority in a highly mobile industrial society employing all manner of high-speed communication tools and holding all forms of historical information in easily available open storage is far from the benighted peasantry of the past. Once knowledge is recognized by any group of Americans as the principal tool for changing society and more immediately the principal weapon for doing battle with management, the determined group will find means to acquire such knowledge.

Thus a conflict between conservation groups and the management of a public resource agency, for example, may escalate through various levels of knowledge power with great expenditures of energy on both sides and culminate in a fruitless stalemate (not unlike the current condition of inter-nation conflict) which could take inordinate time and further energy to resolve productively. Whether it

3. Address by Norman Johnson, Albuquerque, New Mexico, Feb. 24, 1971.
4. *Supra* note 2.

is the Forest Service or the Bureau of Land Management fighting for another road in a wild area, the Bureau of Reclamation or the Corps of Engineers pushing for another recreation-irrigation-flood control-power dam, or the Food and Drug Administration, the Federal Trade Commission, or any department or bureau withholding action on an environmental or consumer issue, each new use of the management information system as a policy tool requires more skill and effort and generates increasing opposition. The opposition will increase as the rate of rising material expectations in our society is achieved and finally surpassed by the rate of rising information and knowledge expectations.

MODIFICATIONS AND FIXES

As we have seen, all management information systems, whether they employ enormous CIA-type surveillance apparatus which supposedly acquires all knowledge and releases nothing, or the modest, part-time services of a few employees who frequently report upwards all of what they hear and transact and regularly but less frequently and more selectively report back to the public what the agency knows and what it is doing, are guided by the same policy of self-protectiveness, secrecy, and elitism which characterizes the closed systems of early societies. If management now actively seeks wide information from below, it is purely from expediency: first, successful operations of public agencies simply require enormous amounts of information; second, action proposals must be fully supported by data before legislators can be induced to appropriate funds and change statutes and enact new ones. The management system of gathering and studying data has nothing to do with any relinquishing of management executive power or sharing of the decision-making authority.

Nor is it reasonable to expect a radical change in information policy when the established information tool begins to decline in effectiveness. What we do find is a series of new appendages designed to overcome whatever seem to be the "minor operational problems." Perhaps the most common "fix" appendage is the citizen advisory board, ostensibly set up to promote public participation. In practice, however, the board is most often placed between the public and the agency and then used to promote management plans and proposals and to discharge public animosity toward the agency.[5] Among their other deficiencies, citizen boards are as a rule unrepresentative of the

5. I am not, of course, thinking of district grazing boards made up of stockmen who use public rangelands. Such grazing boards often become the operating management in their areas, controlling the activities of the government manager and practicing generally restrictive information policies in regard to outsiders.

general community which they are supposed to represent. Yet however selective the membership, the boards are still not privy to much of the information in the hands of the sponsoring agency, either raw or processed information. Members have neither official standing nor frequent or meaningful contact with management. Gradually such boards degenerate to honorary status and are used solely to counter criticism from above that an area or district manager has not consulted the public: "But our citizen advisory board has studied the problem. . ."

The agency ombudsman is another attempt to loosen the flow of information to and from the public without really changing the concept that information is first and last a management tool. Although the ombudsman idea may have historical antecedents in the censor and tribune of Rome and the procurator of the Roman provinces, its direct lineage is the office established in 1713 and updated a century later "as a mechanism in Sweden for defending citizens against official wrongdoing."[6] The office has been naturalized in the United States to serve local governments as the "neighborman" providing information and investigating complaints, as a go-between in military-civilian conflicts, and even as a department store "fix-it" man. In natural resource management the ombudsman and his staff would interpret policy and supply information to the public at local levels and investigate and attempt to resolve complaints about irregular or unfair practices. He would have access to the highest levels of management and at the same time be fully accessible to any and all members of the public.

The practical advantages to management of an ombudsman office are many, especially from the standpoint of gaining public support of general agency activities while retaining complete control of all planning and implementation.[7] For whatever else he seems to be, the ombudsman is always a tool of management. He influences objectives, plans, and policies in his role as public spokesman only in so far as management feels it is desirable and expedient to be influenced.

A third possible appendage to the management information

6. Floyd, *The Ombudsman: The Citizen's Advocate,* Management Information Service, Oct., 1969. Floyd, who was city manager of Savanah when the report was published, explores ombudsman functions in both developed and developing countries with particular emphasis on municipal applications in the United States. Information exchange is not always the primary function of the ombudsman, but it is always significant.

7. I do not know of any natural resource or environmental protection agency in the United States which has an ombudsman at this time. Such offices will no doubt be established after the general concept becomes more familiar in other areas of government. (The complaint-reviewing function of the Army inspector-general's office, though certainly well established, cannot be significant in advancing the ombudsman concept since the military hierarchy controls both the flow of information and the actual physical existence of its soldiers.)

system is the formal adversary process designed "to represent environmental values vigorously in administrative agency proceedings."[8] The environmental adversary, operating within the resource agency, would gather information from management and citizen sources and then prepare and present a strong case for the environment in an open attempt to influence agency policy. Of these three ways of modifying while not fundamentally changing the management information system, the adversary process would probably come closest to satisfying the requirements of informed and militant environmentalists. Yet like the ombudsman, the agency-employed adversary remains an office between the public and the managers and as such would never be fully accepted by those who want direct contact, full communication and exchange of information. What they are seeking is a completely different kind of information policy, one that includes not only an unrestricted information flow in both directions, but also a commitment to share responsibility for setting goals and making plans.

A "PEOPLE'S INFORMATION SYSTEM"

Significant experiments in open information systems are underway in the East Liberty-Garfield section of Pittsburgh and at the executive level in the Commonwealth of Puerto Rico. The Pittsburgh project, called a "people's information system" by Professor Johnson of Carnegie-Mellon's School of Urban Affairs,[9] is designed to make all possible urban information available to any citizen who wants it for whatever purpose and who is willing to go to any of five neighborhood computer data banks to get it. Carnegie-Mellon students gather some of the basic information themselves in neighborhood interviews—youth values, housing, and education information, for example. Other data is obtained from information panels. In both cases citizens may ask questions as well as answer them. Other information, on transportation and economic opportunities, for example, comes from city government sources. Merely going to a neighborhood data center and learning how to get information for personal use from a computer is a valuable experience for the participants, according to Professor Johnson. Besides giving them a certain self-confidence in using the machine, it also gives them a better feeling toward their government than they have ever had. But perhaps most important, by operating from a common data base private citizens know for the first time the views and problems of their neighbors directly, instead of through a management filter, and they can act from knowledge in anything they undertake, be it economic, social,

8. Green, *Book Review*, 172 Science 47 (1971).
9. *Supra* note 3.

or political. Because the citizen now has knowledge he has choice and the beginnings of power.

Puerto Rican Governor Luis A. Ferré and his New Progressive Party are trying out a citizen feedback system as a means of drawing "ordinary citizens into decision making."[10] Telephone-equipped feedback terminals in San Juan fire stations and a mobile unit travelling through rural areas are manned by "citizen aides" trained to handle citizen inquiries, requests, and complaints. Eventually the terminals will have conversational-type computers to speed applications for government services and to feed service performance and other data to the government for use in program correction and improvement. Governor Ferré hopes the system will also "encourage new forms of involvement feedback, such as opinions, suggestions, and volunteering," once the system proves itself by first raising the quality of government service.

MANAGEMENT BY INFORMATION

Applying people's information techniques to natural resource management and general environmental protection will require the same philosophical commitment which has been made by the commonwealth government and the city government of Pittsburgh in undertaking the sharing of information. In its extensive 1970 report to Congress the Public Land Law Review Commission has suggested the first step toward a new information and communication policy— the establishment of widely representative citizen advisory boards to broaden the vision and improve the planning of professional resource managers who may have been too narrowly oriented in the past.[11] But advisory boards have been tried before. The crucial point is that management must be willing to enter into a meaningful dialogue with both regional and local citizen groups (not just economically interested groups, of course) and share with them the information gathering and evaluating programs, the goal-formulating, the planning, the establishment of priorities, and the actual implementation of policies. The function of professionals would be to inform rather than persuade, to educate rather than proselytize, and to honestly

10. Stevens, *A State That Listens To Citizens and Science,* 49 New Scientist and Science Journal 298 (1971).

11. Public Land Law Review Commission, One Third Of The Nation's Land, at 262 (1970). "Citizen advisory boards should be used to advise the heads of land administering agencies on public land policymaking." *Id.* at 289, "To be consistent with the broad role of public land agencies, we recommend that members of each citizen advisory board be chosen to represent a broad range of interest . . . and that representation should change as interest in, and uses of the lands change. We believe the appropriate range of representation includes not just the obvious direct interests, such as grazing, recreation, mining, fish and wildlife, and wilderness, but the professor, the laborer, the townsman, the environmentalist, and the poet as well."

reveal attitudes and conflicts rather than hide and disguise them. Citizen groups and managers working together could then formulate reasonable alternatives for public consideration, rather than take-it-or-leave-it proposals. Public decisions could then be made intelligently and from knowledge, rather than under the guns of imminent disaster.

Such an information exchange mechanism would include an education mechanism the purpose of which would be to involve students and teachers and private groups in participation and learning projects connected with the agency's responsibility. Working on actual resource use and enhancement projects would reveal basic problems to the citizen-students and might also suggest solutions that can only come from the insight of the uninitiated. Specific educational techniques would, of course, be dependent upon the communication resources and patterns established in the area. But in all cases the extent of involvement should be limited only by the imagination and commitment of professional managers. If citizen participation is too restricted because of a too small or too homogeneous population in the immediate area, the education program should be extended to the whole region. In fact, perhaps the most imaginative programs could involve young people from completely different areas of the country.

Besides involving students in resource demonstration projects on public lands, resource managers must also consider ways of bringing their particular resource to urban areas by establishing miniature ranges and forests and microwildernesses, for example, on available open land. The establishment and the maintenance of the area would in itself be an educational process. An equally important function would be to help inner city residents relate to public natural resources.

It would of course be a mistake to throw open a major, controversial public project to a citizen participation mechanism without preparing the participants on small, non-controversial projects and without establishing the credibility of the new management policy. Because of the credibility problem and because of the traditional concepts of management responsibility and authority, implementing an open, people's information system will not be easy. Yet it may be the only way to proceed with conservation and natural resource management programs in the United States in the future. Although all solutions will not follow immediately from the establishment of open communications, and although all solutions that do follow will not necessarily be wise ones from an ecological standpoint, ultimately it is only through citizen participation that our society or any society can truly further the social evolution of its citizens in reasonable harmony with the natural environment.

PUBLIC PARTICIPATION AND ENVIRONMENTAL QUALITY

ARNOLD W. BOLLE†

The environmental crisis calls for new policies. The crisis has established the need for a new set of relationships between the public and governmental agencies at all levels.[1] It is possible that a new set of values can be impressed into the governmental process through greater participation in decision-making at the field level.

There appears to be a breakdown in the normal democratic process through which the public need is translated into law by the legislature and, in turn carried out by administrative agencies. Dissatisfaction is expressed in confrontation, conflict, and lawsuits as means of defending and developing environmental values. Litigation, rarely used in environmental problems until recently, has now become an important means of public access to the decision process of government agencies.[2]

Recent cases have demonstrated the usefulness of the courts in establishing environmental values. But, in the longer run we are going to have to rely most heavily on the legislative-administrative process as it is revealed in the day-to-day decisions of public administrators at all levels. As Tom Wilson puts it:

> It is possible, if not probable, that the present focus on air and water pollution and solid waste disposal will induce the public illusion that the problems can be solved by money and technology, legislation and litigation. The pervasive impact of environmental management on decision-making processes and criteria may remain out of view. But not for long.
>
> It seems more likely that the value changes predicated on the need for environmental management are more likely to emerge from hundreds of separate decisions in public and private life, as one decision after another requiring trade-offs comes up for action.[3]

Such cogent decision-making and problem-solving requires a level of public participation uncommon in public natural resource agencies. The awareness of value changes can emerge primarily through involvement of the public in agency programs at the field level. Citizen involvement in government should be welcomed by the natural resource administrators as evidence of the growing importance of these programs to the American public. Unfortunately,

---

†Dean, School of Forestry, U. of Montana.

1. *See* L. Caldwell, Environment, a Challenge to Modern Society (1970).
2. J. Sax, Defending the Environment (1971).
3. T. Wilson Jr., The Environment: Too Small A View (1970).

the reaction of administrators far too often is resentment. The many and growing instances of conflict between natural resource agencies and their publics are basically breakdowns in relationships because of administrators' lack of genuine understanding of the participation process. This gradual erosion of credibility over the past few years was not recognized by field administrators. Signs of discontent were ignored until an accumulation of micro and macro insults brought open splits.

The problem on the Bitterroot National Forest in Montana[4] is a case in point. Local public dissatisfaction grew from a small local issue to a national issue as the dissatisfied public found it impossible to be effectively heard by local officials.

> Over the past few years management and decisions have frequently resulted in situations that have disappointed virtually all the publics that make use of the Bitterroot National Forest. Frequently this has led to situations in which the land managers have found themselves isolated by these publics, and to situations in which their word with respect to land management policies was substantially doubted.[5]

The disparities in objectives and values between the public and the Forest Service grew as public concern with environmental quality intensified. The public felt isolated from the decision process of the agency which they felt was, in fact, standing between them and the abusers of the environment.

The field administrator was limited in his ability to react to public pressures by the system within which he operated. His bureaucratically determined policies had been established within the context of agency structure, and adjustment to public demands was restricted by procedures and regulations laid down by the Supervisor, Regional Forester, and Washington officials which were all locked into the system. The reward system determined by adherence to the system is not accommodation of the public. The local ranger is "denied the flexibility to meet local issues and problems on an ad hoc basis . . . . his decisions are always predetermined, at least with respect to major issues and problems."[6]

The Washington Office of the Forest Service has recently released an impressive policy statement in an attractive and easily read brochure. Public participation is recognized as an official goal and

---

4. Select Comm. of U. of Mont., A University View of the Forest Service, S. Doc. No. 115, 91st Cong., 2d Sess. (1970).

5. *Id.* at 15.

6. *Id.* at 26.

objective of the Service. Officially, the new statement sets forth that one of the official operating policies of the Forest Service shall be to "Involve the public in forestry policy and program formulation." The statement gives specific instructions to amplify the policy:

> Seek out and obtain local and national views in the process of policy and program formulation.
>
> Discharge our responsibilities in ways that make our management processes visible and our responsible people accessible.
>
> Consult with and seek cooperative action with agencies at all levels of Government and with private groups and individuals, in programs for resource management and economic development.[7]

There appears to be a regrettable gap between stated policy and the practice of that policy. The stated policy is as pure as one of the beatitudes. While consistency may be somewhat difficult to declare, there seem to be enough instances of record at this time to consider the Bitterroot situation more than an isolated case. The study concludes that: "The staff of the Bitterroot National Forest finds itself unable . . . . to involve most of the local public in any way but as antagonists."[8] Because local people do not understand the operation of the agency or the reasons for them, "they feel left out of any policy or decision-making and resort to protest as the only available means of being heard."[9] Official policy charges agency personnel to "[d]ischarge our responsibilities in ways that make our management processes visible and our responsible people accessible."[10] Why is there this great disparity between official policy and practice: possibly a cultural lag between recently recognized need at the top level and customary field practice; possibly a difference between what the field personnel hear and the signals they appear to be getting; possibly disbelief of Washington pronouncements; possibly outright disagreement between Washington and field personnel; possibly simple obtuseness by field personnel amounting to apparent insubordination. Many variations on the same theme are possible—and possibly there is some element of truth in each of them.

The desirable solution could be described as one in which there were, in truth, "a people-oriented approach" one in which the public was truly "involved in forestry policy and program formulation." A program "sensitive to the problems and needs of a changing

---

7. U.S. Forest Service, Framework for the Future: Forest Service Objectives and Policy Guides (1970).

8. *Supra* note 4, at 14.

9. *Id.*

10. *Supra* note 7.

society" and built-in "flexibility to meet those needs." And one in which all the various publics using the forests would be happy and more fully supporting of the agency and its problems.[11]

Some professional employees believe that the problem in the Bitterroot National Forest, for example, was really a failure of the Information and Education Division of the Forest Service. It was the attitude of some of the professionals that if the public relations people had been doing their job correctly, adequately, and professionally, the public would have raised no objection and the foresters could have gone about their proper business of getting out the logs. It seems almost inconceivable at this time that any public employee could be so insensitive to public sentiment.

An attitude expressed at upper levels of the agency was somewhat similar—that the public was unappreciative of the programs of the Service, was irresponsible because it did not accept the country's great need for wood, and seemed totally unwilling to learn. In other words, first the agency was right, second the people were wrong, and third how could the agency get these people to recognize it? The agency had determined the public interest in terms of its own professionalism. This approach provides an almost impossible basis for the public participation apparently desired. The professionalism of the foresters gets directly in the way.

The professional forester apparently accepts certain assumptions which would give him certan fundamental truths believed by him to be beyond the comprehension of the ordinary mortal. These truths are good for people in spite of what they as people might think or feel. These assumptions were found to be at the root of the professional attitude toward the public in the Bitterroot case. They lay in the belief of the primacy of timber as a use of the forest, based on the fear of a wood famine, interwoven with a puritan ethic that utilitarian or commodity uses are always more important than any amenity values. A blind belief existed in sustained yield of timber which, as Duerr put it, remains unchallenged over a period of recent history when even the existence of God has been questioned.[12] Still another belief is the strange assumption of maximum production of timber per acre which then is used to justify a blanket recommendation for intensive management, which in turn leads to totally uneconomic forest practices and destructive uses of forest land. These came as blanket recommendations which ignored local conditions and interests. Unless the forester, and the Forest Service, is

---

11. *Supra* note 7.

12. W. Duerr, *The Role of Faith in Forest Resource Management,* Man and Ecosystem (U. of Vermont, 1971).

willing to depart from these assumptions, or at least permit them to be questioned, any real participation in policy and program formulation is going to be a pretty one-sided business. After all, democracy is pretty difficult. And when you have a priest class in possession of ultimate truth to deal with an atheistic or ignorant public, it becomes not merely more difficult but virtually impossible. If you can't deal with the public on the basis of your preconceived conclusions, how then can you deal with them?

It should be obvious that there is only one real basis for participation, if indeed participation and not some form of acceptance is meant. Participation must mean full participation or else it is no participation in reality. The word participation does not lend itself very well to degrees. Participation implies action by those involved, not necessarily equal action but action and interaction of some kind by both and each. How then can there be mutual action in policy and program formulation?

To answer that question we must examine carefully the decision process. The decision *process*, which is fundamental to policy and program formulation, consists of several steps: problem identification, goal determination, identification and analysis of alternatives, decision, action, feedback and re-analysis, etc. The emphasis is on *process*. But note well, the question is not in which steps of the process the public should participate. To raise that query is ridiculous. If there is participation at all it must be within all the process itself—all aspects of the process or none.

We have had foresters recoil at even the thought, much less the *process*. "We would be abrogating our professional responsibility if *we* didn't work out the problem and present the public with *our* best solution," they say. What arrogant and irrelevant nonsense! To so do they would have to first identify the problem, which involves setting the goals! Foresters are no more competent to set goals for society than any other group of citizenry or citizen. Unless foresters can accept this simple fact they have no basis for participation with anyone, except as professional high priests.

Foresters have a far more important and useful function to perform than to attempt setting goals for society or determining the public interest. The professional has the responsibility to provide the public with the basic information required to understand problems and to recognize what is involved in the decisions that are made. Once the public has set *its* goals, the professional can help by applying technical skills in the attainment of those goals. Unless the professional is willing to assume this role as a contributor to the social process and hence to society, the professional may well be one of society's major problems. Participating starts by attempting to identify the problem.

Problem identification or "definition," the initial step in the decision process, is the essence of participation. A problem exists because the present situation is not the desired situation. A determination therefore must be made of two things. First, what is wrong with the present situation? Second, what is the desirable situation? What is the goal?

Problems of environmental quality involve two main aspects: the physical or biological aspect; and, the human, including as a minimum the social, economic, and political aspects. Agency resource-trained professionals are, or should be, best informed in the physical or biological aspects. Theirs is the responsibility to be expert in these matters. But *only the public* is able to provide adequate and important knowledge and insights into the social or human aspects. The contribution of both provides the basis for problem identification.

A problem identified only as a biological problem may well lead to solutions that are unacceptable to the public. Problems identified in only their human aspects may lead to solutions which might do violence to ecological conditions. Problems identified only in their biological and economic terms might well not meet social needs. Clearcutting, for example, in certain areas has been determined to be justifiable on biological and economic terms, but it offends the public. The feelings of the public are just as important a set of "facts" as the biological or economic facts. The problem solution must take account of these as well.

Once the problem is properly identified, the way is open to recognition of relevant alternatives and satisfactory solutions. In these steps public participation is important and of significant help to the professional; provided, however, that there has been effective meaningful public participation in problem identification. Unless there has been, public participation cannot be very useful later. A special warning must be given against a simplistic problem definition. The biological and particularly the social aspects must be explored in depth. First assumptions of the problem need to be reexamined during later steps in the decision process as further information and understanding are developed.

Often the solution is found to be inherent in the definition of the problem. If the problem is not clearly and properly identified, any solution arrived at is almost certain to be wrong. If solutions are predetermined by national fiat, their chances of meeting local needs are indeed remote. Unless there is freedom to solve resource related problems on a situational basis, there are no grounds for public participation.

There are further advantages to public participation in problem identification. First as well as foremost is the mutual education and understanding by professionals as well as by the public. Probably even more important is the feeling of public involvement and the acceptance of responsibility by the public for the successful solution to the problem. There is recognition and acceptance of the fact that most solutions will be compromises of some kind. There are seldom victories for any "side." In fact, the idea of "sides" or adversary positions gives way to helpfulness, toward a recognition of community and better understanding of all the elements that must be considered. Included is the fact that the agency does have certain limitations within which it must operate.

The attitude with which the professional approaches effective participation may be difficult for him to develop or even to accept. Instead of being *the* expert, *the* man with the answers, he must recognize that he is only a fellow learner with his publics. He does possess certainly some important knowledge to contribute to the identification and solution to the problem. But, so does the public. If mutual recognition of this situation is developed, the road to participation is opened. This, in essence, is the democratic process. "The democrat assumes that men in the aggregate pooling their resources—their shares of the truth, so to speak—will in the long run do a better job of guiding their destiny than will any leader, no matter how able."[13]

How is the public interest determined or protected by this process? Does local public interest become primary at the expense of a broader public interest?

There is no one public interest. One monolithic national interest in environmental quality clearly identified, or determined by Congress, or the administration, or by the head of any agency in Washington does not exist. There are many problems and many public interests. While *general* policies in response to expressed public needs can be set within the legislative-administrative process, the particulars of policy are to be determined through the expressions of public interest at all levels and with the use of the discretionary powers of administrative agencies. Public participation is the key in determining the particular expression of public interest to particular problems.

Public interest in any issue of national scope concerning a local issue is often best expressed by the local public, if it is expressed on an informed and thoroughly involved basis. The participation process

13. Roche and Stedman, The Dynamics of Democratic Government (1954).

lends itself to providing such information through open and frank discussion. The field administrator needs to develop his knowledge and understanding of the local publics in order to recognize to what extent the public with which he deals is expressing a broad interest or merely that of some special interest. This calls for considerable developed skill on the part of the field administrator. A skill which many have developed:

> [T]he field officers of a multi-purpose agency frequently show great talent for counter-balancing one group with another. Where there are numerous interests affected by an Administrative Service there will be great variations in the consciousness and articulateness of interest. Some vocational interests are much more alert than others: they are usually better and more insistently expressed than the more diffused social interests. A skillful field administrator will discover these differing social interests, furnish the inert groups with data revealing their stake in good and honest administration, release tongue-tied interests so they may make themselves heard, sometimes discover ambivalences among even the most active vocational interests which, when brought to consciousness, rob the driving, single-purposed pressure groups of much of their political impetus.[14]

The intent, however, must be participation, to seek, to discover, to find the common interest and to develop the desirable solution, not manipulation to engineer acceptance of preconceived solutions of preconceived goals.

Effective public participation within the decision process of natural resource agencies is vital to environmental quality. Achievement of the necessary public participation is not without difficulties. The achievement requires a new level of understanding of people, of human ecology, of the formal and informal structure of the community, of the lines of communication, of democratic processes. It calls for patience, understanding, and extraordinary sensitivity. It demands inventiveness and the trial of new systems and their continual adaptations.

Systematic, situational resource management requires greater levels of knowledge on the part of field administrators. It requires a new structure and philosophy of operation of the agency. The field administrator must have and develop the freedom to invite and require effective public participation in goal establishment and problem identification and solution. They are necessary ingredients to the achievement of public agency contributions to environmental quality. Effective participation is essential by all affected publics if policy is to be determined without litigation, challenged administra-

---

14. McKinley, *Federal Administrative Pathology,* 11 Pub. Ad. Rev. 17, 25 (1951).

tive fiat, public confrontations, or the continuous processes of public conflict with agency determinations that have dominated the arena within which land managers have found themselves operating. The initiative for change, in our opinion, still lies within the agencies. The changes required will come. The future will tell us whether the agencies will act as the agents of change, or merely be the recipients of the changing social process that characterizes so much of American public life today. The wise foresee the future; it is our hope that public resource agencies find themselves wisely led today.

INTERNATIONAL ENVIRONMENTAL MANAGEMENT: SOME PRELIMINARY THOUGHTS

THOMAS W. WILSON, JR.†

The assumption that rational men could devise and manage institutions to serve successfully the goals of society is embedded in Western liberal thought. At best, this faith has tended to be neglected in recent times and, at worst, has come under direct or indirect challenge. "Establishments" of any kind, including bodies chosen by the electorate, can scarcely be said to enjoy great public confidence these days.

Yet in the face of this, we now confront the novel task of organizing, or reorganizing, international institutions to cope with "environmental management" on a global scale. How?

The idea of "world government" has been nourished during its ups and downs almost entirely by the notion that this is the only sure formula for abolishing war. For those who have dreamed this dream, the answer to recurrent conflict seemed to lie in a "parliament of man" with the authority to pass laws, an executive with the power to enforce the laws, and a judiciary system to settle international disputes on the basis of law without recourse to violence.

The League of Nations undertook certain activities, like narcotics control, unrelated to keeping the peace, but expired because of its failure to prevent more wars.

The opening words of the preamble of the United Nations Charter assert the determination "to save succeeding generations from the scourge of war . . ." The United Nations has had more success in keeping or repairing the peace than is generally credited to it. Yet nothing is plainer than the fact that we still live in a world dominated by nation-states, armed beyond any previous imagination of military power, clinging to nineteenth-century strategic concepts, and accustomed to international competition for control over world resources and trade. The prospect of "world government," to deal with the environment or anything else, appears as remote as ever—regardless of whether it was a good idea in the first place.

At the same time, apart from the General Assembly and the Security Council of the United Nations, an impressive array of international organizations—intergovernmental, nongovernmental, and in a few cases, mixed—have come into being at transnational, regional, or near-global levels during the past quarter of a century. They are an

†Vice-President for Programs, International Institute for Environmental Affairs, Washington, D.C.

important part of what Teilhard de Chardin called the nöösphere and they have been hailed, not without reason, as the foundations for a cooperatively working world community.[1] At this point, several basic things need to be said about the general characteristics of these international institutions:

First, intergovernmental organizations have no resources beyond what national governments agree to delegate to them. Their power is minimal to the task at hand, restricted in scope, and subject to sudden cancellation by withdrawal of national support. Moreover, governments tend to keep their international civil servants on a very short leash and only rarely do the leaders of intergovernmental agencies develop personal influence or following.

Second, international organizations are specialized and have inadequate mechanisms—or interest—in coordination of their work. They pursue their sectoral goals without much attention to the side effects upon other areas of activity and so work, to some extent, at cross purposes.

Third, international organizations—notably those within the United Nations system of agencies—are stuck with the principle of "geographic representation" on both governing bodies and staffing patterns. Most governments want to be represented in the affairs of most international agencies and, as membership in the United Nations has grown, there has been inexorable pressure to expand the size of governing bodies, beginning with the Security Council. Last year the membership of the UN Committee on the Seabeds, for example, was expanded from forty-two to eighty-six nations. Principles of administrative efficiency appear to be in conflict with principles of political representation in international institutions.

These points are made not to *contrast* intergovernmental institutions with national agencies of government, but to say that their problems and shortcomings are highly *analogous* to those of national governments. The similarities of the institutional predicament at national and international levels of organization are especially apparent in the case of environmental issues.

Like agencies of national governments, the agencies within the UN system have been engaged, in some cases for many years, with bits and pieces of subjects now lumped under the rubric of the "environmental crisis"—soil erosion, water pollution, urbanization, population control, etc.

Like agencies of national governments, the UN agencies have been dealing with each of these subjects in a compartmentalized way— indifferent if not hostile to what other agencies, or even other

---

1. Teilhard de Chardin, Man's Place In Nature (1966).

branches within the same agency, were doing within their own specialized bailiwicks.

And like economic agencies of national and subnational governments, the economic agencies of the UN system have been focused on the all-out promotion of growth in economic output, measured by traditional quantitative standards without regard to external economic or social cost. Nor have they seriously questioned the assumption that technology not only is transferable from one geographic and cultural setting to another but that the next stage of technology in any line is automatically better than the last.

All this, of course, simply reflects the thinking of national governments which authorized, financed and shaped the policies of these international activities in the first instance. If international institutions are not well conceived or organized for the tasks of environmental management—nor endowed with an "environmental point of view"—nor prepared for decision-making on the basis of alternatives and trade-offs, it is basically because national governments suffer similar drawbacks.

Is this to say that the existing international structure of specialized agencies, like the Food and Agriculture Organization and the World Health Organization, needs to be abolished in favor of a fresh start? The answer is probably not—again an analogy with national institutions. When the Executive Branch of the U.S. government was reorganized to create two new environmental agencies, old-line governmental departments around Washington were stripped of a large number of their former functions. The Department of Agriculture, for example, was put out of the business of regulating the use of pesticides and herbicides.

But a technically qualified national Department of Agriculture presumably will be needed for the indefinite future—no doubt more concerned with such matters as land use planning than it has been in the past. By the same token, the Food and Agriculture Organization no doubt will continue to exist at the international level—perhaps minus a few of its present functions, perhaps with added responsibilities in such environmentally important areas as planning the stabilization of marginal lands on a global basis.

It is too soon to predict the extent to which the UN system will be adapted in the longer term to cope more effectively with environmental issues. The first test will come at the UN Conference on the Human Environment in Stockholm in June of 1972. That conference is expected to adopt a work program of environmental subjects on which it is agreed that some form of international cooperation will take place in the post-Stockholm years. During the second week of the Stockholm proceedings, one of the three conference committees will debate "the institutional implications" of the package of agreements expected to emerge from the conference. It is the intention of Maurice Strong, Secretary-General of the Conference, to present governments with proposals to vote up or vote down, not only with respect to specified projects for international cooperation but with respect to institutional assignments for work on each problem. The studies and recommendations for institutional assignments, however, are yet to be made.

At this stage it is easy to be pessimistic about the likelihood of a major reform or revival of the UN system to meet the environmental challenge. The difficulties are enormous. Among the most obvious are: resistance to change on the part of existing international agencies; ideological obstacles in the East-West context; suspicions that environmental quality will be pursued at the cost of economic development in the North-South context; a threatened impingement on traditional concepts of "national sovereignty"; a general distaste for international "machinery" on the part of some governments; resource allocation problems which influence governments toward placing priorities on the more parochial manifestations of environmental problems; and funding for what necessarily will be an expensive business.

Yet there are countervailing factors at work. For one thing, there is no possibility that the environmental issue will go away; one of its essential characteristics is that the problem is now permanent.

Another thing is that at least some aspects of the environmental crisis—notably atmospheric and oceanic pollution—are so inherently global that the option of national action does not realistically exist. International cooperation is literally the only way to cope.

What's more, concern for environmental quality has powerful public support. And this is what stirs and stiffens the political will of bureaucracies—whether they be international, national or local, public or private.

If public support is aroused only in highly industrialized countries, it is those countries which supply most of the political leadership within the UN and almost all of its technical and financial resources.

Finally, the environmental issue almost certainly is going to prove to be a powerful instrument for social reform—from the recasting of values and priorities to the redesign of mechanisms for decision-making. Such reforms no doubt will move at different paces in different societies but must at some point reach the international community.

In the short term, it would be sheer guesswork to predict how the world is going to be organized for environmental management. And it is important to note that any intelligent institutional arrangements will be consciously open-ended and transitory if they are to be capable of adaptation to an environmental situation in a constant state of dynamic change. Indeed a case can be made for avoiding commitments on institutional questions in favor of a deliberately experimental approach, on the grounds that so little is known about the environment that institutional design must await greater knowledge.

Yet for the longer-term, it is not quite so difficult to perceive the general directions in which institutional arrangements on environmental questions are likely to move at the international level. Six such trends are suggested here:

First, the traditional institutional boundaries between governmental and nongovernmental, physical and social sciences, professional, technical, legal, academic, and public interest organizations will be criss-crossed and blurred if not eliminated. One result will be to draw wider segments of society into an interdisciplinary process of decision-making and significantly strengthen the roles of nongovernmental institutions.

Second, new institutions will tend to take the form of "centers" serving as hubs for "networks" of institutional constituents. They will be headquarters or service centers for federations or working alliances of more traditional, more specialized institutions.

Third, international organization for environmental tasks will move in the direction of the "task force" approach—*ad hoc,* problem-oriented concentrations of people and resources with specified jobs to do within specified periods of time, after which they will be disassembled, perhaps to be replaced by other groups.

Fourth, information systems—gathering, processing, analyzing, distributing and storing data—will tend to be near the functional heart of environmental institutions.

Fifth, there will be a trend toward new and/or adapted international regional organization—less along the lines of regions defined by present political groupings and more along the lines of environmentally-related regions such as river systems, airsheds, watersheds and biomes.

Sixth, the permanent bureaucracies within international environmental organizations will tend to be the minimum required for administrative continuity; the bulk of professional personnel will serve for relatively short periods of time.

These trends probably will characterize international organization to research, study and analyze environmental issues that are poorly understood today. But this leaves in limbo the question of a more formal, more central, more continuous institutional instrument for environmental policy direction at the international level. Before drawing organization charts and raising jurisdictional issues, it would be well to pause and consider the basic approaches that might be taken toward such an instrument by institution designers.

One approach is to begin by looking upon environmental degradation as a threat against which the world must adopt a policy of defense. This leads directly to discussion of the need for "monitoring" or "surveillance"—and to talk of "standards" and "controls" and "enforcement" and "dispute settlement machinery." At this point the whole affair begins to look like a police function in an adversary setting. This approach, I suggest, would maximize political, ideological, emotional and semantic obstacles to getting on with the job.

Alternatively, one could back off and run at the problem from a diametrically opposite approach: what kind of institutions are needed to direct a positive, constructive enterprise *to improve the human environment?* How can we *develop* the environment and raise the productivity of the ecosystem for the benefit of man and nature? This approach would lead to emphasis on intensive international searches for, say, a harmless substitute for nitrogen fertilizer, etc., etc., etc.

If development of a healthy, productive environment is the dominant theme of the enterprise, it should attract leading scientists, researchers, planners and specialists from around the world. Whatever monitoring might be necessary could be subordinated to the role of supporting research, not that of a dominant policing system.

Such an approach would minimize the difficulties inherent in international agreements and the widespread suspicion that environmental management is anti-development. It might also go a long way toward offsetting the inherent lack of power of international organizations tolerated by nation-states still zealous of their independence.

An institution with a name such as the Environmental Development Authority would be operating on the leading edge of knowledge. It could acquire an international analytical capability and bodies of data available in no other place. From this would flow the prestige of authority—a kind of authority which may well be more influential in the world of tomorrow than more traditional forms of power associated with sovereign states pursuing their "interests" in a competitive setting.

ENVIRONMENTAL POLICY AND INTERNATIONAL INSTITUTIONAL ARRANGEMENTS: A PROPOSAL FOR REGIONAL AND GLOBAL ENVIRONMENTAL PROTECTION AGENCIES

ALBERT E. UTTON[†]

It is fair to say that present international arrangements for protecting the environment are inadequate.[1] The daily news headlines clearly indicate the problems. We are told of black snow falling in Sweden—snow which has been polluted presumably by industrial air pollution which has crossed Sweden's national frontier from some other nation. In this case, it is guessed that England is the culprit, and that the pollution may have emanated from its black industrial belt in the Midlands. On the Riviera—the Cote d'Azure—the French claim that Italian wastes are polluting their beaches.[2] Although the estimates differ, we are told that annually 1,000,000 metric tons of oil are spilled into the sea as a routine part of the sea transportation of this energy source.[3] A recent study finds that the national regulation of coastal states controlling offshore drilling are uniformly inadequate, and that safeguards are nonexistent.[4] The Santa Barbara spill and the Chevron Gulf spill supply dramatic corroboration of these inadequacies.

The inadequacy of international machinery is no better illustrated than the nerve gas dumping incident of August, 1970. The citizens of the Bahamas were just as interested as the citizens of Florida—in fact, the dumpsite was slightly closer to the Bahamas, but the Bahamas could act only through diplomatic channels; there was no international machinery through which the Bahamas could put their case and question. This undeniably was a matter of international concern, it was not a private matter, nor a national matter.[5] Yet, there was no adequate international mechanism available for interested parties.

[†]Professor of Law, University of new Mexico School of Law. B.A., University of New Mexico, 1953; M.A. (Juris) (Oxon.), 1959.

1. For recent discussions, *see* Kennan, *To Prevent A World Wasteland: A Proposal,* 48 Foreign Affairs 401 (1970); Burke, *International Cooperation to Curb Fluvial and Maritime Pollution,* Proceedings, Colum. Univ. Conference on Int'l. & Intrastate Regulation of Water Pollution 73 (Mar. 12-13, 1970); R. Falk, This Endangered Planet: Prospects for Human Survival (1971).

2. New York Times, July 19, 1970, at 3, col. 5.

3. Schacter & Server, *Marine Pollution Problems and Remedies,* 6 J. Am. Int'l. L. 84, 89 (1971).

4. Utton, *A Survey of National Laws on the Control of Pollution From Oil & Gas Operations on the Continental Shelf,* 9 Colum. J. Transnat'l. L. 331 (1970).

5. *See* Brown, *International Law and Marine Pollution: Radioactive Waste and Other Hazardous Substances,* 11 Natural Resources J. 221, 249 (1971).

This is not to say that there are no international organizations or treaties, concerned with protecting the environment. For example, by 1970, there were at least 15 international organizations concerned with or having some obligation with regard to air pollution,[6] and the Intergovernmental Maritime Consultative Organization has succeeded in establishing the 1969 Brussels convention, which imposes liability on ship owners for spills of oil and other hazardous materials into the ocean,[7] but no one would disagree with the assessment that these are merely first steps, and that international machinery designed for protecting the environment is either non-existent at worst, or inadequate, at best.

As in the area of air pollution, where we have 15 international organizations dealing with the same problem, the major defect with international environmental efforts is that of divided authority; the authority is divided between national and international agencies, or between international agencies, or is divided between national and local agencies, and the usual rule of thumb is that divided authority leads to lack of action—paralysis. A recent example that can be cited is that of the city official of Genoa who closed the city beaches because of pollution, only to be overruled by a national official, who said the beaches were so badly polluted that only a national official could act.[8] As Oscar Schacter recently said, "On the international level authority is not so much divided as non-existent."[9]

We are at the threshold where we must ask the question, how do we organize institutionally on the international level to protect the environment against pollution which is no respector of artificial national political boundaries? Do we organize globally, so that one all encompassing environmental protection agency has jurisdiction over all environmental threats for the entire globe? Or is that too ambitious, and should we organize regionally? Or should we organize functionally—that is, establish agencies according to the function they are to perform; an air pollution agency to control air pollution, and a marine pollution agency to control marine pollution, and a fluvial pollution agency for rivers, streams, and lakes. Or, there could be combinations of these various approaches. There could be a global air pollution agency, or a regional air pollution agency, or a global agency which was comprehensive in its jurisdiction and covered all

6. U.S. Dep't of Health, Educ. and Welfare, Profile Study of Air Pollution Control Administration in Foreign Countries, First Year Rep. 171 (1970).

7. International Convention for the Prevention of Pollution of the Sea by Oil, [1954] 12 U.S.T. 2989, 17 U.S.T. 1523, and I.M.C.O. Document A VI/Res. 175, 9 Int'o Legal Materials 1, 47, 48 (1970).

8. New York Times, July 17, 1970, at 3, col. 5.

9. Schacter and Server, *supra* note 4, at 104.

environmental considerations, or we could organize regionally and give each regional agency comprehensive jurisdiction. The options are many, the alternatives are numerous, but the agony of construction and decision is imperative.

Another question which must be faced in this effort, if, in fact, we do organize internationally, is what sort of power should the international organization have; should it have coercive power, or simply persuasive power? George Kennan argues for a blue ribbon international agency which would be a model of persuasiveness, and which would achieve its goals through persuasion, example, and prestige.[10] Professor Kennan draws upon his long diplomatic experience to outline the political difficulties in establishing international machinery for environmental protection,[11] and there can be no doubt that any attempt to give coercive power to an international body will be met with strong national resistance; and that the usual pattern is for treaties simply to be the lowest common denominator to which various states can agree. Given the difficulties and uncertainties faced by policy makers in establishing machinery for the protection of the environment, nonetheless, the broad outlines of what we need are beginning to emerge.

1. The environmental protection agency should be environmental and not developmental in orientation. Those agencies, national or international, which have had as their tradition the development and exploitation of resources are not by professional conditioning the best ones to supervise and control these same developmental activities in order to protect the environment.

2. It needs to set limits of what is permissible and what is impermissible.

3. It needs to enforce those limits as a policeman for the environment, or, if its authority is only persuasive, it needs to serve as a conscience for the environment.

REGIONAL AND GLOBAL AGENCIES

The pivotal question then arises as to what the jurisdictional limits should be. What should the aerial limits be? A possible strategy would be to use two different institutional approaches simultaneously. One could establish regional agencies which would have comprehensive authority over environmental supervsion within defined

10. "A third function would . . . extend advice and help to individual governments . . . . It is not a question here of giving orders . . . . the function is in part an advisory one and in part, no doubt, hortatory . . . . It's responsibility should be . . . to exert itself, and use its influence with governments . . . ." Kennan, *supra* note 1, at 404-05, 409.

11. *Id.* at 408.

regions. Possible regions might be the North Sea countries, the Mediterranean Sea countries, or a Western European region, a South American region, a North American region, a Southeast Asian region. At the same time, international agencies could be established over the great international media such as the high seas, the stratosphere, and perhaps the Arctic and Antarctic.

The regional agencies thus would be established in areas where there are existing national land bases with administrative and legislative machinery in being. The argument against such a regional approach is quite cogent and is to the effect that pollution does not recognize regional boundaries any more than it recognizes national boundaries. However, on the other hand, pragmatic political reality indicates that it may be easier to reach agreement on higher standards within a region with common problems and a common perspective than would be the case with an attempt at global approach. Also, the regional approach would bring government closer to the people it affected and, therefore, make the imposition of environmental standards more palatable and responsive to the people of that region.

INTERNATIONAL MEDIA

Those international media, such as the stratosphere and high seas, and perhaps the Arctic and Antarctic, would be more amenable to an international global approach, since the standards would not be imposed within existing international boundaries in most cases. The method of operation of the regional agency as opposed to the international agency would vary also. Since the regional agency would deal with the territory of sovereign nations, it probably would be most effective using a persuasive approach. It could be composed of prestigious members of the scientific community from the various countries of the region, as suggested by George Kennan,[12] and use its influence to encourage the nations within the region to bring their environmental quality standards up to those found to be technically feasible and advisable by the regional environmental protection agency. This would permit considerable flexibility since the regional environmental protection agency could constantly be upgrading the permissible standards as dictated by the "state of the art." The regional agency would be comprehensive in establishing the environmental standards for the entire spectrum of environmental concerns, such as air, and water, and pesticides. The world-wide environmental protection agency for the high seas, stratosphere, arctic-antarctic,

---

12. *Id.* at 411.

should have coercive power, since there is no legislative or administrative machinery in being to cover those areas. Therefore, this agency must have power to promulgate rules and enforce them in those areas. This should be possible, again, since there would be no sovereign states into which the international agency would be intervening. This dual approach calling for the establishment of two different types of environmetal protection agencies at the same time, of course, would be merely a beginning, but it would be a large step over the almost nonexistent institutional situation we have at present. It would be more closely tailored to meet the political realities of the present world community, using existing administrative machinery where possible, and using new international machinery where possible. By establishing regional agencies closer to the disparate citizenries of different countries, with the different perspectives of different cultures, highest environmental quality standards possible could be developed region by region. Likewise, the agency concerned with the international media would not have its standards pulled down to the lowest common denominator that all regions could agree to.

Thus, rather than putting all our environmental eggs into one administrative basket, perhaps we should simultaneously pursue two distinct paths, one leading to a variety of regional agencies, and the other leading to international global agencies.

TOWARDS A NEW METHODOLOGICAL APPROACH IN ENVIRONMENTAL LAW

DANTE A. CAPONERA†

Environment protection raises a host of questions involving practically every discipline—political, technical, social, economic, legal and institutional. The extent to which each of these disciplines predominates in any one country is determined by a number of factors at work. Among these factors are those relating to the conditions of nature with regard to the quantity, quality and degree of exploitation of the available natural resources, to the level of economic development, to the financial means available, to social needs, to the population growth and to its standard of living, to the level reached by science, technology, industrialization and urbanization and to the characteristics of its legal and institutional framework.

At the national level, from the legal and institutional point of view, several problems of major importance are encountered. In the first place, there is the problem of the internal administrative subdivisions which, being created by man and thus artificial, rarely fit to perfection the needs of nature. Then there is the problem of the functional attributions of different administrations with sectorial jurisdictions rarely showing adequate coordination or liaison among themselves. Lastly, since the ecological and natural environment embrace practically all the exigencies and spheres of human activity, there is the problem of the "vertical" functionality of any given new administration set up for the purpose of preserving the environment vis-a-vis other existing sectorial government departments.

The same kind of legal and institutional problems met with at the national level are, of course, met with also at the international level. Here again, the political frontiers created by man seldom coincide with the imperatives of nature, which, while they may vary between states and continents, are still part of the biosphere in which all

---

†Chief, Legislation Branch, FAO Legal Office; Chairman, Executive Council of the International Association for Water Law (AIDA); Chairman and Rapporteur, Working Group on Administration of International Water Resources Law of the International Law Association; Member, International Environmental Law Council. The opinions expressed here are the author's own, and in no way imply endorsement by the bodies mentioned.

human, animal and plant life goes on. Accordingly, if a solution is to be found, it is essential to consider the various possible legal and institutional alternatives at any required level, *i.e.*, at the national, regional, continental and worldwide levels, provided that such solutions respect as much as possible the imperatives of nature.

A further question concerns the methodology to be followed regarding the legal and institutional aspects if a solution is to be found for the many problems posed by the degradation of the environment. We are up against a novel state of affairs, and the prevailing methodologies do not answer present-day needs. These problems have been tackled in the past following the traditional subdivisions of human activity: agriculture,[1] industry and commerce,[2] services and transport,[3] population,[4] etc., and on the basis of laws and institutions dealing with each of these fields of activity. Occasionally, laws and institutions also refer to products which directly or indirectly pollute or degrade the environment.[5]

In view of the complexity and interdependence of the problems needing to be tackled, the traditional legal-institutional methodologies are somewhat ineffective, or difficult to apply. It has thus become necessary to develop new methodological concepts in order that the problems we have described may be tackled in an organic, rational manner. One of these methods is to consider the problems before us not by economic sectors but in terms of natural resources, first one by one, and then taken together.

The causes determining the degradation of human environment, as people have recently come to realize, are innumerable and closely interconnected. Bad management, improper administration, and unsound use of resources, whether by individuals or by nations, are chief among them. Until recently, the main aim in the development

---

1. Agricultural production, for example, may give rise to harmful effects directly (the use of pesticides, weedkillers, fungicides and chemical fertilizers destroys ecological systems) or indirectly (when contaminated meat or vegetables are ingested). Agricultural production suffers, in turn, from the pollution caused by industry, where water and the air are concerned, or from soil degradation as a result of the encroachment of new industries and human settlements over agricultural lands.

2. Increased industrial production leads to pollution of the air, the soil, and water, and to the disappearance of the plant cover, forests in particular, and fish.

3. Expansion in transport reduces agricultural and industrial areas, and pollutes the air, water and the soil.

4. Population growth, progressive urbanization, the flight from the land—all these, in their turn, lead to the degradation of the soil and to water pollution. They are responsible for the cutting down of forests and the disappearance of green areas, with harmful effects on ecosystems.

5. Such is the case of laws on fertilizers, pesticides, hydrocarbons, inorganic residues, mercury, and waste (automobile wrecks, containers and other materials, etc.); or on secondary products, such as carbon monoxide, organic acids, and nitro-compounds, etc.

and exploitation of these resources was economic. Historically speaking, there may have been some justification for this. But today there is none, for the insurgence of other factors renders the re-appraisal of present legal and institutional structures imperative. Among these novel factors are those with social implications in the clash between individual, or sectorial interests, with the collective—national or international—interest. Added to these are the scientific and technological advances in which development has gone so far as to permit changes hitherto unthought of.

The problem, as it is now realized, is one of control or monitoring: control in order to secure the rational use of natural resources. But before we attempt to develop a new methodology, we must first be clear as to what we mean by these natural resources. The scientists and the technologists have their various types of classification for resources. On the one hand we have the distinction between renewable natural resources and non-renewable natural resources. The non-renewable kind are those that become depleted with use, as is the case with minerals, which once extracted, cannot be replaced by natural means; this category is further subdivided into resources not subject to natural depletion or deterioration (coal and most other minerals) and those so subject, the depletion and/or deterioration often being accelerated by human interference (oxidation of minerals, erosion of the soil, evaporation of water, nuclear decay in the case of radioactive materials, and so on). Renewable resources may be divided into those where human intervention has so far not caused irreparable damage (solar, and cosmic radiation, and to a larger extent, air, water) and those where a "critical level of use takes place," beyond which the depletion or deterioration process becomes "irreversible," and regeneration, by that token, impossible (animal or plant species now extinct or in danger of extinction, groundwater resources, resources in the form of scenic beauty, etc.)[6]

Any conservation policy must aim at two things: first, to arrest or slow down the natural process of depletion or degradation of non-renewable resources and, secondly, to prevent or keep at arm's length the *critical level of use* of renewable resources.[7] In such cases, the critical level becomes the norm in reference to which conduct is prescribed or prohibited: it represents the "safe minimum standard."

6. Schemes are under way to replace or increase natural resources, notably in the use of nuclear, geothermal and solar energy, desalinization of sea water and the tapping of fresh-water sources below the seabed. Then, in agriculture, there is the trend toward high-yielding varieties; in fisheries, the attempt to increase stocks and the exploitation of marine plankton.

7. For a general description of conservation economics, *see* S. V. Ciriacy-Wantrup, Resource Conservation: Economics and Policies (3d ed. 1968).

Other scientists speak today of ecological systems. Thus, where two or more resources unite or are living together (micro-organisms/soil; man/air; animals/water/plants, and so on), they form an ecological system. For the conservation of such systems a number of authors advocate a policy of ecomanagement.[8] All ecosystems, moreover, are constituent parts of the biosphere—that part of the universe of nature that supports all life on earth.[9]

Yet other scientists, and many technologists with them, refer to ecocyclic systems—vital, natural systems affecting a particular resource: thus, the oxygen cycle, the carbon cycle, the nitrogen cycle, and the hydrological cycle whereby water evaporation from the sea, for example, ultimately finds its way back there.[10]

In short, in tackling these varied technical and scientific problems, we may broadly take the resources concerned to be air, water, soil, mineral and the so-called bio-resources, *i.e.*, resources that are living: flora and fauna, and man among them.

From the standpoint of the present legal and administrative framework one may note that the laws and the agencies dealing with the control and administration of natural resources are, in nearly all countries we care to mention, "use-oriented," or concern one or more harmful effects of the resources themselves. What are needed, however, are *resource-oriented* laws and institutions.

To make the distinction clearer, we may take the example of water. Without water, animal, plant or man's life is impossible. It is therefore an essential, indispensable, yet limited element There are three main types of problems where water is concerned: water, in the first place, may be put to beneficial use—livestock watering, domestic needs, irrigation, industry, hydro-power production, navigation and the rest. Generally, there are a plethora of institutions and laws controlling the beneficial uses to which this single resource is put: irrigation laws, electric power generation laws, navigation laws, industrial water use laws, navigation and floating laws, and so on. Secondly, there are the harmful effects of water to be considered; if water is inadequately controlled (whether from the technical or the legal and institutional standpoints), harmful effects ensue, such as floods, erosion and the salinization of the soil (in, say, tropical countries). Here, too, there is a diversity of laws governing these harmful effects, sector by sector and with separate administrative authorities

8. J. Mayda, Environment and Resources: From Conservation to Ecomanagement (1968).

9. The term biosphere was first used by the Austrian geologist Eduard Suess in 1875; *see also* C. I. Vernadsy, La Biosphere (1929, translated from the Russian).

10. 223 Scientific Am. (Sep. 1970). A special number on cycles in the biosphere.

providing for the control over those same harmful effects. The third and last type of problems concerns the health aspects—quality control, usually—of water. It is at this point that the question of water pollution comes into the picture. And so it is that water pollution—the pollution of one of the several resources listed earlier—is but one sectorial aspect of that series of problems arising from the use of one and the same natural resource.[11] And the inadequacy of the legal and institutional framework where water is concerned is reflected to the full with each of the other natural resources.[12]

The foregoing analysis of the existing state of affairs regarding the legal and institutional provision for the control of natural resources calls for certain remarks before the discussion is taken further. In the first place, the technical, scientific, economic and social aspects of the problems calling for solution are largely unknown to the lawyer and lawmaker whose task it is to provide precisely that solution. Both need to be informed, at least in broad outline, on all these aspects and problems which, when all is said and done, must be solved by legislative and institutional means. Again, the scientists and technologists, who are intimately acquainted with the problems created by the bad management of natural resources, are not usually the ones best able to propose the requisite legislative and institutional remedies, the latter entailing, as they do, the devising of novel methodologies, legal frameworks and government organization. The lawgiver called upon to introduce new laws and the creation of new institutions has his hands tied by an electorate that is usually unaware of the problems at issue. And so it is that, without the stimulus from the "grass roots," he puts off again and again the consideration of those same problems. And then, the reforms that

11. Even in the single sectorial field of water pollution there are special laws designed to secure control of those aspects of pollution associated with the various uses of water or specific applications (pollution due to urban, industrial, commercial, waste discharge, etc.). Thus, various institutions exercise (or are supposed to exercise) control over water quality on the one hand, and over water pollution, on the other—each institution responsible for a different aspect of one and the same problem. Examples of this division of responsibility are the public health authorities, local authorities, the Ministry of Public Works, and so on.

12. In the case of the air, both the law and the institutions are at the present time use-oriented: the air law concerns itself with air transport and navigation and the relevant institutions whereas air pollution due to industrial activities comes within the purview of other institutions and other laws—industrial or commercial; other uses such as artificial rain (cloud seeding) are governed by yet other laws and institutions. The same may be said of both the law of the sea, which concerns itself primarily with shipping, while fisheries and resource conservation are covered by legislation administered by different bodies, and of the law where the mineral resources of the seabed are concerned. Likewise, land, as a resource, is governed and administered by different laws and institutions such as agricultural, agrarian and forestry law, town and urban planning, zoning laws, industrial laws, transport laws, amenities laws, etc. . . .

are needed are of such scope and are so much at conflict with vested interests, that any attempt at changes calls forth massive resistance from economic and other sectors. Lastly, existing legal disciplines and institutional organizations are in need of major reform and bringing up to date. Thus the task is an extremely complex one.

Given the nature of the problem, the only possible approach to the protection of man's environment is the interdisciplinary one, in which all aspects—technical, scientific, economic, financial and social, and not only legal and institutional—are taken into account.

Where the technical aspects are concerned the legislator needs the collaboration of those who can explain to him the consequences of, and the interconnection between man's activities when he exploits or uses natural resources. It is necessary to consider aspects of the biosphere, ecosystems, ecology and natural resources in the broadest sense. Again, any solution, whether it be technical, scientific or legal, has economic and financial implications which cannot be ignored; the cost of the essential technical and scientific measures to be taken and the financial resources that must be drawn upon for the purpose must also be taken into account.

Then, there is the conflict between the concepts of development and conservation. Until recently, the main concern has been the development and the exploitation of resources: today conservation is on everybody's lips. If development *per se* may bring in its wake loss, damage and harmful effects, whether direct or indirect, this very fact may induce some people to emphasize conservation at the expense of development, thus closing the road to progress. The solution therefore must be sought in a balance between these two concepts.

Insecticides, for example, are dangerous and cause alterations in the ecological milieu but it is equally true that a country may need insecticides and fertilizers to intensify its agricultural productivity. One also must remember that laws and institutions are not ends but means—means of implementing policy decisions; and the decisions in this case, *i.e.,* where the environment is concerned, are better appreciated by the scientists and the technicians than by the lawyers and the politicians. There is a scarcity of lawyers in the natural resources field, a circumstance due, at the present time, to the fact that in this specialized sector the "user" can only be states or international organizations. Again, there is the pressure of vested interest of the economic and industrial operators, often in conflict with social considerations. A policy of environmental conservation inevitably implies a renouncement to a certain immediate utility by our generation for the benefit and survival of future generations. New legal and institutional concepts are needed, and precedents are lacking. In this connection, the distinction is sometimes made between the Western and the socialist countries, private ownership surviving in the former and not in the latter. The distinction, however, is out of date in many respects: in the United States, for example, one may read articles affirming that one may one day come to the point where all natural resources will have to be state-controlled, if not declared the property of the community altogether.[13] Now, these novel approaches call for novel legal and administrative structures, whereby resources may be looked on as the birthright of all generations, both present and future. Therefore, it is necessary to create— for each resource, and not, as in the past, for sectorial beneficial uses (harmful effects and quality control)—those kinds of legal and administrative institutions that guarantee the rational use of natural resources, compatible with the need for their conservation.

We have seen how the existing legal and institutional framework at the national level is largely "use-oriented," or geared to the "abatement of harmful effects" or to the control of quality of natural resources. We have considered the need for the replacement of those structures by others which should be "resource-oriented;" we shall try to demonstrate the validity of this statement in order to reach the final aim towards "rational" resource use.

Nowadays all countries have progressed from the sectorial use phase to the more comprehensive approach referred to as economic planning. Any planning of natural resources requires the fullest knowledge of: a) the abundance and availability of the respective resource, b) the existing uses and the users of the resource in question and, c) the future needs, due consideration being given to the population growth and demands. Under present legal and institutional systems, it is not usually possible to have a clear knowledge of these three fundamental data, despite their being an essential prerequisite of any planning worthy of the name. Thus, as regards their abundance and availability, the relevant data, surveys and inventories of the individual resources now available are in the possession only of the sectorial institutions concerned with their particular use of the resource. Existing laws do not oblige the sectorial government departments to supply each other with those data; still less do they make for centralizing such information as exists. It is rather as though individual banks knew their respective financial resources without there being a "super-bank" informed as to the total financial resources possessed by all the banks together. Generally, in most

13. Burhenne & Irwin, *The Coordination of Legislative Policy and the Regulation of Private Interests: Some Suggested Pragmatic Principles for Environmental Policy,* 11 Natural Resources J. 455, 458 (1970).

countries total financial resources are known to the central or issuing bank, and yet there is no analogous arrangement where natural resources—water, soils, minerals, fauna, flora, etc.—are concerned.

An entirely similar situation—of the sectorial and fragmentary approach—is encountered where present use patterns and the users themselves are concerned. Each individual institution has control through its particular sectorial legislation over resource uses and users—whether as regards the volume exploited or as regards the type of use in the more specific sense of the word or with regard to the type and number of users, but the law rarely prescribes the bringing together in a central register the various types of uses and of users of the same resource. To return to the analogy of the bank, it is as though there were no information constituted in an organic and centralized form as to who holds cheque books, who signs cheques, and how much money is being used in this way. If this were the situation in the banking world, the financial consequences would be disastrous. And yet it is just such a situation that happens where the use of natural resources is concerned.

Coming, now, to the questions of future needs, again we encounter the same difficulty: since the two sets of data we have already discussed—regarding availability, existing uses and users now in being—are inadequate, any calculations made of future needs are bound to be incorrect, even though statistics, with its special techniques can, to some extent, come to the rescue.

In practice, it is the individual, sectorial institution that sees to the inventory of the resource with which it is concerned, to the granting of permits and authorizations (again on a sectorial basis) and to future planning, per force sectorial. With current legislation, it is not possible to have a complete overall picture for the resource or comprehensive control over its use. This makes it excessively difficult to develop an overall policy for the rational use of natural resources. An attempt to remedy this situation is to be found in the formula of inter-ministerial committees, but frequently committees of the kind are not vested with the necessary powers to impose a determinate policy. Furthermore, the inevitable resistance and rivalry between ministries or agencies are only aggravated by the greater number of the sectorial economic and financial interests involved.

If, contrariwise, laws and institutions were "resource-oriented," it would be possible to make decided progress in the direction of the harmonious planning of natural resources. Moves are already being made in this very direction, and in several countries we may find the formula of Ministries established for a given resource[14] or of a

---

14. In Argentina, China, Iran, Lebanon, Mexico, to mention only five countries, there is

Ministry of natural resources.[15] Thought is being given to the possibility of enacting consolidated or unified natural resources codes or laws.[16] It is essential, however, that such a Ministry or institution should limit its powers to those of a regulatory, monitoring, or licensing nature (regulatory or monitoring agency) and not be itself the user or developer of the resource in question; it should be vested with powers to regulate licensing of all uses, harmful effects and quality control aspects of the same resource, of coordination, inspection and enforcement. The actual utilization of the resource should be left, subject to the conditions contained in the license, to users whether these users are individuals, associations, communities, corporations or development Ministries or agencies.

A "resource-oriented" administration of the kind backed by appropriate legislation would be in a position to facilitate the solution of problems posed by the protection of the environment.

Even at the international level, one encounters difficulties similar to those at the national level. An example of piecemeal responsibility may be cited in the case of water. Thus, where the question is one of water use for agriculture, the component agency is FAO; for industrial uses, UNIDO; when studied from the scientific standpoint, UNESCO; when it is a question of groundwater in connection with mining activities, the United Nations would be the appropriate body; for atmospheric water, WMO; while water for domestic uses would come within the sphere of WHO. But, the United Nations and the Specialized Agencies are no more than the resultant of their Member Nations, each of these in turn being the expression of the human community making up the particular state and engaging in the activities in question.[17]

Coming now to the protection of the environment, a major program is now under way involving the United Nations and all other

a Ministry of Water Resources; in Venezuela, a Ministry of Mines and Hydrocarbons; in Botswana, a Ministry of Commerce, Industry and Water Resources, in Uganda, a Ministry of Mineral and Water Resources; in India and Pakistan, a Ministry of Water and Power.

15. A Ministry of Natural Resources can be found in some states of the United States of America, in Honduras, Kenya, Malawi, Mauritius, etc. *See also* the recent proposal of President Nixon to bring together in a new Federal Department of Natural Resources several of the present Departments. Herald Tribune, 29 Mar. 1971. In many cases, however, these Ministries, etc., for natural resources imply no more than the addition of yet another institution to the list of those already in being, without thought for divesting the latter of their regulating powers. For this reason, the newly created Ministry often does not function properly.

16. For individual resources (Water Code—France, Nicaragua, United Kingdom, China, etc., some of the United States of America), or for all resources together: Natural Resources Code.

17. The problems of coordination between the programs of the United Nations agencies are dealt with by an inter-agency coordination body (the Administrative Committee on Coordination), which has various subcommittees on resources or activities.

Specialized Agencies. A Secretariat has been set up to prepare for the United Nations Conference on the Human Environment, to be held at Stockholm in 1972.[18] Heading this preparatory body is a Secretary-General. The Stockholm Conference will be a meeting at the world level, attended by representatives of international and scientific organizations. It will have an action-oriented program. A United Nations declaration on the Human Environment is currently being drafted. All the international organizations of the United Nations family are preparing studies and contributions for this conference and also for such action as it may take.

Since FAO is concerned with the flora and fauna, soils, water, inland and sea fisheries and the farming populations, it directs its attention to most of the resources of nature, with the exception of minerals and air (which is of interest to FAO under certain aspects only). Nor is it concerned with urban populations. An interdepartmental committee has been set up within FAO with the participation of experts of the various divisions concerned for coordinating the work in view of the Stockholm Conference. The study of environmental problems, in fact, comes under one of the five "areas of concentration" that constitute FAO's current strategy, namely, "war on waste." Again, during the second Development Decade, which began in 1970, one of the items singled out for attention was precisely the protection of the human environment. The programs designed to put these intentions into practice are implemented both at Rome, where FAO has its Headquarters, and in the field, as part of the technical assistance programs that FAO executes in various parts of the world. Special effort is to be directed to mass information and involvement. FAO's main areas of operation are: development, administration and conservation of water resources, soils, plants, forests, animals, including wildlife and fisheries, and the study of the legal and institutional implications of such resources.

At the request of the Secretary-General of the United Nations Conference on Human Environment, "Methods to expedite the adoption and implementation of international rules and standards for environment protection" has been prepared.[19] Also in preparation for 1972 is another publication on the legal and institutional aspects of environment protection. At the United Nations Secretariat, the Social Development Division, the Centre for Housing, Building and Planning, the Resources and Transport Division, and the Public Administration Division, not to mention the regional economic

18. G.A. Res. 2398.
19. U.N. Doc. A/Conf. 48/PC(II)/Conf. Paper No. 3 (1971); *see also* Contini and Sand, *Methods to Expedite Environment Protection,* 66 Am. J. Int'l L. (Jan. 1972).

124

missions,[20] all have under way programs for environmental protection. Thus the United Nations Development Program supplies financing for technical assistance in this sector to developing countries either through the United Nations' own operations or through the Specialized Agencies which carry out the programs falling in their respective spheres of competence.

Thus, too, UNESCO concerns itself with marine science, hydrology, earth sciences, ecology and social science and has programs for the conservation of monuments, the development of tourist activities and the protection of man in the biosphere.[21] The World Health Organization (WHO) defines environmental standards for human health protection, identifies hazards and studies effects deriving from environmental changes. The World Meteorological Organization (WMO) is responsible, in this connection, for the application of meteorology to aviation, marine navigation and agriculture and also the solution of problems where atmospheric water resources are concerned. The Inter-Governmental Maritime Consultative Organization (IMCO) deals with problems connected with the pollution of the sea, land and air by ships, and with the preparation of conventions designed to prevent such pollution.[22] The International Atomic Energy Agency (IAEA), in cooperation with other international organizations, has a program concerned with aspects of the radioactive contamination, caused by the peaceful uses of atomic energy, of plants, water, soils, etc. . . . The International Civil Aviation Organization (ICAO) is to contribute to a program concerned with noise in the vicinity of airports and with the "sonic boom," both problems having been aggravated by the advent of supersonic aircraft. The legal services of the United Nations and of FAO are very active in the study of the legal and institutional problems of environment protection at the international level. All the works described converge on the preparation of the 1972 United Nations Conference on the Human Environment.

Another interested international organization which has its own program on the protection of the environment is the Council of Europe. It was the Council that, in fact, convened a very important conference which led, in February 1970, to the declaration on the administration of the human environment in Europe. Activities of

20. ECLA, ECAFE, ECA and, in particular ECE (Economic Commission for Europe), which organized a conference on the human environment at Prague in 1971.
21. *Cf.* Conference on the Resources of the Biosphere, 23 U.N. GAOR (1968).
22. *E.g.,* International Convention on the Prevention of the Pollution of the Sea by Oil, 1954; International Convention Relating to Intervention on the High Seas in case of Oil Pollution Casualties, 1969; and the International Convention on Civil Liability for Oil Pollution Damage, 1969.

the Council are directed towards the coordination of national activities, the harmonization of European laws, the formulation of minimum safety standards, the creation of a European agency for pollution control and, again, towards the constitution of a European fund for pollution control. In 1968, a convention for the restriction on the use of detergents was also adopted. The European Economic Community (EEC), the Organization for Economic Cooperation and Development (OECD), the North Atlantic Treaty Organization (NATO), the COMECON and the Warsaw Pact Organizations, have also undertaken studies on enviornment protection. A number of non-governmental organizations pursue similar objectives.

The International Union for the Conservation of Nature and Natural Resources (IUCN) has appointed a Council on environmental law and, in 1968, cooperated in the preparation of the African Convention on the Conservation of Nature (fauna, flora and other natural resources); in addition, it has prepared two draft conventions for the conservation of natural resources and for the administration and protection of the environment. In the countries of Northern Europe, a draft convention is being prepared for the protection of the environment. The World Peace through Law Center has two similar projects under study.[23] The International Law Association has set up an expert committee for the study of the legal aspects of environment protection.

At this point, it will be appropriate to make a rapid survey of the activities undertaken and the solutions proposed at the national level. Here again, the preoccupation with the protection of the human environemnt is, from a historical standpoint, of very recent date. The problem is particularly acute in the industrialized countries, where the consequences of human interference with nature are much in evidence and weigh heaviest. The situation is still fluid, and the legal and institutional movement already under way, albeit of very recent date, is gathering momentum.

In the light of the experience of the individual nations and of the solutions proposed, one may summarize by saying that attempts at control and regulation are being channelled along four main directions, thus: A) the setting up of environmental coordinating committees between ministries and specialized institutions responsible for activities touching the human environment; B) the creation of a ministry, department or agency, responsible for the protection of the human environment; C) the enactment of laws for the protection of

---

23. World Peace through Law: Draft Convention on Environment Cooperation among Nations, 1971, and Draft Convention on Weather Modification, 1971.

the human environment; D) the mobilization of public opinion and the action resulting therefrom. These may now be examined in turn.

A. *Setting Up of Environmental Coordinating Committees*

Coordinating committees between ministries and institutions responsible for sectorial aspects affecting the protection of the human environment have been set up in many countries.[24] The powers vested in these committees vary from one country to another, but generally are higher than those of the ministries whose activities they coordinate. In addition to coordination, the purpose usually is to approve and control all activities and products at the *planning stage, i.e.* before plans are finalized. In this way, the creation of acquired rights is avoided, such rights being difficult to remove once the projects have been carried out. In a number of countries, it is necessary to obtain for such projects a prior authorization by a Secretary appointed to implement the policy of the co-ordinating committee. Authorizations, concessions and licenses of this kind usually lay down the measures and conditions designed to prevent the degradation of the human environment.

B. *Creation of an Environment Ministry, Department or Agency*

Several countries have created overall ministries or departments or other responsible institutions directly in control of those activities which may lead to the degradation of the human environment.[25] Thus, in the United States of America, there was set up, in July 1970, the Environmental Protection Agency, following the signature by President Nixon, on 1 January 1971, of Public Law 91-70, declaring it to be the national policy to encourage the protection of the environment and the conservation of natural resources. This law, then, enshrines a determinate environment policy, sets up an Environmental Quality Council, which acts as advisor to the President, and places under the jurisdiction of the new Agency all problems concerning the control of air and water pollution, pesticides, radiation and the disposal of solid waste. In the United Kingdom, in September of the same year, a Department of the Environment was

---

24. Among these are the following countries: Austria, Bulgaria, Chile, Czechoslovakia, Denmark, Finland, Hungary, Iran, Poland, Turkey, USSR.

25. Such is the case at present in about 15 countries, *i.e.:* Australia, Canada, Chile, Finland, France, German Democratic Republic, Greece, Japan, Malta, New Zealand, Portugal, Senegal, Sweden, United Kingdom, USA. Other countries which are considering the setting up of such environmental agencies include: Ceylon, Cyprus, Denmark, Germany (Fed. Rep.), Hungary, Iran, Italy, Ivory Coast, Malaysia, New Zealand, Philippines, Poland, Portugal, Singapore, Sweden, Switzerland, Turkey.

set up with wider powers than the component ministries. This is a kind of super ministry to which, for the moment, other ministries must report, and under which will later be brought together the Ministry of Public Works, Town and Country Planning, Health and Transport. In France, in January 1971, there was created a Ministry for the protection of nature and the environment, reporting to the Prime Minister direct. In Canada, the federal government has created a Department of the Environment, to be responsible for renewable natural resources and taking over important powers as regards water resources, fisheries, etc., hitherto under the control of other ministries or departments.

These environmental institutions have the powers necessary to enforce control over plants and projects likely to cause degradation of the human environment. The actual control is exercised at the planning stage and takes the form of the granting of authorizations. In States with a federal system of government, control is exercised also through financial policy in the allocation of funds for development or environmental protection purposes. In these countries, the problem of coordinating inter-state activities is obviously much more difficult.

C. Enactment of Environmental Protection Law

The third type of action that States have undertaken consists in the promulgation of laws for the protection of the human environment: this has taken the form of either an overall and comprehensive environmental law or of legal enactments concerned with sectorial aspects of a whole resource, or of a type of use of a resource, or of a particular product.

It should be realized, that, in most countries, there are already laws which concern sectorial aspects of environmental protection. However, the legislation in such cases, having accumulated over the years, usually lacks an organic structure, does not meet present-day needs, and fails to take into account the interconnections between a multiplicity of environmental factors. Lastly, such legislation makes no provision for financial assistance from the State. Antiquated legal systems and traditional water and land rights constitute a bar to the rational use and the conservation of natural resources. Often, any regulation for the protection of the environment is regarded as an unjustified limitation on human activities, for people do not yet understand that such laws are an integral part of the long-term and harmonious development of the rational exploitation and the conservation of resources. During recent years, a number of countries have introduced sectorial laws for pollution control:[26] United Kingdom,[27] France,[28] United States of America,[29] Czechoslovakia,[30] Hungary,[31] Italy,[32] Germany,[33] Bulgaria,[34] and many others.

However, more recently, the need has been felt in certain countries to deal with environmental protection problems by means of organic and comprehensive enactments.

Sweden, in 1969, introduced a basic environmental law.[35] This law deals with water, soil, dwellings, air, noise and vibrations; it sets up a collegiate body for the granting of concessions wherever the human environment is involved, the body in question being assisted by an executive organ—the Nature Conservation Office, which also provides the Secretariat. A regulation lists activities subject to the control by the new institution, which is responsible for the coordination, supervision, licensing and inspection.[36]

Other countries have or are considering the introduction of similar organic laws for the protection of the environment.[37]

The current trend in law-making, which has thus gathered momentum in our days, is one oriented largely towards the concept of subjecting to control and to minimum safety standards those products which be be deleterious to the ecology. Control generally concerns the production, marketing, and use of such products. In this way, the use of non-biodegradable detergents has been pro-

26. This legislation has grown in piecemeal fashion and covers such fields as air, water, soil, etc.

27. Clean Air Act 1968; Radioactive Substances Act 1960; Water Act 1963; Noise Abatement Act 1960; Waste Disposal Act 1967, etc.

28. Law on Pollution and Water Control, 1964; Decree of Feb. 28, 1960, on the Pollution of the Atmosphere; Decrees on Central Heating (1963-69), on Automobile Emissions (1954-59), on Noise (1962-69), on Parks (1960-67).

29. Clean Air Act, 1963, *as amended* (1965); Air Quality Act, 1967; Federal Water Pollution Act, 1956; Water Quality Improvement Act, 1970; Federal Insecticides Act, 1965.

30. Law on the Elimination of Solid Waste, 1965, etc.

31. Water Conservation Act, Pure Air Bill; National Building Construction Act, 1967, etc.

32. Town Planning Act, 1960; Law No. 615 on the Air Pollution, 1966; Ministerial Decree No. 1444 of 1968 on Green Areas; Law of 1967 on the Economic Development Plan; Circular of July 23, 1966, of the Ministries of the Budget and of Public Works, on the Appointment of Regional Economic Planning Committees (CRPE) and so on.

33. Laws on Physical Planning, Apr. 8, 1965; on Building Construction, June 23, 1960; on Water Conservation, July 27, 1957; on Detergents, Dec. 1, 1962; on Hydrocarbon, Dec. 23, 1968; on Air Pollution, May 17, 1965; and so on.

34. Law on the Protection of Nature, 1966; on the Protection of the Air, Water and the Soil, 1963; on Cultivable Areas, 1967; on Town Planning, 1970; on Forests, 1958; on Water, 1969.

35. Law No. 378 on the Protection of the Environment, June 24, 1969.

36. Crown Order No. 388, of May 29, 1969, on the Protection of the Environment.

37. Such is the case of Mexico (Federal Act, Mar. 11, 1971), Honduras (Regulation Jan. 22-27, 1970); USA (P.L. 91-190 of 1969, etc. . . .)

hibited in many countries, or their prohibition is being contemplated. Among the countries in question may be mentioned Finland, the Federal Republic of Germany, Sweden and the United States. Most European countries have recently been added to the list. A number of insecticides are prohibited in some countries (United States, Netherlands). Sweden, for example, has subjected to strict control the marketing of motor fuel, which may not contain lead in excess of certain standard levels.

D. Mobilization of Public Opinion and Action Resulting Therefrom

In many countries, especially industrialized ones, there has been a growing awareness of the importance of mobilizing the public opinion through the press, radio, television and the school, as a means of ensuring that the community is informed of the problems connected with the degradation of the environment by man. Such mobilization of opinion is extremely useful in achieving a number of important goals where legal and institutional aspects are concerned. Among these goals there is that of creating public awareness of these problems and encouraging people to act in such a way as to avoid activities likely to degrade man's environment. Thus, citizens will think twice before discharging indestructible waste, destroying fauna and flora, and before polluting the air, the water, the land and the sea, and will come to respect green and protected areas. In this way, too, they will find it easier to comply with legal provisions (even where they are outmoded) and will help, indirectly, the existing institutions responsible for control over resources. This public participation and awareness will also justify and facilitate the acceptance of new laws and administrative prescriptions as well as the restrictions imposed on human activities which are harmful to the human environment. In this way, too, the population itself will spur legislators to introducing the necessary reform.

The mobilization of public opinion also constitutes an important stimulus for local authorities in restricting or prohibiting activities which cause damage to the environment through the enforcement of existing—though archaic—laws. As an example may be cited the proceedings instituted by magistrates against persons responsible for pollution,[38] and the direct interventions of local authorities to reduce activities that degrade the environment.[39]

---

38. Examples may be cited of the proceedings recently instituted by certain local magistrates (*pretori*) in Italy against industries and firms causing pollution.

39. *Cf.* orders recently issued by a number of mayors in Italy prohibiting the use of nonbiodegradable detergents. Another example of this type of action is that recently taken at Los Angeles (USA), where a commission composed of experts and police officers went to

The mobilization of public opinion has also, in certain cases, developed an individual consciousness tending to consider the right to a wholesome and decent environment as one of the fundamental and inalienable rights of man, even if it is not yet generally recognized in constitutions and current legislation. Thus, a recent Federal Court in the United States authorized the City of New York to sue for damages those automobile manufacturers who had failed to mount anti-smog devices on their products. According to this ruling, any individual or undertaking or government authority able to prove grievance as a consequence of air pollution caused by automobiles may recover damages from the automobile industry.[40] In Michigan (USA), the fact that certain individuals initiated judicial proceedings against polluters led to the promulgation of a state law, in 1970, recognizing the rights of citizens to individually initiate proceedings against persons causing the degradation of the environment. In this way, there was recognized for the first time the right of every individual to a wholesome environment. As a result of the above-mentioned law introduced by Michigan, Senator Cranston and others tabled a resolution for an amendment of the Federal Constitution in order to include in it an article to the effect that every individual has an inalienable right to a wholesome environment and that the United States and each State guarantee such right.[41] The same right is recognized in certain States such as Switzerland, but only to associations and not to individuals.

Lastly, mobilization and participation of public opinion generate a collective conscience whereby the respect of the environment is recognized as a duty of the community; such a collective duty should be manifested at all levels—individual, local, national and international.

The rights and duties of the individual, of States and of the international community with respect to the environment are not yet recognized in national and international law.

In conclusion, it may be said that the problems concerning the protection of the environment are new problems everywhere in the world, and that the existing legal and administrative structures preclude rapid and whole embracing solutions. The task of the legislator is a hard one indeed due to the technical, scientific, economic, financial and social implications of the problems he is up against, but

the airport and, having established that jet engines caused pollutant emissions and noise, imposed fines and other sanctions, to the extent of temporarily bringing air traffic to a halt there.

40. International Herald Tribune, Sep. 19, 1970.
41. S. Res. No. 169, 91st Cong., 2d Sess. (1970).

also due to the ignorance of the masses and the fact that they do not participate directly in these matters. What is needed is to develop and bring into being new legal and institutional tools whereby a rational exploitation of the available natural resources, compatible with their conservation can be secured. Only in this way, an awareness and a sense of responsibility can grow in our generation, and that is essential for the survival of future generations in a decent environment.

Due to the complexity and the interdependence of the problems raised by the need to protect the natural ecologic environment and the lack of precedents in all countries (as they have just begun to face them), it is necessary to proceed cautiously before introducing new legal and institutional structures, though it is essential to make a start with the necessary studies. It is important not to create institutions and government departments which may indeed be suitable for dealing with present impelling needs and yet may well be quite unsuitable for dealing with those of the future.

Where the future is concerned, action might be divided into two main parts: one, an examination of existing laws and institutions in any interested state and in other countries to determine their functional value, and then, to seek those overall solutions for which present laws and institutions may not be adequate; and the other—which is more immediately needed—the study and enactment of new laws regulating those products which cause the degradation or pollution of the ecological environment, particularly with respect to their standards, quality, manufacture and marketing. Even if action of the kind will be still sectorial in character, it could be introduced rapidly and without it being necessary to conduct a foregoing review of the existing legal and institutional structures; and it will make it possible to deal with the most critical and immediate aspects of the problems, leaving time for the study of those necessary reforms for which our present legislation and departmental structures stand in need. It is important, however, that the control and regulating powers vested in existing institutions should be clearly defined and coordinated with those of other sectorial and interested institutions. Every institution made responsible for a different sector should be in a position to prescribe the control of products, plans, and the activities which may degrade the human environment—a control which must be applied at the planning stage, before the products are manufactured or sold. The respective laws must contain provisions on cost, taxation, financial or other contributions, or subsidies needed in order to put an end to or to restrict activities responsible for pollution or the degradation of the environment.

Meanwhile, the need clearly exists to consider the possibility of evolving new legal and institutional structures designed in such a way as to deal with each and every natural resource in its entirety and in each and every aspect—knowledge of total availability, existing uses, future needs, and, consequently, to bring under a centralized regulatory control at any appropriate level (basin, region, nation or otherwise), depending on a resource (or on other circumstances), all beneficial uses as well as harmful effects, and quality control. This may be achieved either through the prescription of minimum standards and/or the granting of licenses or concessions whereby all aspects of a particular utilization of a given resource should be considered. From the standpoint of legislation, something might be gained by simplifying and consolidating existing laws into codes to deal with the natural resources, lands, water, air, minerals, flora and fauna. Since many legal and institutional aspects of natural resources are common to all of them, a regulatory natural resources authority could be set up to control all uses. A single code of natural resources could be enacted to be administered by such authority. However, a natural resources regulatory authority should take over only those functions which concern the regulation, coordination, licensing, control, and inspection of resources use while leaving to individuals, associations, corporations, local authorities or to sectorial agencies or to other ministries, the functions of promoting, utilizing and developing different uses of the same resource. Regulatory functions presently exercized by a multiplicity of sectorial institutions and which often are combined with development functions, could perhaps be taken away and centralized into one or more resources regulatory institution, in order to prevent overlapping and interagency rivalry. A regulatory institution should maintain close contact with local and intermediate authorities and all interested sectorial groups in order to encourage popular participation and involvement.

Lastly, it would be well to consider the possibility of creating new legal and institutional structures able to recognize and define the rights of each individual and of the community at large to a decent environment as one of the basic human rights.

The evolution of new legal and institutional structures at the national level will contribute greatly at the international, regional or world-wide levels to the solution of problems arising in connection with the protection of the human environment, and will have additional repercussions on international institutions and international law in those cases where the demands of environmental protection, transcending national frontiers, call for international solutions and action. Such solutions are needed particularly in the case of atmospheric resources, international basins, the sea and its resources, migratory fauna, the flora in frontier areas and, finally, as regards international transport and trade where those resources and the products obtained from them are concerned.

THE CHANGING STRUCTURE OF INTERNATIONAL POLICY: NEEDS AND ALTERNATIVES†

LYNTON K. CALDWELL††

Whatever their scientific and technical content, the tasks of environmental protection, restoration, and management are social. They are, therefore, institutional because human societies cooperate only through established sets of relationships and procedures. Individual responsibility and effort are needed, but there is little that individuals can do unaided to solve the larger problems of man-environment relationships.

Social effort that regulates human behavior and requires public expenditure implies governmental action. Man's effort to bring his environmental behavior under control necessitates an expanded role for government. But nongovernmental and voluntary organizations also have important contributions to make to environmental protection. Governments normally move slowly and cautiously into new areas of policy. Nongovernmental groups may anticipate a need for new policies and new decisions—they may alert the public and its official representatives to a need for action. These groups may monitor public action, serving as a kind of organized public conscience. Throughout the world there are growing numbers of such voluntary groups at all political levels—national, local, regional, and international. The operational tasks of environmental protection, however, are governmental, and it is, therefore, largely through governmental organization that we will find the means to action on matters of environmental policy.

The governing of man's impact upon the biosphere poses the largest and most complex challenge that has confronted the peoples and nations of the Earth. It is a challenge to all nations capable of altering the biosphere significantly because the scope of the problem cannot be less than the biosphere itself. It embraces the crucial sub-

†This article is based upon remarks presented by the author to the Conference on the Environmental Future sponsored by the Government of Finland and held at Helsinki and Jyvaskyla, June 27-July 3, 1970.

The author wishes to acknowledge his indebtedness to the Committee on International Environmental Programs of the National Academy of Sciences for stimulus, inputs, and criticisms of ideas contained in the paper.

††Arthur E. Bentley Professor of Political Science at Indiana University; Chairman, Commission on Environmental Law, Policy and Administration, International Union for Conservation of Nature and Natural Resources; and Chairman, Panel on Institutional Arrangements, International Environmental Programs Committee, National Academy of Sciences (U.S.A.).

problem of the numbers and distribution of human populations and is closely related to that other great problem of our times—that of world peace. Effective means of action toward coping with the problem of man's impact on the biosphere must be appropriate to the problem; but the problem is not primarily the natural processes of the biosphere, but is man himself—his attitudes, behavior patterns, and institutions.

Man could not organize himself to govern successfully his impact upon the natural systems of the Earth until an adequate concept of these systems and of their interrelationships had been developed. The concept of the biosphere as an evolving, complex, and integrative total system has only recently emerged as a manageable body of scientific propositions. The philosophic origins of the biosphere concept are old, but we owe its formulation in systematic scientific terms to V. I. Vernadsky, published in Paris in 1929 under the title *La Biosphere.* The elaboration and refinement of the biosphere concept is a continuing task for science. Nevertheless, we know enough about the nature of the living Earth to understand how man's behavior is jeopardizing its integrity and viability and endangering not only man's survival but the continuity of life itself.

Unfortunately, man's social, economic, and political institutions have not developed in a manner consistent with the realities of the biosphere. Man's present institutions have not been designed to protect the self-renewing capabilities of the Earth. Within a single human generation man's explosive growth in numbers, in technology, and in demands upon all aspects of the biosphere have brought him to a circumstance in which control over his impact upon the biosphere has become essential to his future. But the *means* to this control have not evolved with the necessity for them. Modern society must therefore match its scientific and technological inventiveness with social and political inventions. A part of the price of survival, and of an environmental future, will be the reshaping of institutions at all levels of human organization to cope with the problems of man-environment relationships that man himself largely has created.

Regarding the development of these institutions, the following propositions seem valid:

(1) Because modern society and the biosphere are changing, and because we do not know precisely the kind of arrangements that will be most effective or acceptable, *institutions for the administration of environmental policy (at all governmental levels) should be flexible, and capable of growth and transformation.*

(2) Because modern society already has many institutions governing special aspects of man-environment relationships, a major part of

the task is to strengthen these institutions for environmental protection, bringing them into more consistent and mutually supportive relationships.

(3) But *the novelty of the task and its worldwide character may require the creation of certain institutions that do not now exist.* Most important of these are international bodies, or agencies, politically and scientifically competent to help national governments and international organizations develop goals, criteria, and programs of cooperative action for protection of the biosphere.

(4) Finally, because man's behavior in relation to his environment involves all aspects of his life, environmental policies and programs should not (indeed cannot) be developed in isolation. *Environmental considerations cannot be made effective unless they are built into, and thus modify, man's so-called "development" activities.* There are obvious risks in attempting to integrate developmental and environmental programs of national and international levels. Environmental values could be unduly subordinated to economic and short-run considerations. But it is through development efforts, promoted by governments and assisted by international organizations, that the environment is now being shaped and substantial environmental damage is being done.

Environmental policy at any level, to be effective, must be related to development efforts in a constructive manner, especially to modify them where necessary on behalf of ecological sanity and, in some cases, to prevent the adoption of ill-conceived development plans. The best development may sometimes be no "development." Environmental needs and values should have a strong and independent voice in governments and in the United Nations system. But the relationship of environmental and developmental objectives should be structured to ensure, so far as possible, that what is done by way of development will enhance and not diminish the environmental future.

The institutional means to action must almost certainly be a coherent, flexible system—developed largely out of existing organizations, but with a few important additions and modifications. This system must, if it is to be effective, contain the means for its own evolution and growth. We should learn from the experience of past efforts, particularly within the United Nations system, what to do and what not to do in the designing of new arrangements.

The varied conditions and constitutions of individual nations preclude any but the most generalized observations regarding action at the governmental level. The actual administration of environmental policies and programs is largely a task for national governments. But protection of the biosphere requires concerted action among all nations, and our attention therefore may most usefully be focused upon the structure of action at the international level. The basic elements of this structure already exist in the United Nations system, supplemented by nongovernmental scientific and professional organizations especially the International Union for the Conservation of Nature and Natural Resources (IUCN) and the International Council of Scientific Unions (ICSU). Let us briefly consider how this structure might be reinforced and reshaped for the purposes of environmental protection, restoration, and management.

A central intergovernmental body for policy analysis, formulation, and review is needed at the highest levels of the UN system to assist national governments, the General Assembly, and the Specialized Agencies to develop consistent priorities and programs. The membership of this body should not be too great for deliberative purposes and should involve qualifications that justify confidence in the competence and objectivity of its recommendations. The precise legal status of this body is less important than its reputation and its effective relationship with governments, the General Assembly, and the Specialized Agencies. It could be constituted in several alternative ways as an environmental council, commission, or committee—initially perhaps by resolution of the General Assembly or, perhaps, by continuation of the 27-member preparatory committee for the 1972 United Nations Conference. Permanent status as an independent council might require revision of the UN Charter, but this difficult procedure could be deferred, or could move forward, while the new body was being organized and was beginning to function on an interim basis. Without such a body at highest levels, it is difficult to see how any coherent or continuing world effort on behalf of the biosphere could be sustained.

The effectiveness of this deliberative body would depend upon the continuing availability of a high-quality supportive staff. Accordingly, an office might be established within the UN Secretariate to undertake the tasks of administration, communication, and policy analysis that the effective functioning of the intergovernmental body would require. And, because the effectiveness of this body over time cannot be assured, an alternative focus for policy formulation and review should be provided in the UN Secretariate, an officer for environmental affairs with the rank of Under-Secretary-General. This officer, although appointed by and administratively responsible to the Secretary-General, would necessarily have to be acceptable to at least a strong majority of the members of the intergovernmental body.

There is no way by which the working relationships between the Under-Secretary-General for environment and the intergovernmental council could be fully determined with certainty in advance of actual experience. Personalities and politics are unpredictable influences. A general specification of relationships would be required, but they need not be provided here. A structure that would permit the shifting of initiative between the UN office and the intergovernmental body contains some apparent hazards to harmony and responsibility. But it avoids the hazards of reliance upon a single UN entity to advance the cause of global environmental protection. It is more important to optimize the options for the development of effective international action on behalf of the environment than to adopt organizational relationships that, although logical in principle, do not correspond to the realities of human behavior.

Coordination is an unhappy word in any decentralized organization. Within the UN structure there is need for more effective coordination on environmental (as on other) issues, but there is also vigorous resistance to being "coordinated." It would be excessively optimistic to assume that a UN office or intergovernmental body could directly "coordinate" the Specialized Agencies. But the proposed intergovernmental body, linking the UN Secretariate with national governments, might contribute significantly to the coordinative process. If this body were to agree upon a need for coordination and were to present this need to its member governments, these governments, some of whom would be influential on the governing bodies of the Specialized Agencies, could promote coordination directly within these Agencies. Under the present structure of relationships within the UN system, this may be the most promising and realistic approach to a problem that has no ideal solution.

A third modification in the UN system might be the enlargement of the activities or competence of the International Court of Justice to settle disputes over environmental issues. The Court, through its power to establish special chambers for particular classes of issues, could respond to needs for more specialized and less formal procedures where controversies arise among nations over environmental rights and obligations. But the World Court does not adjudicate issues involving nongovernmental agencies, nor does it perform the informal negotiating functions of an *ombudsman,* able to take rapid and informal action short of adjudicative or arbitration procedures. But such a function might be associated with the Court or, alternatively, with the UN office and the Under-Secretary for environment.

A global monitoring network for environmental surveillance has already been proposed by the Scientific Commmittee on Problems of the Environment (SCOPE) of the ICSU. Other aspects of monitoring have been under study by a number of scientific organizations, including several groups of UN agencies, IUCN, and independent scientific projects such as the 1970 M.I.T. Study of Critical Environmental Problems (SCEP). No single all-inclusive organization for environmental monitoring is feasible, but a major center (or centers) for the assembly, collation, analysis, and interpretation of cumulative data does appear to be feasible and necessary. These functions might appropriately be performed either in the UN environmental office or in the research center which will next be described. A related, but separate, task is the review and evaluation of the monitoring system, and it should be performed by qualified scientists who are independent of the monitoring operations and agencies.

Several proposals for a world center for environmental research have been advanced. Among them are the ICSU International Center for the Environment, United States Senator Warren G. Magnuson's World Environment Institute, and a survival center proposed by former United States Secretary of the Interior, Stewart L. Udall. The greater part of environmental research will, of course, continue to be performed in the academies, institutes, universities, and governmental and industrial laboratories of the world. But a central agency for the marshalling of scientific information, collation of data, and tho organization of long range global research projects may be needed. Although such a research agency should be protected from political bias or interference, its financial needs and its needs for access to all nations and regions of the globe suggest an intergovernmental status. It is especially important that the less-developed nations feel some sense of involvement in its activities, and that their nationals receive training to participate in its investigations.[1]

Closely related to this research facility, and one of its principal reasons for being, would be a proposed environmental science advisory board or council. This body within its field of competence, broadly defined, would serve the United Nations and its environmental office in a manner similar to that provided to national governments by national academies of science. Unlike the UN intergovernmental council, or committee, the science advisory body would be independent of the UN system and would consist of scientists and other experts on environmental problems instead of

1. Initiative in the establishment of this agency might appropriately be taken jointly by the ICSU, the IUCN, and other international scientific organizations, possibly including several of the U.N. specialized agencies.

governmental representatives. Members could probably be nominated by academies of science or comparable bodies. The board, or council, would be responsive to requests for advice and information from governments, regional organizations, and UN agencies. It would require the limited research capability that has just been described.

Because two major world conferences relating to the oceans will be held in 1973,—one sponsored by the International Maritime Consultative Organization (IMCO) on pollution and another by the United Nations General Assembly on the Law of the Sea—, it may be premature to dwell at length on institutional arrangements for the oceans at this time. We are confronted by a paradoxical circumstance that, although there is widespread agreement that some type of effective international regime is needed to protect the high seas and control exploitation of the deep-seabed, there is also widespread opposition to additional UN agencies. A strategic alternative might be to replace IMCO with an International Maritime Organization representing all nations and to give it certain specified jurisdiction over that 70 per cent of the Earth's surface where national sovereignty does not now exist. Its functions would be largely those of resource allocation and policing. Responsibility for food from the sea might be retained by FAO and scientific investigation and monitoring developed through an expanded WMO, perhaps reconstituted as the World Geophysical Organization.

A final element in this projected system for the environment is a mechanism to better ensure the protection of man's heritage in historical and artistic monuments, in cultural and natural landscapes, and in the preservation of plant and animal species and their natural ecosystem habitats. The Population Trust Fund, established in association with United Nations Development Program (UNDP), may provide a useful model for what might be done. Nations with exceptional richness in artistic and historic structures, or in wildlife, are often least able to protect and maintain them.

There are two aspects to the need for international funding for the environment, and either a dual fund or two separate funds may be required. Proposals for a World Heritage Foundation are being formulated for presentation to the Stockholm Conference in 1972. The IUCN, UNESCO, and several international nongovernmental associations concerned with monuments, landscapes, and historic sites are contributing to this effort. There is also need for aid to the less affluent nations to assist them in meeting the short-range and incremental costs of environmental quality. These are costs which some nations may be unable, financially or politically, to meet in the critical years just ahead. They include the added costs of environmental protection and amenities in development projects, development of environmental awareness and education programs, and establishment of offices for environmental protection and management with supporting research capabilities. The question of one versus two or more international funds for the environment may possibly be answered by political convenience, but it is of greatest importance that aid in adequate amounts be forthcoming at an early date.

The establishment and activation of this structure could be built into the program of a World Environment Period which is presently being considered as a means toward implementing such constructive proposals as may be generated by the Stockholm Conference on the Human Environment. A two year preparatory phase followed by a five year period of project implementation is now being considered by several international organizations, notably by ICSU and IUCN. A structure such as has been outlined here might be constructed and fully functioning by this period (*e.g.* by 1980).

Only very recently such a structure—modest as it is—would have been considered utopian. Today, it is not only practical, it's urgently needed if any effective control is to be exercised by man over his use of the Earth. No system can be devised for which defects and objections cannot be found. But a perfect system cannot not be developed by imperfect men—and in any event, whatever system was agreed upon would not remain indefinitely "good." What is important is that we now match the functioning structure of the biosphere with a coherent system of institutions capable of enabling man to govern his behavior in relation to this biosphere—which has been epitomized in the expression "Spaceship Earth." We should not be deterred from this challenging effort by the inevitability of some mistakes or by differences of viewpoint over nonessential details. What is imperative is that we begin as soon as possible to build the structure for the tasks of environmental protection and restoration that must be accomplished if mankind and his fellow creatures are to have a future.

ENVIRONMENTAL POLICY AS A WORLD ORDER PROBLEM†

RICHARD A. FALK††

> Now I could accept the cutting of wood out of need, but why devastate the forests? The Russian forests are groaning under the ax, millions of trees are being destroyed, the dwellings of wild beasts and birds are desported, rivers are subsiding, drying up, wonderful landscapes vanish never to return, and all because lazy man hasn't sense enough to stoop down and pick up fuel from the ground. . . . One would have to be a reckless barbarian to burn this beauty in his stove, to destroy what he cannot create. Man is endowed with reason and creative powers so that he may increase what has been given to him, but up to now he has not created but only destroyed. There are fewer and fewer forests, rivers are drying up, wild life is becoming extinct, the climate is ruined, and every day the earth gets poorer and uglier.

So speaks the visionary doctor, Mikhail Lvovich Astrov, in Anton Chekhov's *Uncle Vanya,* a play written sometime around the year 1900. Such a set of perceptions indicates an early appreciation of the destructive relationship between man and nature that has dominated the growth of industrial society. Only recently have we been becoming additionally aware that as men we are ourselves not apart from but rather a part of nature. Man is victim, as well as exploiter. This realization, however dim, generates a sense of urgency because it is accompanied by the further awareness that the extent of interference with natural process is becoming so great as to imperil the quality and even the very basis of life on earth. As we grow richer, we become poorer; as we gain more mastery over nature, we become more vulnerable to natural catastrophe. By these paradoxical rhythms the modern encounter between man and his environment can be measured. This article shall explore one aspect of this encounter—its international, or better, its global side, as interpreted from a legal angle of perception.

Only very recently have international lawyers conceived of environmental problems as falling within the province of their professional concern. The subject-matter remains largely over the horizon and reflects the more general neglect of the international side of the recent upsurge in emphasis upon environmental quality.

The United States government, too, reflects this tendency to conceive of environmental policy as a domestic question. Indeed, there

---

† Lecture given at University of Maryland School of Law, Nov. 10, 1970.
†† Milbank Professor of International Law, Princeton Univeristy.

has been a tendency to locate much of the work on this matter within the Department of the Interior and the first year's report of President Nixon's Environmental Quality Council was almost exclusively confined to domestic discussion. Of course, there is no doubt that the most manifest impacts of environmental problems are currently found on the domestic level, but these are not potentially the most serious for either the United States or for the world. The growth and spread of industrial society in a world of rising population and increasing GNP per capita places ever-increasing pressure on the life-support systems of the earth, air, and water that makes this planet habitable. Nothing less than the survival of life on earth is endangered by present patterns of land, water, and air use throughout the world, but especially in the rich, populous, high-GNP countries. The extent of danger and its immediacy are subject to controversy, but not the basic contention that we are using the earth in a manner that is threatening in numerous ways the delicate balance of natural forces that provides the climate, the oxygen, the food, and the energy we need for life. Also not subject to controversy is the assertion that the absence of global regulation results in a variety of damaging uses of the world environment, ranging from the continuing testing of nuclear weapons in the atmosphere and underground, to the large-scale spillage of oil into the oceans, to the increasing concentrations of DDT (and related compounds) in the bodies of all animal species, including man, to the disposal of highly toxic nerve gas in the oceans in containers that may or may not leak, and so on. The agenda of environmental issues with an international aspect is limited only by the knowledge and fortitude of the compiler.

The basic reorientation of the understanding that is needed involves an acceptance of what might be called "the ecological imperative." Franklin Frazer Darling has said that people are growing tired of the word "ecology" before they know what it means. And although one can find some encouragement in the fact that the DAR and other ultraconservative groups have started to attack the environmental movement as unamerican, there is still a real danger that the unquestionably faddish quality of the sudden upsurge of interest will draw attention away from the very real seriousness of the situation. For as Senator Gaylord Nelson put it so well ". . . it can't be a fad, because it becomes more difficult to breathe each day." Essentially, the ecological perspective emphasizes the delicate interdependence of natural processes at all levels of life activity, from a single organism, to a lake or stream, to the world itself. Such a perspective entails an emphasis on the wholeness of view and encourages those who propose interferences with life systems to comprehend and assess the whole set of displacements caused. Translated into political terms, the ecological imperative requires coherent and overall management of all systems of life activity, institutions with the knowledge and powers to uphold the balance of the ecosystems, and a reorientation of human loyalties and political priorities to entrust such institutions with the resources and respect that are needed to do their task. The international order, based above all on competing and unequal sovereign states, has a structure and a set of traditions that are peculiarly inimical to giving any effective reality to the ecological imperative. Very briefly the international order rests on an operative set of assumptions that presuppose the rationality of minimal encumbrance upon sovereign initiative:

> The assumption that human and industrial activities carried on within national territory are not dangerous to the world community as a whole;
> The assumption that the permissive use of the oceans and airspace serves the general interest of mankind;
> The assumption that land use and ocean use are generally compatible;
> The assumption that various ocean uses are compatible with one another;
> The assumption that oceans and the atmosphere are so large that they can absorb all wastes of human endeavor;
> The assumption that misuse of the environment is reversible and is, at worse, local in its impact;
> The assumption that all governments have a shared equivalent interest in maintaining and restoring environmental quality.

In my judgment each of these assumptions is incompatible with the development of an adequate structure of control and guidance with respect to environmental subject-matter. The significance of this incompatability is of very recent origin and has basically to do with the *scale* and *scope* of human activities pressing up against the tolerance limits of these basic life support systems and is, in this sense, different from the spiritual and aesthetic concerns evident to Chekhov's character, Dr. Astrov.

It is against this general background that I would like to address myself to the role of international law in this area. The capacity of international law to operate successfully in the world as now structured depends on its ability to develop norms, procedures, and regimes that serve the perceived interests of most governments on most occasions. In other words, there needs to be a *consensus of governments* that rests largely on the perception of *common* or *reciprocal* interests. The accentuation of this *voluntaristic* basis of international legal order has been a byproduct of the declining utility of military power as a source of general order within international affairs. A combination of prudence, arising from the dangers of large-scale warfare, and of normative change, arising from the movement to eliminate colonialism and to outlaw intervention, has virtually eliminated the police role of the great powers in world affairs outside the realm of strategic geo-politics [*i.e.,* sphere of influence interventions]. Such a development, largely unnoticed but highly significant, can be illustrated by the unwillingness and inability of capital-exporting or investor countries to use force any longer to protect their investments from confiscatory expropriation or the inability of the United States to impose its will on Chile, Peru, or Ecuador with respect to the seizure of fishing vessels far from their shore. Rather than alienate these Latin American allies there has been an internal political compromise struck—the fines imposed on our fishing vessels are paid but reimbursed by the U.S. Government, that is, by taxpayers. The same change in world context was evident in the unexpectedly strenuous protest by African governments against the so-called Stanleyville Operation in 1964 when the United States, the United Kingdom, and Belgium cooperated to rescue approximately 1000 white hostages being held in the course of the Congo Civil War. The point, then, is that outside of high politics, international legal order depends for its effectiveness more than ever on its capacity to serve the *common interests* of mankind as these interests are understood and perceived by governmental leaders around the world.

In approaching environmental questions this issue is of great importance because perceived interests as of now are largely *antagonistic.* Leaders from poor countries see the environmental agenda as a subtle way to deprive them of the wealth and power that have accrued to the advanced industrial societies. Furthermore, these governments, regardless of vast differences in ideological outlook and domestic situation, all share an emphasis on maximum economic development in a minimum period of time. If environmental prudence will inhibit agricultural and industrial growth it will be seen as an interference with basic national aspirations. These governments also tend to define the environmental situation in light of its domestic impact, and therefore confronted by a hungry, expectant, and growing population their leaders agree that the immediate need is to generate pollution, so to speak, by stimulating growth, rather than protect the environment through costly anti-pollution procedures. From a Third World perspective, then, the problems associated with environmental degradation, to the extent that they exist, should be dealt with in such a way as to avoid any interference with prospects of economic development. Such an attitude also has been evident in Third World reactions to proposals that hard pesticides such as DDT be banned; here, the situation is further complicated by the role of DDT in fighting tropical diseases such as malaria and in the need for massive reliance on pesticides to make viable "the Green Revolution." In sum, given the fantastic disparity in per capita GNP between rich and poor countries and the extraordinary pressures that exist to alleviate mass misery throughout Asia, Africa, and Latin America, there is no basis for concluding that common interests exist with respect to the new ecological agenda. Surely on high levels of abstraction—just as with human rights—rhetorical affirmation of environmental quality has been solicited and will be achieved, but such an affirmation does not produce the real structures of *regulation* and *control* that are so urgently needed.

Of course, it would be a grave distortion to pretend that the principal resistance to a rational policy on the international environment comes from Third World capitals and the diversity of perception that truly exists on these matters. More consequential by far are the competitive dynamics of the relations among the principal industrial states, relations that rest on rivalry and an overriding concern with self-interest. The emerging world trade war, the rebirth of protectionism, is but one dramatic indication of the extent to which the general welfare continues to be sacrificed on behalf of well-organized sub-national interest groups. Therefore, even though the interests among developed countries are convergent in relation to environmental quality, the prospect of an *implementing* (as distinct from a *pious*) *consensus* on action remains poor. Just as with disarmament, perhaps even to a greater extent, the dynamics of competition lead to an endless search for *relative advantage,* to distrust of rival proposals, and to a self-interested set of perceptions that induce contradictory assessments of what constitutes a reasonable adjustment. Surely environmental defense of any adequate sort requires that major economic burdens be shouldered. However, the extent of these burdens and their allocation is exceedingly difficult to agree about in a world system that exhibits such strong tendencies toward national egoism and nationalization of truth.

Let me restate the argument up to this point—international law works where perceived common interests stimulate voluntary action or where coercive pressures can promote the position of the stronger side in situations of adverse interests and impose an involuntary solution. Environmental use has been successfully regulated on an international basis up to recent times by a reliance upon territorial sovereignty to regulate land use and permissive community arrangements to regulate ocean and airspace use. Such permissiveness has been accompanied by a legislative assertion of special claims ranging from the right to use the high seas to test nuclear weapons to the already mentioned claim of some Latin American countries to close off large portions of the high seas as territorial waters (that is, by assimilating the *permissive community* regime of the oceans into the *exclusive sovereign* regime of land territory). This kind of guidance setup cannot meet the emerging needs for regulation given the agenda of environmental problems. This agenda can be broken down into four categories of issues:

Category I: ultra-hazardous activity such as tanker collisions, radioactive and nerve gas waste disposal, nuclear testing;

Category II: cumulative hazards to climate and resource purity arising from sustained patterns of human activity such as burning of fossil fuels, discharge of mercury, lead, DDT, and oil;

Category III: mounting dangers of extinction to animal species arising from excessive exploitation, such as to the species of the great whale, the Arctic polar bear, and a variety of fish;

Category IV: allocating rights among incompatible uses such as between ocean mining and fishing or as between economic gain and aesthetic quality of nature.

Most environmental problems on an international level fall into one of these four categories of concern. Unregulated permissiveness poses the problem and therefore is not likely to lead to a solution. The world-order challenge for international law depends on the capacity of the system to generate *cooperative regimes* in situations of competitive use and inconsistent interests and priorities. These cooperative regimes can be of three broad types, each of which can be briefly illustrated: *Voluntary Special Purpose Regimes, Tradeoff Regimes,* and *General Purpose Regimes.*

A. *Voluntary Regimes*

These regimes depend for their viability on discovering and clarifying a common interest of a specific sort and imposing reasonable conditions for its fulfillment. They can be expected to work where the governments primarily involved do have a reasonably common position and a reasonably shared perception of interest. The United States has put forward recently a proposal at a NATO conference to ban all international ocean spillage of oil by the mid-1970's. Compliance would require new ship designs in which the mixture of oil and water in ballast was eliminated. Such actions would impose fairly heavy additional operating costs on shipping interests and oil companies. Any one country has an incentive to get all the other countries to adopt such anti-pollution standards but not to burden its own operations. The dynamics of self-interest lead to the paradox of aggregation whereby the sum of separate assessments of self-interest produces a community disaster in which each actor shares in the loss. Such a situation also exists with respect to endangered ocean species of whale, seal, and bear; the *individual* incentive to maximize self-interest by earning the highest possible annual profit produces a lower and lower aggregate yield. Voluntary regimes of restraint have not operated very successfully where strong individual interests to violate exist. The regulatory weakness can also be illustrated by attempts to impose collective economic sanctions and by efforts to restrain the sale of arms to foreign countries. Whenever the costs of compliance seem merely to transfer the benefits of the market to a competitor, the incentive to violate is strong and can only be fully frustrated by a regime of uniform enforcement that treats all actors alike and makes them all bear equally the burden of serving the common interest. Therefore, it seems unrealistic to rely on the efficacy of *voluntarism* to serve the community concern in Category II or Category III situations, although such standard-setting regimes may work reasonably well in relations to Category I or Category IV situations. It is not surprising, therefore, that such halting progress has been made in securing ratification of the 1969 Amendments to the 1954 International Convention for Prevention of Pollution of the Sea by Oil. (Sixteen gallons per nautical mile; no ratifications to date.) Governments are reluctant to impose costly unilateral restraints under any conditions, but especially in the absence of assurance that they are not merely making more profitable the conditions of operation for rival governments.

B. *Trade-off Regimes*

In these regimes there is some acknowledgment of diverse interests and some conscious effort to create a uniform incentive by building explicit tradeoffs or positive payoffs for each set of interests into the structure of the agreements. The idea here is to replace the permissive consensus—that is, wherein each government can do as it likes—with a regulatory consensus in which stability of expectations and other gains are substituted for the loss of freedom. President Nixon's path-breaking seabed proposals for May 23, 1970, are an exceptionally interesting example of an attempt to establish a trade-off regime based on forging a new set of reciprocal interests. Mr. Nixon's language of presentation is worth quoting because it represents such an explicit attempt to meet the challenges of the ecological age with the resources of the present world-order system:

> The nations of the world are now facing decisions of momentous importance to man's use of the oceans for decades ahead. At issue is whether the oceans will be used rationally and equitably and for the benefit of mankind or whether they will become an arena of unrestrained exploitation and conflicting jurisdictional claims in which even the most advantaged states will be losers. The issue arises now—and with urgency—because nations have grown increasingly conscious of the wealth to be exploited from the seabeds and throughout the waters above, and because they are also becoming apprehensive about the ecological hazards of unregulated use of the oceans and seabeds.

The substance of the Nixon proposals are really beside the point here, but briefly they seek to establish three zones of control which provide: (1) special status to coastal interests up to an ocean depth of 200 meters; (2) a trusteeship regime for an intermediate zone to the edge of the seabed (the so-called "continental margins") in which coastal states, organized world community, and developing countries share the proceeds; and (3) an international community regime with complete authority over activity on the ocean floor.

Such an approach contrasts with the unilateralism and exclusivity of the series of claims, initiated by the Truman Proclamation of September 28, 1945, to exercise national jurisdiction over the resources of the continental shelf. (These claims were later given international recognition in the Geneva Convention of 1958.) Such a change in initiative is of profound significance in attempting to test the limits of the existing world-order system to sustain regimes of common interests in (a) situations where ecological management is needed; (b) situations where major economic resources are involved; and (c) situations where the interests of governments—because of access, capability to exploit, and distinct resource bases—are clearly diverse. The seabed solution—or its eventual failure—provides a major test-situation of the *reformist* capabilities of the international legal system. To quote Mr. Nixon once again ". . . the stark fact is that the law of the sea is inadequate to meet the needs of modern technology and the concerns of the international community. If it is not modernized multilaterally, unilateral action and international conflict are inevitable." The preliminary problem, of course, is to secure some kind of consensus as to what is a reasonable tradeoff among the diverse interests and then to evolve the kind of international machinery that implements the consensus in reliable fashion. It remains to be seen whether rich countries and poor countries can converge sufficiently on a common perception of reasonableness to bring tradeoff regimes of this sort into being by agreement and to sustain them thereafter. The failure to achieve such a consensus—and there are internal as well as international diversities of interest that block progress—will almost certainly intensify the destructive character of competition in all major arenas of international life and will accentuate the inequality of benefits deriving from the new frontiers of human technology.

C. General Purpose Regimes

The final reformist possibility is to establish a central guidance apparatus for environmental matters on a global level. There are proposals by George Kennan, U Thant, and Lynton Caldwell for a World Environmental Authority. In essence, the call is for a new international institution, probably loosely affiliated with the United Nations, to be given a comprehensive mission in relation to environmental policy. Although I think such a development is both desirable and likely to take shape in some form—perhaps as a result of recommendations to be put forward by the 1972 UN Conference on the Human Environment in Stockholm—it should be understood that it is not likely in the immediate future that such an institution will be given a strong independent role. Such an institution may be able to gather and disseminate information bearing on principal environmental concerns, thereby helping to clarify and sustain a common interest in taking various curative or preventive actions. But for reasons already indicated, the prevalence of competitive relations among the states and the traditions of self-interested decision-making make it highly implausible to expect a voluntary international association of governments to have more than nominal powers in an area of diverse interests and highly divergent perceptions as to the seriousness of the alleged problems. As with such other areas as human rights and disarmament, where abstract sentiments of agreement often obscure concrete divergencies, there is little prospect of moving the world community into a position to set environmental policy and bind governments to adhere. Yet, as argued at the outset, the interdependence of action and the paradox of aggregation make such a regulatory effort essential. The thrust of my argument is that a general purpose regime on environmental policy is helpful and may be established in the next few years, but that its capabilities are almost certain to be severely curtailed by the realities of the international setting, most especially by the absence of a consensus on policy and action that moves beyond a vague rhetoric of concern and aspiration. Therefore, the role to be played by such a general purpose regime will be confined to information-gathering and monitoring, rather than extending to the restoration of balance and quality to the world environment. Such a conclusion prompts a certain despair because the problems are growing more serious at a far greater rate than is the emergence of a consciousness or a world structure of authority that would allow for their solution.

CONCLUSION

The analysis above leads inevitably to the conclusion that the present international legal system can generate, at best, stop-gap measures that will defer the day of ecological reckoning, but that there is no realistic prospect that the conditions giving rise to this dangerous situation can be eliminated by reforms of the sort described above that involve the establishment of new international law regimes. The fundamental environmental pressures are consequences of the way in which domestic societies are organized and interact with one another. Put more plainly, the world-order system is constituted by states in very different circumstances, each seeking to maximize its gross national product and competing with each other for as large a share of the gross global product as possible. The counter-structures of restraint and coordination are weak both within national bureaucracies and at the international level. The over-riding need of mankind is to confront the reality of an organizational crisis in human affairs. The system organizing human loyalties, security, and material well-being under the institutional control of the sovereign state cannot cope successfully with the strains caused by the modern interplay between high technology and expanding population. Only a more centrally conceived and constituted world-order system can hope to deal with this new agenda of challenge. Whether such a central solution comes about primarily by consent or coercion, or as the alternative to rather than as the aftermath of catastrophe are among the great unanswered questions of our time. What is clear is that unless a world-order movement with this general vision emerges in the next few years in the principal portions of the world, the prospects for further ecological deterioration will become increasingly certain and the prospects for human survival will become increasingly uncertain. In Buckminster Fuller's apt summation, the choice is literally one of "utopia or oblivion." Such a world-order movement will have to struggle against the forces mobilized by entrenched interests and values; that is, it will be necessary to overcome the reaction of the DAR or the derision poured upon so-called "prophets of doomsday" by soft-headed optimists and dreamy-eyed technocrats who continue to believe that science can undo what science has done. The main terrain of struggle is in the human spirit and in the accompanying effort to establish a new orientation toward the relationship between man and nature, and a new and realistic sense of the world as an isolated island space, and a new set of global institutions and values to sustain the new vision.

International law has two principal roles to play in this central drama of human experience:

First, international lawyers can clarify common interests in relation to regimes designed for environmental defense, whether these regimes are of the special purpose, tradeoff, or general purpose variety.

Second, international lawyers can establish models of future world-order systems that seem to meet the functional needs of the day without building a gigantic prison for the human spirit; the depiction of models and the specification of the transition strategies to move from here to there are part of the initial task of mobilizing popular support for the urgent need to recast the world-order system of sovereign states in the form of a community-oriented central guidance world-order system.

Of course, the task is far away, and that is why we have to begin now, like the retired French general who, when told by his gardener that an exotic Oriental fruit tree he wanted planted wouldn't take mature shape for thirty years or so (or long after his death), replied "in that case, don't wait until this afternoon to plant it."

But the task is broader, of course, than the skills of the lawyer; it needs to be informed by a positive vision of what the world could be like, nothing less than a rebirth of confidence in the future of mankind. I conclude where I began, with another quotation from *Uncle Vanya*, this time from a character who reflects upon Astrov's strange crusade for environmental quality:

> Every year Mikhail Lvovich plants new forests; he's already received a bronze medal and a citation. He makes great efforts to prevent the old forest from being laid waste. If you listen to him, you'll fully agree with him. He says that the forests beautify the earth, that they teach man to understand beauty and induce in him a nobility of mind. Forests temper the severity of the climate. In countries where the climate is mild, less energy is wasted in the struggle with nature, so man is softer and more tender; in such countries the people are beautiful, flexible, easily stirred, their speech is elegant, their gestures graceful. Science and art flourish among them, their their philosophy is not somber, and their attitude toward women is full of exquisite courtesy. . . .

POLLUTION & LIABILITY PROBLEMS CONNECTED WITH DEEP-SEA MINING

L. F. E. GOLDIE†

The sanction underlying the threat of liability, especially strict liability, may not provide the only, or even the relevant, deterrent to pollution of the sea. Regulation and control of uses of the sea and of the land, including the outright prohibition of some activities and substances, surveillance, experimentation and the search for antidotes or alternative beneficial uses, and their imposition when proved, are also necessary. In this wider context liability merely becomes a peripheral and incomplete means of enforcement, just as it must always remain a less than one hundred percent satisfactory remedy for the injured. This article is intended to bear upon the liability issue, remembering its standing as a relatively inferior, insensitive and unsatisfactory weapon in the armory of remedies and controls.

Analysis of the problem will be served by identifying some examples of emerging deep-sea mining activities which will increase the hazards of pollution and connected harms, and by identifying other emerging or possible maritime uses which may be more than usually vulnerable to those harms. It will then be possible to indicate liability issues in terms of conduct which operates expropriatively by throwing the burden of risks onto others as contrasted with conduct which is vulnerable to expropriation through the creation of risk by others.[1]

EMERGING TECHNOLOGIES AND INCREASING RISKS OF HARM

A. Examples of Deep-Sea Mining and Related Activities Which Increase Risks to Others

Many large-scale ocean enterprises functioning on the frontiers of science and technology engage in operations with a high degree of cost and risk. They would all appear to have one thing in common. They illustrate how some of the emerging scientific uses of what the ocean has to offer, these being generally justified by man's scriptural

---

†Charles H. Stockton Professor of International Law, Naval War College, Newport, R.I. (1970-71); Director, International Legal Studies Program, Syracuse University College of Law.

1. This thought was basic to this writer's *Liability for Damage and the Progressive Development of International Law,* 14 Int'l & Comp. L.Q. 1189, 1222-24, 1254-58 (1965) [hereinafter cited as *Liability for Damage*]. Many of the thoughts in this earlier study will be central in the pages which follow.

mandate to exercise mastery over nature and as serving the general benefit, may greatly threaten the environment and bring waste, poverty, and misery in their train. They may, indeed, constitute not merely a risk of economic loss, but at times a possibility of bodily harm and even of sudden death. Economies which may seem attributable to technological breakthroughs and to size may, on a more careful review, come to be seen, at least in part, as savings made at the expense of third parties or the environment. Such economies will precipitate increased hazards of pollution. These two items, cost and risk, may, furthermore, be seen as reciprocal. The more an enterprise is called upon to shield third parties and the environment from the risks of disasters which may result from its operations, the higher its operating costs tend to become. Conversely, the more such an enterprise is permitted to expose third parties to harm, or the environment to devastation, the more it will be in a position to reduce its operating costs. The costs of protection, however, still remain; they become "social costs"[2] and are merely transferred from the enterprise to the environment or to society. Enterprises which enjoy the privilege of passing on their costs clearly increase the risk of harm to other users. In doing so, the risks they deliberately create effectively expropriate from members of the public the expectations that they will continue to enjoy security of person and property and the environmental amenities of life. Examples of this group of expropriative activities include the winning of minerals from the sea floor and related activities.

1. Mineral Resources from the Ocean
(a) Fossil Fuels under the Seabed

For a considerable time oil has been won from shallow seabed areas. But recent improvements in technology have allowed economically feasible oil drilling to take place beyond the two hundred meter bathymetric contour line[3] (the outer limit of the legal continental shelf as defined in terms of depth[4]). This tech-

2. For a discussion of this issue, and the thesis that throwing the costs of extra-hazardous activities onto the shoulders of those who are exposed to the risk of harm should provide a basis for compensation, see *Liability for Damage, supra* note 1, at 1189 *passim* and *especially* 1212-13. *See also* Goldie, *Responsibility for Damage Caused by Objects Launched into Outer Space,* British Institute of International and Comparative Law, Current Problems in Space Law 49, 54, 56-57 (1966).

3. For an outline of this trend off the coasts of the United States, *see* Goldie, *The Exploitability Test—Interpretation and Potentialities,* 8 Natural Resources J. 434, 434-36 1968), *especially* notes 1 and 2 and the accompanying text and Appendix I.

4. *See* Convention on the Continental Shelf, *done* April 29, 1958, [1964] 15 U.S.T. 471, T.I.A.S. No. 5578, 499 U.N.T.S. 311. The other conventions which the 1958 United Nations Conference on the Law of the Sea at Geneva produced were: Convention on the

nological trend[5] will become intensified as demand increases.[6] Thus *Our Nation and the Sea* tells us:

> Twenty-two countries now produce or are about to produce oil and gas from offshore sources. Investments of the domestic offshore oil industry, now running more than $1 billion annually, are expected to grow an average of nearly 18 per cent per year over the coming decade. Current free world offshore oil production is about 5 million barrels per day or about 16 per cent of the free world's total output.[7]

As claims to develop more offshore oil and gas resources go out into deeper and deeper regions, they will inevitably give rise to even more acute problems of polluting the seas and the coasts.

More injurious to the environment than such dramatic blowouts as those in the Santa Barbara Channel and the Gulf of Mexico, and such massive oil spills from giant tanker casualties as those of the *Torrey Canyon,* and the more recent collisions in San Francisco Bay and the English Channel, are the day-to-day minor spills and leaks of oil from a multitude of activities. Thus:

> Pollution of the marine environment through massive oil spills has received increasing public notice because of several recent dramatic situations involving damaged tankers. These occurrences highlighted

Territorial Sea and the Contiguous Zone, *done* April 29, 1958, [1964] 15 U.S.T. 1606, T.I.A.S. No. 5639, 516 U.N.T.S. 205; Convention on the High Seas, *done* April 29, 1958, [1962] 13 U.S.T. 2312, T.I.A.S. No. 5200, 450 U.N.T.S. 82; Convention on Fishing and Conservation of the Living Resources of the High Seas, *done* April 29, 1958, [1966] 17 U.S.T. 138, T.I.A.S. No. 5969, 559 U.N.T.S. 285.

5. Already experimental drillings have been conducted through over 11,000 feet of water into the sediment beneath. *See, e.g.,* the report of the *Glomar Challenger's* drilling through 11,720 feet of water and a further 472 feet of sediment in the Gulf of Mexico to discover oil in submarine salt domes, N.Y. Times, Sep. 24, 1968, at 44, col. 2. *See also, id.,* Nov. 26, 1968, at 28, col. 2. For a report of discoveries by the U.S. Navy research ship *Kane* of clues to "oil rich salt domes" in the deep ocean off the west coast of Africa, *see, id.,* May 13, 1969, at 29, col. 1. For reports on oil exploration plays on the continental shelf and slopes of the United States and Canadian Atlantic coasts, *see, id.,* Aug. 30, 1968, at 25, col.

6. These include: (1) permits have been issued for the exploration of 260 million acres or nearly 410,000 square miles of seabed; (2) the Shell Oil Company will use a semi-submersible rig, the *Sedco H,* which will drill as deep as 25,000 feet while sitting on the seabed under 100 feet of water, or afloat through 800 feet of water; (3) most of the areas now being explored are within 200 miles of the largest cities of the United States, while other areas are close to major Canadian cities; and (4) like the North Sea, and in contrast with the Gulf and Southern California coasts, most of this area is extremely turbulent.

6. For projections of increases in both demand for and production of offshore oil "twenty years from now," *see* U.S. Commission on Marine Science, Engineering and Resources, Our Nation and the Sea 122-30 (1969) [hereinafter cited as Our Nation and the Sea.] In addition to Our Nation and the Sea, the Commission has published three volumes of Panel Reports: 1 Science and Environment (1969); 2 Industry and Technology: Keys to Ocean Development (1969); 3 Marine Resources and Legal-Political Arrangements for Their Development (1969) [hereinafter cited as Panel Reports and prefixed by the appropriate volume number].

7. Our Nation and the Sea, *supra* note 6, at 122.

the ease with which natural resources and the economic life dependent upon them could be wiped out by one unfortunate incident, and focused attention on the possibility of other such incidences. Yet the most pervasive pollution comes not from headlined oil spills but from the many activities that take place every day underwater. There are about 16,000 oil wells off the continental United States, and the number is increasing by more than one thousand a year. There is rightful concern that oil well blow-outs, leaks in pipelines, and storm damage can cause pollution that could ruin large parts of commercial fisheries, sports-fishing, and recreational areas.[8]

(b) Surficial Deposits

Some seven years ago Dr. John Mero told us:

[S]ubstantial engineering data and calculations show that it would be profitable to mine [from the sea] materials such as phosphate, nickel, copper, cobalt and even manganese at today's (1964) costs and prices. And I firmly believe that within the next generation, the sea will be a major source of, not only those metals, but of molybdenum, vanadium, lead, zinc, titanium, aluminum, zirconium, and several other metals as well.[9]

And added:

But most important, the sea-floor nodules should prove to be a less expensive source of manganese, nickel, cobalt, copper, and possibly other metals than are our present land sources.[10]

Although these minerals may be increasingly won from the sea, they undergo a cycle of constant renewal[11] which, as far as can be foreseen, will continue to add a greater quantity of nodules to the store already on the seabed than will be taken for human use.

These possible future sources of wealth and well-being, however, may, like the winning of oil and gas from the subsoil of the deep oceans, carry risks of polluting the environment[12] if their waste products, including acids and other processing chemicals, should be dumped into the sea by the mobile processing ship.[13] A number of

8. 1 Panel Reports, *supra* note 6, at III-52 to 53.

9. J. Mero, The Mineral Resources of the Sea 275 (1965).

10. *Id.* at 280. *See also* Mero, *Review of Mineral Values on and Under the Ocean Floor*, in Marine Technology Society, Exploiting the Ocean 61 (Transactions of the 2d Annual MTS Conference and Exhibit, June 27-29, 1966) [hereinafter cited as *Mineral Values*]; 1 Panel Report, *supra* note 6, at I-32; 3 Panel Reports, *supra* note 6, at VII-106 to 171; and C. Troebst, Conquest of the Sea 180-93 (B. & E. Price transl. 1962) [hereinafter cited as Troebst].

11. *See, e.g., Mineral Values, supra* note 10, at 76.

12. 2 Panel Reports, *supra* note 6, at VI—184 to 186; Our Nation and the Sea, *supra* note 6, at 134-35.

13. *But see* 2 Panel Reports, *supra* note 6, at VI-188 quoting W. Hibbard, Director of the Bureau of Mines, as saying:

Research on the problems of waste disposal. . . . [U]nwise dumping of the

such ships could turn sea areas (possibly of no great extent initially) into maritime equivalents of slag heaps, thereby causing very considerable ecological change and deleteriously affecting the food web.

2. Transportation

Winning petroleums and other mineral wealth from the sea floor is but the first stage in the development of the raw materials into the commodities which enhance life; they will need to be transported to centers of population. The logistical means of bringing oil and other maritime resources to shore may remain, at least for this century, giant tankers.[14] Pipelines may well eventually come to provide means of transporting the great bulk of gaseous, liquid and fine-grain materials from seabed operations in the deep ocean,[15] but this mode of transportation faces not only great technological problems, but also problems of the political stability of the coastal states upon whose lands the pipelines encroach. Giant tankers, nuclear-propelled cargo ships,[16] submarine trains and pipelines present international lawyers with hard problems of pollution liability.

The economies of scale these modes of transportation provide also increase the hazards of pollution. These will be commensurate with the increase in the size of the tankers and submarine trains and the diameter and length of the pipelines. As new modes of surface and submarine cargo carriers increase in size and speed, they will create very important problems of safety. The risks their speed and power

tailings, if not carefully planned, could quickly foul a mining operation. Furthermore, the compatability of a marine mining operation with exploitation of the other resources of the sea, particularly the food resources, will depend principally on the effectiveness of the tailings-disposal system.

14. For a projection of the growth of tankers and bulk carriers over the period 1970-2000, *see* Table 4, 1 Panel Reports, *supra* note 6, at III-67. *See also* the textual matter accompanying that Table.

15. *See* Troebst, *supra* note 10, at 97-98, where the author projects the following possible developments in ocean transportation:

Eventually man will use regular convoys of submarine barges, towing behind them a chain of enormous, sausage-like containers. The United States Rubber Company and several European firms have already designed rubber containers for surface transportation of various liquid cargoes. Bigger versions, 20 feet in diameter and 360 feet long, would be ideal for high-seas traffic. Every "rubber sausage" of this size could hold 182,000 gallons of freight and several of them could be towed by a single submarine tanker. Admiral Momsen is convinced that by 1980 such submarine barge trains will be almost a mile long, transporting some seventy-five different liquids ranging from oil, petrol, alcohol and acids to fine-grained materials like cement or grain. One great advantage would be that no reloading would be necessary if the purchaser was located inland. Tugs could continue to convey the goods by river to the point nearest the final destination.

16. *See Shipping Faces the Rapids,* 235 The Economist, Apr. 11, 1970, at 51.

will create constitute yet another threat to their potential victims and to the environment.

B. Some Examples of Risk-Exposed Activities

1. Development of Biological Resources

Edible fish constitute perhaps the oldest, and certainly the most valuable, of the biological resources of the sea. But, from the most far-off times to the present, mankind has had only one approach, the most primitive, to the winning of this resource—that of the hunter and collector. Mankind may eventually need, in order to survive, to change his means of gathering food from the sea, from the hunter of fish to the herdsman and shepherd of some species and the farmer and cultivator of others, thereby changing fundamentally his ecological, social, economic and legal relations to the sea.[17] It may well become necessary for him to cultivate and process algae and plankton, even if only to feed the fish and animals which he himself will eat. These activities could clearly qualify for a very high level of protection from exposures to harms, since they are especially vulnerable to destruction by pollution and to risk-creating preemptive activities generally.

2. Health, Therapy and Recreation

In addition to winning drugs from the sea,[18] mankind may also use its surface and volume for health, therapy and recreation. Dr. Cousteau has described how cuts and sores, which proved obstinate and hard to cure on account of the heat and other adverse conditions ashore, healed in 48 hours or less under the Red Sea in Conshelf II.[19] Perhaps hospitals for personal injury and accident victims and major surgery cases might be beneficially established underwater. In addition, psychotherapy may develop concepts, arising from the universal symbolism of the sea, calling for restful sanatoria, especially for hypertension and anxiety cases, to be developed in the volume of the oceans or on the seabed.[20]

With the spread of leisure, of education, and of the popularity of scuba diving, underwater activities—no less than such surface recrea-

---

17. Experiments are already being conducted into fish farming by analogues with battery methods. *See On Flatfish Farm,* 234 The Economist, Jan. 24, 1970, at 51.

18. *See* 2 Panel Reports *supra* note 6, at VI-190 to 197.

19. J. Cousteau, *Working for Weeks on the Sea Floor,* 129 Nat'l Geographic 498 (1966).

20. For an interesting confirmation of this theoretical possibility, *see* Wilford, *Learning from a Sojourn Under the Sea,* N.Y. Times, July 12, 1970, § 4 (The Week in Review), at 10, col. 1.

tions as sailing, surfing, speedboat racing and cruising—may become increasingly popular. The appeal of underwater hobbies and interests may even come to exceed that of the surface, since they offer an intellectual dimension lacking in surface water sports, while they also possess an equally physical dimension in the form of exercise and excitement. Scuba-diving amateur naturalists could become interested in being observers of, reporters on, and important contributors to, the many nascent underwater sciences. Can we not foresee mass production of inexpensive underwater recreation and research vehicles and vessels? What would be the liability of extrahazardous submarine enterprises such as deep-sea well heads, to those engaging in underwater naturalist and observation activities? What precautions should be demanded?

3. Scientific Research

The marine sciences are developing very rapidly, but their burgeoning may well become a basis for one of the major confrontations of exclusive and inclusive claims by users of the oceans' volume and floor. At a time when more and more countries have scientific research ships flying their flags—whether owned by universities or private or government laboratories[21] —many coastal states are seeking more than ever before to restrict scientific research activities off their shores.[22]

Increasingly, ocean and outer space research activities may become intimately connected in a number of ways. The ocean seems to provide a location for the recovery of space vehicles on their return to earth. Reciprocally, space vehicles have enormous ability in monitoring the state of the oceans. In addition, large floating platforms may well provide valuable links in combined ocean-outer space research and communications activities. However, their functioning is predicated on an environment kept relatively free of pollution.

On the other hand, the freer marine scientific research is allowed to become, the more likely pollution, radiation, eutrophication, ecological imbalance, and other man-made abuses of the sea may be discovered and rectified. Claims made in this connection may well vie with many of the most time-honored uses of the sea—including its treatment as the ultimate depository of all kinds of garbage and as

21. *See, e.g.*, list of scientific research ships registered by the maritime nations of the world in 1 Panel Reports, *supra* note 6, at I-14. For a survey of the growth of marine science research activities, *see, id.* at I-2 to 3 and I-13 to 19.

22. Papers delivered by William L. Sullivan, Jr., Department of State, and Daniel S. Cheever, Director, Department of International Affairs, University of Pittsburgh, at the Law of the Sea Institute's Fourth Annual Summer Conference on National Policy Recommendations (Kingston, Rhode Island, June 26, 1969).

the "ultimate sink." In evaluating a viable system of priorities it will be necessary for international law to determine the protections it will accord to research—an inclusive use of the sea—and to the pre-emptive, exclusive uses which may curtail it.

POLLUTION AND LIABILITY

A. Absolute Liability—A Proposed Definition

Professor Winfield has pointed out that the exculpating rules which the courts have developed to mitigate the rigour of the defendant's liability under such rules as *Rylands v. Fletcher*,[23] render the adjective "absolute" something of a misnomer; hence the phrase "strict liability" has come to be preferred. I would like, how-ever, to revive the term "absolute liability," not in order to enter any debate with Professor Winfield, but to indicate a more rigorous form of liability than that usually labeled "strict," as for example, that formulated in the nuclear liability treaties.[24]

It would be more exact to say that absolute, rather than strict, liability was imposed in the international agreements on liability to third parties in the field of nuclear energy which have just been indicated. Those agreements utilize the principle of channeling,[25] which traces liability back to the nuclear operator, no matter how long the chain of causation, nor how novel the intervening factors (other than a limited number of exculpatory facts). They also admit of fewer exculpations than does the rule in *Rylands v. Fletcher*[26] and similar rules.

B. Proposed Perspectives for Liability Doctrines

Even though I welcome the advent of strict and absolute liability in international law, I do not look forward to the elimination of the

23. L.R. 3 H.L. 330 (1868).

24. These treaties are: (1) International Convention on Civil Liability for Nuclear Damage, *done* May 21, 1963, Int'l Atomic Energy Agency Doc. CN 12/46, 2 Int'l Legal Materials 727 (1963); (2) Convention on the Liability of Operators of Nuclear Ships, May 25, 1962, 57 Am. J. Int'l L. 268 (1963); (3) Convention on Third Party Liability in the Field of Nuclear Energy, *done* July 29, 1960, O.E.E.C. Doc. C (60) 93, 8 Eur. Y.B. 202 (1960); and (4) Convention Supplementary to the (O.E.E.C.) Paris Convention, 1960, *done* Jan. 31, 1963, 2 Int'l Legal Materials 685 (1963). There is a fifth embryonic agreement, a draft sponsored by the Inter-American Nuclear Energy Commission.

25. "Channelling" in this context denotes the tracing of liability for nuclear injuries back to the operator of a nuclear ship or reactor notwithstanding the length of the causal chain or the intervening acts—except the willful acts of the plaintiff. *See, e.g.,* Vienna Convention Art. 2, § 1, 2 Int'l Legal Materials 727, 730-31.

26. Illustrative of the limitations which its many exceptions place on the rule in Rylands v. Fletcher, *supra* note 23, is the fact that Winfield lists eight. P. Winfield, Winfield on Tort 417-32 (8th ed., Jolowicz & Lewis, 1967).

less stringent doctrines from the areas of their appropriate application. The strictness of the liability to be imposed should depend upon the type of activity causing the harm, the type of activity harmed, and the juxtaposition of the operator and the injured.[27] A scale of liability, reflecting the degree of preemptiveness of the activity to which liability is attached, and exemplified in five social situations and their consequential regimes[28] may be proposed. These have not, it should be emphasized, been developed in order to render the question of liability dependent on the location of the accident (*i.e.*, in exclusive zone of coastal state jurisdiction or on the high seas), but on the activities giving rise to the ensuing injury—that is on the social relations created by the incident. These five exemplifying social situations and their attendant levels of liability are:

(i)   When harm to a coastal population or to its livelihood is occasioned by a use of the sea which gains economies from exposing others to increased risks, absolute liability, channelling accountability to the operator (possibly subject to a maximum limitation of liability sum) should be imposed on the risk-creating operator for causing the harm;

(ii)   When fish-farming, including intensive or "battery" fish farming activities, health (including submarine therapy), submarine recreation and scientific research activities are harmed by the types of activity indicated in (i) above, absolute liability, subject to a maximum limitation of liability figure, should be imposed;

(iii)   When harms caused by activities in (i) above are suffered by other activities in the same category, then the injury calls for no higher level of compensability than that given by fault liability;

(iv)   When traditional maritime activities, for example fishing with trawls, lines and nets (including purse seine nets) cause injury to such activities as those in (i) above, for example, submarine pipelines or tankers, or mining activities, then the liability applicable should be in terms of fault; but negligence should be presumed. The actor, for example the fisherman, should be permitted to exculpate himself on such grounds as want of notice and knowledge on his part, due care, or inevitability. When traditional fishing activities are the immediate cause of

27. This concept of the relativity of liability in international law to risk creation, exposure, and social desirability was first outlined by this writer in *Liability for Damage, supra* note 1, at 1220-24, 1254-58.

28. The concept of "regimes" used here and elsewhere in this essay is taken from Goldie, *Special Regimes and Pre-emptive Activities in International Law,* 11 Int'l & Comp. L. Q. 670 (1962). *See also* McDougal, *The Prospect for a Regime in Outer Space,* Law and Politics in Space 105, 106-109 (Cohen ed., 1964).

harm in traditional fishing grounds, or under other circumstances where the operator of the tanker, submarine or other risk-creating activity, knowingly increases the risk to others, the fisherman may show that those facts represent an assumption of risk by the operator of the pipeline, tanker, mine or other technologically advanced artifact involved in the casualty. Indeed, the application of channelling proposed in (i) above may well leave the operator of the risk-creating enterprise as the party liable rather than the fisherman whose net or trawl may have been the immediate cause of the harm;

(v)   When traditional maritime activities such as those indicated in (iv) above are the agents of harm to the vulnerable types of emerging activities, for example those indicated in (ii) above, then liability should be strict in the traditional sense; but not absolute.

Each of the five sets of social relations inherent in these different classifications of liability varies from the others in terms of the balance of risk and power to inflict harm while remaining free from physical injury or financial loss, and with the degree of effective expropriation which the creation of risk in each relationship entails. Thus, the regime appropriate to each set of social relations, by adopting the appropriate concept of liability on the total scale from absolute to fault liability, should be viewed as restoring the balance of risk and power, so that one group of interests is not permitted to take risks, or carry on its operations, at the expense of others. On the other hand, those "others," while entitled to protection, should be protected against the consequences of risks, which, as a result of their own prior conduct, they might well be viewed as being under a duty to shoulder. Furthermore, their own protection should be in terms of the risks to which they expose their own operations, their social desirability, their relative immunity from harm, and the risks they create for yet other activities. In this way each set of social relations which is brought into being by the creation of risk is seen as being subject to the degree of liability appropriate to the exposures it creates for others, to its own social value, and to its own vulnerability to harm. This thesis looks to the adjustment of the balance of risk and to the advantage in each special social situation which may be gained by the creation of risk as a form of expropriation.

THE RESOLUTION OF UNCERTAINTY

HAROLD P. GREEN†

Environmental abuse is a consequence of human activity, particularly the use of technology. Every human activity—even basic biological functions—takes place within man's environment and involves the use of the environment. It is meaningless, therefore, to speak of preservation of the environment, since all human activity to some degree changes the environment in proportion to the scope of the activity. The more dynamic our society, the greater will be the impact of human activities on the environment. Environmental change can be minimized only in a static society. The real question, therefore, is what environmental change will be accepted as a consequence of man's aspirations for a better life.

All human activities also take place within the framework of our political, social, economic, and legal systems. These systems are inter-related; a basic thread running through all of them is that people are free to act as they please, subject only to restrictions imposed by law. In the economic sphere, our system contemplates that government and law will be neutral in the first instance; that in the absence of some regulatory law, people will make decisions on producing, using, and selling products and services in terms of their own self interest as determined through their own personal value judgments. Products and services come into existence because a market exists for them at the prices at which they are offered. In a real sense the market is made as people vote with their dollars for the products and services they want. As is well understood, economic activities sometimes result in environmental abuse because the costs of such abuse are not internalized so as to be reflected in the prices for products and services, the production or use of which causes the environmental injury. When abuse of the environment is found to be unacceptable, the remedy lies in the making of laws which regulate the activities causing the abuse or which impose liability for the abuse, thereby forcing an internalization of environmental costs.

The present automobile internal combustion engine is a good example of this. Development of the automobile was a tremendous boon to our society and was enthusiastically accepted in the market place. No attention was paid to the fact that its exhaust fumes might be injurious to the environment. It was assumed that the environment had a virtually infinite capacity to absorb these fumes. Only in recent years have we recognized that this is an intolerable pollution

†Professor of Law, George Washington University

of the environment and adopted laws requiring automobile manufacturers to incorporate in their products devices to minimize this source of pollution and to consider alternatives to the present internal combusion engine. These corrective measures will, however, undoubtedly increase the costs of automobiles and in turn decrease the attractiveness (*i.e.*, the benefits) of the vehicle to consumers with possible major consequences to the economy of the country.

The recognition that automotive exhaust fumes have an intolerable effect on the environment and must be minimized has come at a very late date. Incalculable harm to the environment and to life has already resulted and will continue at least until the present generation of motor vehicles passes out of existence. There are, moreover, immense practical difficulties in eliminating such a well-established source of pollution because of the dislocations which corrective measures involve affecting not only the automobile manufacturers, but also their employees and the general public which will be adversely affected by increased costs. The case of the automobile is by no means unique. The same situation applies with respect to other sources of today's pollution such as sulfur dioxide from industrial plants and the use of pesticides and herbicides.

This suggests the necessity not only for eliminating known, existing sources of pollution, but also the necessity, if we are serious about having environmental quality, for prevention of future pollution before technological sources of such pollution become well established, with strong vested interests in the production and use of products and services associated with the pollution, and before substantial environmental abuse has become a *fait accompli*. It is important also that pollution attributable to future technology be arrested before it develops because of the simple fact that successively new sources of pollution are likely to be much more destructive, much more quickly, than their predecessors.

The problem of stopping pollution before it begins is a difficult one, especially when the pollution consists of materials discharged into the environment in small quantities. Frequently, adverse effects on the environment cannot be predicted or verified on the basis of laboratory research and experimentation because the effects are creeping and cumulative over a long period of time. In such cases, the pollution does not become observable until the polluting activity has been conducted on a sufficiently broad scale over a long enough time span to permit ascertainment of injury through use of statistical techniques. It is doubtful, for example, that the injury caused by automobile exhaust fumes could have been ascertained until automobiles were used in such quantities and concentrations, and under such circumstances, as to produce the smog effect. Similarly, it is doubtful that the environmental impact of DDT could have been recognized until DDT had been in actual use for a considerable period of time. This is particularly true where the adverse consequences may result from a synergistic combination of the material with some other material in the environment.

The determination that environmental consequences constitute unacceptable pollution and that they must be eliminated is not a scientific determination. True, scientific data is an important element, but these determinations in a democracy are essentially political judgments reflecting public sentiment that additional costs should be imposed and benefits foregone in order to have a higher degree of environmental quality. The making of such political judgments in a timely manner so as to prevent pollution from developing and becoming entrenched involves substantial difficulties. Even in the early stages of development of a technology, its benefits are obvious and relatively immediate. The benefits will always be effectively and vigorously articulated by the cohesive and well-financed sponsors of the technology. Moreover, the public is always eager to enjoy the benefits of new technology. On the other hand, the potential adverse environmental consequences are usually, if perceived at all, relatively remote and speculative; and there rarely are individuals who have sufficient interest or resources to articulate the risks to the environment in an effective, or even minimally adequate, manner. It is to be expected, therefore, that in any assessment of the benefits and environmental costs of a new technology the conclusion will be that the relatively immediate benefits outweigh the speculative potential costs, thereby flashing a green light for development and use of the technology. In effect, such conclusions reflect the optimistic presumption that experience will ultimately resolve the uncertainty through demonstration that the effects are not injurious, or are at least tolerable. The companion assumption is that if the effects prove to be intolerably injurious, it will be time enough to impose social controls when the fact of injury has been authoritatively established. It is doubtful, therefore, that even a law requiring prelicensing, based on research and testing of all new technologies, would be effective in forestalling pollution.

The basic need is to develop political institutions which will tend to give potential adverse environmental effects time, dignity, and attention more equal to that given to benefits. In other words, the existence of unresolved uncertainty should in itself be regarded as a substantial environmental cost of the technology. This approach can, however, be carried to an untenable extreme. If laws were enacted in effect banning introduction of new technologies in the face of unresolved uncertainty, the consequence would be that no new technologies could be introduced and the uncertainties would never be resolved. This would place an intolerable brake on progress. On the other hand, if the fact and the implications of uncertainty were adequately articulated in the political arena, the public, and legislators responsible to the public, would have the opportunity to make judgments in each case as to whether development and introduction of the technology should be restricted. These judgments would, of course, be based, in terms of the public's values, hopes, concerns, and fears, on what technological benefits the public wants and what environmental risks, including risks incident to uncertainty, the public is willing to accept in order to have these benefits.

At the present time, availability of information as to the environmental consequences of technology is limited by the internal processes of the scientific community. The existence of uncertainty is rarely explicitly articulated in public forums. For example, until Rachel Carson's *Silent Spring,* DDT had been in widespread use without any public recognition that there was uncertainty as to its environmental effects. The fact of uncertainty emerges into public view only when scientific research produces an inkling of adverse consequences which finds its way into the press. Thereafter, as scientists pursue this initial lead through their cautious and objective processes of research and publication, the uncertainty is slowly resolved, but not without friction and dispute as the vested interests in the technology seek to rebut the scientific critics. The identification of pollution as a predicate for political decision as to what should be done about it is, therefore, tied to the principles of scientific objectivity, and remedial action is usually not forthcoming until a scientific consensus has emerged.

The effect of this is that environmental issues do not become ripe for political debate until the scientists have resolved uncertainty to the point that environmental risks have been identified. There are, of course, exceptions to this, as in the case of political debate on the supersonic transport plane in which the existence of uncertainty as to environmental effects, despite the establishment scientists' optimism that the uncertainty would be favorably resolved, led to defeat of the proposal in the Congress. This was, however, an atypical situation involving complex political questions over and above environmental concerns. In the usual case, there is no effective mechanism through which unresolved uncertainty can be recognized in itself as a risk requiring early limitations on technological development so as to forestall potential pollution.

It seems to be contrary to principles of democratic political philosophy to permit the scientific community in effect to control the nature and level of political debate on public policy issues related to technology. Scientists can tell us a great deal about the potential beneficial effects of a technology and also about its risks. They have no special competence, however, to determine whether the public will regard particular effects as a benefit, i.e., something the public regards as worth the price which must be paid. Nor do they have any special competence to determine what risks—including risks incident to uncertainty—the public is willing to assume.

This suggests the necessity for building into the political process some device for identifying and pressing upon the public, in a form comprehensible to the public, the fact that uncertainty exists as to the potential environmental effects of technology. As a corollary, this device should also press upon the public early intimations that there may in fact be adverse consequences, even before these intimations have been confirmed. True, an effect of this procedure might be to create "undue" alarm and "premature" controls, and create a situation in which public debate and public policy are out of phase with scientific reality. On the other hand, the negativism engendered by such a procedure would be more than counter-balanced by the barrage of authoritative rebuttals which will emerge from the scientific establishment and the technology's vested interests. The public, with access to both sides of the story, can reach its own conclusions just as it does with all other issues of public policy. The fact that "erroneous" political decisions may be made is not a valid argument against this procedure. In a democratic society, we recognize the inevitability, and indeed the utility, of erroneous judgments. Scientific questions, no less than economic and social questions, should be resolved in the crucible of uninhibited political debate in the faith that a democratic people is entitled, rationally or irrationally, to the public policies it wants, and that in the long run truth will prevail.

THE HUMAN ENVIRONMENT: PROBLEMS OF STANDARD-SETTING AND ENFORCEMENT

DR. IAN BROWNLIE†

MAJOR STRATEGIES OF CONTROL AND ENFORCEMENT

The strategy which comes most readily to mind is the global or comprehensive approach. Both from a scientific and organizational viewpoint this makes the best sense. The collection and interpretation of data, and the effectiveness of measures of regulation, are better managed within a pattern which is comprehensive and integral. But a thoroughgoing global approach has implications which need to be considered. The logic of creating a pathology of conservation, environmental control in general, and population management involves major issues concerning the sufficiency of the system of international relations we have. A well-reasoned case can be made for saying that the existing system cannot cope and also for saying that the system we have is positively well-suited to the creation of waste and over-consumption in certain zones of the world, a process dignified by the term "economic development" and buttressed by sermons to the havenots about restraint in general and population control in particular.

If we tackle the environment agenda realistically, then, it should extend to population studies and problems of conservation of all resources: but these items lead on inexorably to sharp political issues relating to appropriate sharing of resources and decisions on priorities.

Thus the global approach may take on a fundamentalist form and there is the risk of frightening governments and others without any compensating advance. We have to accept that the present state system and stock of available types of international institution will continue in the foreseeable future and, therefore, have to be reckoned with. We have to make advances without raising too many issues at once. The best form of comprehensive approach would seem to be to combine specialized responses with certain agencies responsible for co-ordination: and so to have a general strategy which permits sensitive reactions to special problems and local developments.

There is a rather different issue of strategy. The present drive is toward the Stockholm Conference on the Human Environment. In order to establish the importance of an issue, a suitable category or institution is employed. In organizational and publicist terms this is

†Professor of Law, Wadham College, Oxford.

inevitable. However, the single category focus or separate agenda approach should not be allowed to detract from certain humdrum points or premises.

In the first place, however many organizations may be created, enforcement involves very considerable reliance upon the application of national legal controls. The arrest and punishment of offenders and the general enforcement of standards are placed in the hands of the agencies of individual states even when the standards are created by international conventions. The better examples of international systems of supervision are dependent upon realistic assumptions about the respective enforcement roles of national and international agencies.

The second humdrum premise is this: much effort is spent deploring the existince of national sovereignties. Yet, as I have just emphasized, much enforcement is reliant on national legal systems. Many inadequacies of enforcement stem from inefficient aspects of *national* legal systems. On the scale of big politics, the persistence of the U.D.I. regime in Southern Rhodesia is a test not only of the efficacy of the U.N. system but also of the United Kingdom system of law and public order. Closer to the subject of protection of the environment, the ineffectiveness of the Convention for the Prevention of Pollution of the Sea by Oil of 1954 is due in part to the inoperation of national legal constraints.

The "effectiveness" of enforcement is a major problem in all legal regulation.

The matters on which the guidance of scientists will be of special value include the selection of environment issues which are (a) urgent and (b) involve situations in which a low incidence of non-compliance would cause irremediable degradation or serious hazards. Examples of this would include the copper needles or dipoles experiment and the mounting of nuclear tests which could activate earthquake zones and fault movements.

The third humdrum premise is the statement that social control is rarely if ever successfully achieved by use of a single program or vehicle. This must be particularly true of the protection of the environment. Thus care should be taken to conserve and develop a variety of techniques. A good number of specialized institutions and techniques exist already and should be made more effective. They should not be overshadowed by new labels. If we are to create new agencies these should be geared to the specialized roles of filling gaps and of co-ordination. Otherwise, we are resorting to the special department approach. By this I am referring to the diversionary and conscience-salving effects of creating a new institution which allows politicians and others to say that we have "recognized" a particular problem and, in some sense, are dealing with it.

Whatever problems of scale and categories may exist, multi-lateralism is to be preferred to reliance on the outcome of initiative by States acting individually. Unilateralism may be based upon short term domestic policies and is less likely to be related to a broad-based scientific consensus. Technical and scientific considerations are not merely important in themselves. Presented independently by respected and efficient agencies, such considerations have a beneficial influence on the political process. They can produce mediating and cooling effects. Unilateralism may spark off a generalized dispute with other States and obstruct co-operation in various fields. Functionally, unilateralism is patently inadequate, for example, in tackling pollution in the Baltic or the Great Lakes of North America.

Of course, even multilateral institutions may have a club aspect and it would be unfortunate if agencies were set up exclusively by groups of Western nations or other industrialized nations.

OBSTRUCTIONS AND COMPLICATIONS

The most obvious obstacle to effective international co-operation is, or is commonly said to be, the division of the world into national sovereignties. I have already pointed out that certain issues can be raised relating to the structure of international relations. My own feeling is that the harmful effects of sovereignty are overstated in two respects. First, because the amount of political sovereignty most States have is curtailed in practice by the actual circumstances of international life. The world is littered with examples of the difficulty of drawing a line between the status of partner, ally, subordinate and puppet. Secondly, it is simply not the case that if, for example, Latin America or Africa were federal unions the problems their peoples face would take on a different dimension. One may look at the affairs of the Indian sub-continent. At any rate in our thinking we have to accept the world of formal parcels of sovereignty and try to mould it to the purposes of conservation.

A further complication is the fact that States will often act with a mixture of motives and as a consequence of lobbying and pressures based upon both self-interest and references to the general interest. Perfectly benevolent structures and schemes can be used for purposes collateral to their advertised and ostensible objects. Many claims to fishery conservation zones involve extension of national jurisdiction over areas which the majority of States regard as high seas open to all. In all such cases the conservation objective is linked with problems of reservation of fisheries for Coastal States. Conservation is thus linked with a claim to divide resources in a particular way. The Canadian Arctic Waters Pollution Prevention Act contains admirable provisions aimed at preventing disasters of the *Torrey Canyon* type in the Arctic area. However, the background to the Act makes clear the fact that Canada is anxious to preclude certain American activities which might challenge Canada's general political and legal interests in the whole area of seas, sealanes, straits and islands.

Some further examples of the relation between neutral rules and special interest may be drawn from the International Labor Organization. The effective application of labor standards and the resulting increase in operation costs is one aspect of the conflict between European and American shipping interests in relation to the use of flags of convenience. In the field of human rights and labor standards there are a number of partly hidden and unresolved issues of capability and economic context: in other words, the possibility that superficially equal legal burdens may fall unequally because of local economic and social conditions. We must face the possibility that in setting conservation standards the same type of problem will occur.

I have already remarked on the reliance which international regulations place upon enforcement through national legal systems. Since this form of mechanics will continue to be used it is necessary to pay attention to the particular inadequacies of state legal systems, apart from the general question of state sovereignty. State regulation may be superficial and concerned with policies which have an independence of any policy of effective exercise of control and jurisdiction. The classical but nonetheless relevant example is that of the national registration of merchant ships under flags of convenience. The *Torrey Canyon* was Liberian registered. The offer of a flag of convenience to foreign owned shipping is normally based upon (a) the fiscal advantages to the flag state; and (b) the low operating costs of vessels not subject to rigorous control in matters of safety and labor standards. Much of the shipping under flags of convenience is American-owned and the national advantages to the United States are well known. They are: low operating costs in face of European competitors, and the existence of a reserve of shipping for use in time of war when requisition may occur in pursuance of existing agreements by American owners of the ships with U.S. Maritime Administration. These problems involving flags of convenience illustrate the difficulties of operating through national enforcement systems precisely in the context of pollution hazards from large tanker fleets.

It is common knowledge that States place some priority on the mechanism of taxation and control of capital movements across frontiers. It is in such areas of interest that States may be expected to show maximum efficiency in enforcement. Yet in face of multi-national companies it is known that the normal fiscal control mechanisms do not work well or at all. The picture is drawn clearly by Christopher Tugendhat in his recent book *The Multinationals* (1971). The total annual sales of General Motors is greater than the individual gross national products of Belgium, Switzerland, Denmark and Austria. The operational capabilities of several hundred corporations taken individually are greater than those of nine-tenths of the States existing today. Such corporations make major economic decisions, decide on resource priorities and evolve new techniques. The issue of control is not merely a matter of the economic power of the large corporations. There is the further problem of tracing the real sources of control and underlying interests.

One point remains in considering the weaknesses of national legal systems as enforcement agencies. Underdeveloped States have low grade administrations barely capable in some cases of carrying the minimal burdens of government. At the same time States may be tempted to ratify regulatory conventions when performance cannot match aspiration. Some States may not even take the trouble to bring their internal law into line with the requirements of the conventions—to which they are formally parties. Clearly there is a connection here with the question of aid and particularly technical aid and advice to underdeveloped States.

The lawyer appears rather as a technician, engineer and mechanic. He can operate only when others, the politicians and economists, have established certain priorities. Many issues of control are intimately bound up with risk and social cost calculations. The consumer and the armed forces in Western societies want cheap petrol and oil supplies. Governments therefore take the key hazard creating decision: cheap bulk oil transport in tankers which by reason of their bulk and small clearance create serious risks, however well designed the ships may be. What we should do is investigate the real social cost, in terms of risks and actual pollution damage, of large tankers and deal with risk creation at the source.

Weapons testing and fishery conservation involve similar risk calculations and national choices. Other types of choice may have to be made. For example, population control and even pollution control may involve measures which infringe or qualify human rights to marry and found a family and to own and enjoy property.

I turn now to a specialized aspect of control and enforcement. Valid controls must be based upon the collection of data and the monitoring of the environment on a day to day basis. This process is straightforward, in the legal sense that there is a liberty to act, in relation to outer space and the high seas. In the case of the continental shelf, the interests of the coastal State must not interfere with "fundamental oceanographic or other scientific research carried out with the intention of open publication." In the case of research undertaken at the shelf, the consent of the coastal State is required. The general feature of course is that the territory, territorial seas, and airspace above both, are open to monitoring and so on only with the permission of the territorial sovereign. There is the added difficulty that oceanographic and other environmental data may have a military significance.

INTERNATIONAL STANDARDS AND CONTROLS

The nature of standard-setting must vary with the subject matter. Specific activities may be straightforwardly prohibited or prohibited with exceptional powers in emergencies to deviate from the standard. The standard-setting will frequently take the form of requiring parties to a treaty to change their legislation in such a way as to control a particular activity or promote a conserving process. The standards may themselves be programmatic; for example, involving an obligation on the State to take steps "to the maximum of its available resources," "with a view to achieving progressively the realization" of certain purposes.

What if the types of sanction allowed breaches of legal provisions? On the level of State relations, sanctions tend to be confined to a claim for reparation if some damage can be ascribed to the breach, and denunciation or suspension of the treaty depending on the nature of the breach. The essence of the situation is reciprocity, but this can result in a general acquiescence in some level of negligent enforcement. The sanctions applicable to individual operators are varied. Individuals and firms may be punished but there is doubt whether the fines normally imposed amount to more than a tax on profitable risk-taking in most cases. Conditions and standards may be attached to systems of registration or licensing of enterprises or installations, or to provision of development grants or state subsidies. An effective sanction and a simple one at that is refusal of facilities to vessels which do not comply with certain safety standards or are guilty of pollution.

Associated with sanctions are the devices for loss distribution. The United Kingdom Merchant Shipping (Oil Pollution) Act provides for compulsory insurance. International conventions establish a strict or so-called absolute liability for damage caused. The Brussels Convention on Liability of Operations of Nuclear Ships created such liability up to a limit of approximately $100 million. The Brussels Convention on Civil Liability for Oil Pollution Damage, signed in 1969, is concerned with compensation to persons who suffer damage caused by pollution resulting from the escape or discharge of oil by ships. The definition of "pollution damage" includes the costs of preventive measures taken by any person after an incident to prevent or minimize pollution damage. The owner of a ship at the time of the incident bears liability for pollution damage though he is exculpated in certain defined cases, for example, if the damage were the consequence of the deliberate act of a third party. A limit is fixed to the owner's liability (Article V, para. 1). While the effect varies, there is little doubt that the need to insure to cover such liabilities is a useful control provided the underwriters take some informed interest in the risk.

The previous experience of international organization has developed a variety of techniques for supervision of the implementation of standard-setting treaty regimes. The experience relates to conventions concerned with labor standards, the work of the I.L.O. in general, fishery conservation arrangements and human rights, in the latter case both within the U.N. system and on a regional basis.

Very commonly provision is made for periodical reports by governments on the implementation within their spheres of competence of the particular convention. The I.L.O. Constitution requires members to make annual reports on measures taken. Another device is the fact-finding body. It sounds simple enough but if the fact-finding is authoritative it can have a general ameliorating effect on a crisis in State relations. Moreover, in many situations action taken without prior investigation of an appropriate type can produce harmful consequences out of proportion to the original incident.

Of particular value are complaints procedures which provide elements both of monitoring and dispute settlement whilst avoiding the cumbersome qualities and sometimes exacerbating effects of full adjudication. Complaints from individuals, non-governmental organizations and governments may provide evidence on which an organ may take appropriate action even when, taken individually, the complaints have no status which would justify or require consideration or action. One may refer to the present and increased powers of the Human Rights Commission in the U.N. system. Complaints by States may be given a formal status. A committee may be given a competence to consider complaints made by States as of right against other States also accepting the jurisdiction of the committee. The object of a complaints procedure is primarily remedial action based upon investigation of some kind rather than a legal contest leading to an award of damages. Judicial supervision of a very formal nature may be provided for by conferring jurisdiction on the International Court in respect of the subject matter.

Inspection procedures are of particular relevance to protection of the environment. The concept of inspection by an impartial agency is to be found in the Statute of the I.A.E.A. and in the Treaty establishing Euratom. Adversary inspection, or the reciprocal right to investigate the other party investigating suspected violations, appears in the Antarctica Treaty, various conventions concerning high seas fisheries and bilateral agreements for co-operation in the peaceful uses of atomic energy. An organ may have inherent powers of investigation not dependent upon the complaint or initiative of individual governments. Examples are provided by the International Narcotics Control Board and the Councils created by the various international commodity agreements.

A critical feature of enforcement is efficient detection of wrong-doing or abnormality. Existing treaties concerned with oil pollution at sea make no provision for identifying offenders. In the case of major disasters like the wreck of the *Torrey Canyon* there is no problem, but many deliberate or accidental discharges are not always attributable to a particular vessel. In the Oxford Pugwash Study Group a suggestion was made that each load of oil in tankers could be labelled by radio-active tracers in a way which would provide a "signature" in oil found polluting the sea or beaches. At the moment oil can be identified only by reference to its general origin, *e.g.* that it is from the Venezuelan field. Clearly there is a need for technical work and co-operation leading to detection techniques which treaty provisions could utilize in due course.

Simple pollution situations may lead to the making of an international claim under general international law by the State suffering harm against another State. The possibility of such claims or representations anticipating threats of pollution may lead to a higher standard of care and also to regional forms of pollution control. However, the emphasis must be on planning and prevention and the claims situation is not of particular interest, although it should not be forgotten.

By way of conclusion it must be emphasized that legal standards, procedures and institutions are only effective if the politicians, the administrators and the public are convinced of the importance of protection. As in the case of race relations, legal intervention must be part of a well-developed economic and social program, accompanied by well-informed persuasion.

GLOBAL POLLUTION AND HUMAN RIGHTS

ABEL WOLMAN†

The title of this article poses a contradiction in terms. Some 37 years ago, an eminent philosopher[1] in the law commented upon the dilemma implicit in our subject, in these words:

> The craving for absolute moral distinctions and the confused effort to apply them to practical life—the source of so much of our spiritual grandeur and misery—appear nowhere more clearly than in the history of the law. . . . Law, philosophy, and social justice have thus become merged in an absorbing theme of reflection.
>
> But in law as in other social fields the very vitality of our interests makes us passionately espouse half-truths and zealously exclude the vision of those who see the opposing and supplementary half-truth.

The rediscovery of the environment in the 1960's, and the assumption in high places that no pollution abatement occurred prior to the Water Quality Act of 1965, are rich grist for the sociologic research mill for many years to come. Regardless of the causes of interest throughout the world, the phenomenon has endowed the word "pollution" with a conceptual entity which seems to place it in juxtaposition to man and his inalienable rights. We must be reminded that man is at the same time the creator of wastes, as well as the beneficiary of those systems which create them. More important, he is both the plaintiff and the defendant in the world court of the environment. In fact, on different days the Sierra Club member may serve on the Board of Directors of the Manufacturers Association. The lion lies down with the lamb only when the issues concern neither of them very much.

Thus, when we counterpoise "pollution" with "human rights" we place ourselves in a legal paradox. Wherever and whenever man breathes, works, plays or eats he modifies the ecology of the earth. How and whom he affects is a matter of time, place, concentration, and even one's philosophy of the ingredients of a satisfactory quality of life. The canoeist has little regard or even friendliness for the speedboat artist, although they may both desire the reservoir, that recreational Garden of Eden. Provided, of course, each possesses it for himself.

The ecologist reminds us, too, that, even if man did not exist on the earth, equilibrium between species of animal, plant and mineral is rarely permanent.

---

†Professor Emeritus, The Johns Hopkins University.
1. M. Cohen, Law and the Social Order (1933).

This long preamble appears necessary, after wading through thousands of pages of congressional hearings, of hundreds of pages of new curricula in law, engineering, economics, and political science, and dismal repetitive half-truths in newspapers and television. Throughout this deluge of the last decade, reason has given way to non-reason, intelligent interest to hysteria, and positive action to non-action. It is well to recall that "the function of intelligence is not only to recognize but also to evaluate opposing forces, and to determine their resultant with the highest obtainable accuracy."[2]

The problems of the environment are essentially those with which man has struggled for centuries. These have been qualitatively and quantitatively intensified by the almost universal population explosion, industrialization, urbanization and the precipitous advances in science and technology. If any, or all of these, are morally bad, socially objectionable and hostile to health and welfare, they are all man-made and, at least in theory, controllable by man.

If one were to single out that area of greatest promise in reducing environmental ills, it would undoubtedly focus on excessive rate of growth of population—whether in so-called developed or developing countries. Yet, law curricula on the environment or pollution are strangely silent on this score. If we really mean to protect man against himself and his doings, what promise is there in a legal attack against this "cottage industry" of population explosion?

The further pursuit of priorities in the fight against pollution would undoubtedly disclose, with respect to the air, that the automobile is par excellence the primary offender. It has to its debit, also, that it kills and cripples more people each year than almost any other weapon. Yet, few march, with wind swept banners, demanding the protection of the rights of man against these undertakers' certificates. Although these are "socially acceptable," they far outnumber "the unknown diseases of unknown origin" so diligently pursued by some. What can the law offer in this environmental field, where man's decisions daily violate his own and his neighbors' right to survive. Can society provide the curbs to the automobile, either by modifying its unrestrained use or by changing its motive power? We may well be on the road to doing both—but, as always, long after necessity warrants severe legal and technologic action.

In the water pollution field, the first priorities may be equally divided between public and private contributors. The great urban centers, growing day by day throughout the world, generate proportionate increases in domestic and industrial wastes. The speed

2. *Id.*

with which these areas have grown resulted in the problems outstripping the correctives in waste collection and treatment. This is the case with respect to liquid, gaseous and solid materials. In most of these situations, technologic solutions are at hand. The blocks to abatement have rarely been attributable to the absence of law. With few exceptions, the delays are due to failure of the public to provide money and to develop managerial institutions appropriate to the complex overlapping political units. The gap between public propaganda for abatement and public appropriation of funds for the purpose is wide. It is likely to continue to be wide throughout the globe under the inflationary pressures on the dollar, the rupee or the peso. In addition, the other significant demands of society, such as the ghetto, the food supply, the transportation, enter the competitive field for the public and private budget. There is no escape from the fact that no country is rich enough to do everything for everybody simultaneously, and this covers the United States of North America as well.

At the same time as these restraints operate, life goes on. Industrialization moves forward. Metro areas proliferate. Encroachments on open land proceed apace. Hence controversies will continue between preservationist, expansionist, exploiter and beneficiary. Decisions, as they now materialize, or, more often, are deferred in a morass of confusion and bitter controversy, are rarely satisfactory to all the adversaries. It is improbable that they ever will reach a state of perfection, no matter by whom defined. Perhaps, Francis Bacon's[3] dictum of 1627 will prevail, when he suggested for his New Atlantis: "The effecting of all things possible."

The law may very well facilitate an approach to perfecting our environment, by the strengthening of the "trust doctrine," by a new look at the balance between "jus privatum and jus publicum," by simplifying the method of participation legally of the citizen in such adjudications. How successful these efforts turn out to be will depend in no small measure on an objectivity of legal approach, the existence of which is not too obvious in many of the legal discussions of the last few years. The bias is frequent toward the frank and militant preservationist, perhaps because the "climate" of today blows the winds in that direction. The risk inherent in any bias is that "climate" is fragile, reversible and unpredictable. Decision making which is too one-sided, even when reversing an early pendulum swing, undoubtedly brings counter action in its wake.

---

3. Address by Sir Peter Medawar, *The Effecting of All Things Possible,* British Association for the Advancement of Science, 1969.

Many of the efforts of recent years to meet the problems of environmental quality, by more stringent laws, by the creation of new principles in law, by strengthening and extending administrative practice and responsibility and by promoting more effective people participation, will rise or fall depending upon the validity of the assumptions which guide them. Some examples of current environmental issues may illustrate the pitfalls to which all of us are exposed. Fulfillment of the desire to provide logic and wholeness of perspective in public policy, so wisely pressed for by the ecologist, is most difficult.

EARTH AS SPACE-SHIP

Much of the concern regarding the deteriorating quality of the environment stems from the analogy, used by many authors, that, not only does the earth have a finite capacity for people, but that this capacity is rapidly being approached! In simplest terms, it is said that density of living is approaching a level of danger and urban growth is encroaching excessively upon available land. How true are these charges? Is the earth really analogous to a space-ship?

The long experience of Europe has some lessons in this connection. Holland and Belgium, with a combined population of 22,232,000, have managed to get along reasonably well on 25,275 square miles. England and Wales provide a viable society of 48,391,000 people on an area of 58,348 square miles. The amount of land surface there available per person is two-thirds of an acre. France has three acres per person, while the U.S.A. has over 12 acres per person.

The relative density of population in Europe versus that in the U.S.A. is 800 to 900 as against 66 persons per square mile. In addition, the urban population of the U.S. now accounts for less than two percent of the land area of the U.S. continent.

Europe and the U.S.A. may be moving toward a "space-ship" reality, but hardly at a break-neck velocity. Time is amply available to use and deploy our resources with wisdom and safety—without resorting in too great a hurry to transporting our people to the moon.

CAN THERE BE A POLAR PLAN?

For the purposes of this discussion, it is fortunate that we now have an opportunity, as well as a challenge, to bring to bear all our wisdom upon the development of public and private policy in a relatively virgin area. Several years ago, in a session on Arctic problems in Fairbanks, I voiced the view that little time would be available in Alaska to work out a viable policy for development. Such a policy would be required to assure that, if resources were to be tapped, procedures to do so would have to be consistent with the preservation of wilderness areas and for the protection of significant ecological balances. The task would not be easy, but the time for crystallization of views was around the corner.

Since that time, meetings of interested agencies, individuals and private groups have been convened. They have so far produced much acrimony, few original proposals for new legislation and no acceptable consensus. In the meantime, large oil resources have been discovered, and other natural resources appear to be in rich potential supply.

The dilemmas posed by the Arctic are familiar ones. The areas involved are under multiple national jurisdictions, *e.g.,* Canada, U.S.A., Norway, Sweden, Finland, U.S.S.R. Each of these sovereignties has long-standing administrative structures and experienced personnel to deal with polar problems. None have so far evolved joint institutions, of all the interested nations, which might lead to concerted policies best calculated to preserve the interests of all. The issues, of course, are simple to state and most difficult to resolve.

The views of the responsible authorities in the U.S. and Canada make clear what these conflicts are. It is equally manifest, that the resolutions of the conflicts are already being made in economic, political and cultural arenas rather than in law. Administrative agencies, endowed with powers initially prescribed by law, are forced into decisions by pressing circumstances. The bases for their decisions, guaranteed to be unacceptable to some, may be gleaned from their recent pronouncements.

At a 1969 conference,[4] the U.S. Secretary of the Interior, Walter J. Hickel, spoke as follows:

> The North is beginning to undergo the most rapid and profound changes ever seen in any wilderness region in world history. It is unlike any other region in the world in many other ways. All of us, throughout the world, who work with the Arctic must find new ways to meet this unprecedented challenge. We need new ideas, new techniques and attitudes, perhaps even new institutions, and we need them in every nation involved in the Arctic. Knowledge of the world's polar regions will change not only the countries bordering on the Arctic—it will change economic, social and cultural conditions throughout the world.

4. Polar Plan Conference, Sep. 29 to Oct. 2, 1969 (Arctic Institute of North America, Washington, D.C.).

Aside from this over-elaborate statement of problem and effect, the Secretary, under the pressures for immediate action because of thy discovery of oil, permitted the construction of hundreds of miles of pipeline through hitherto undisturbed Alaskan terrain. In spite of elaborate precautions to minimize ecologic disturbance, the decision has stirred up a massive hornet's nest among preservationists. Would new law or re-interpretation of the old assist the Secretary in avoiding such heated attacks—unless, of course, his decisions were always in favor of one side or the other. His attempt to sail safely through the treacherous waters between Scylla and Charybdis will never be a fully happy one.

At the same conference[5] John H. Gordon, Assistant Deputy Minister, Department of Indian Affairs and Northern Development of Canada, apparently intends to meet the issues in more forthright language. Realistically, he knows that change will occur and prepares to meet it, in the following terms:

> Time, however, is very definitely not on our side. Developments and events are accelerating and progressively constrict the time frame within which decisions must be taken. I think it is very clear that the allocation of resources, of time, of money, and of able people to these urgent problems must be sharply increased. Otherwise, it appears inevitable that we shall face, and many of the indigenous people will be involved in, major problems of alienation and of social degradation in the very centre of developments which could be a golden opportunity for them. This very real danger defines an obligation which certainly cannot be discharged by transfer payments. The need is to ensure that the residents of these territories have an opportunity to work, to participate, and to share in the decisions affecting their future. Otherwise, their culture and their dignity as men and women are in very great danger of being destroyed.
>
> Turning to the physical environment, the prospects of new mines opening, developments in petroleum, gas, forestry, and construction are exhilarating. At the same time we are very much aware of the responsibilities that we have for preserving the fragile ecology in the North, for the preservation of its natural beauty. The very success we are attaining poses serious dangers in this respect. The need is to find a balance between the continuing and increasing development of northern resources and the protection of the land. It is a critical problem.
>
> Public opinion all over the world has become more urgent in its pleas for conservation and preservation. At the moment, Canada north of 60° is relatively untouched by industrial pollution and

5. *Id.*

disturbance. What policy should the Federal Government evolve? It appears to me there are two sides, two extreme positions.

There are those who would exclude man from the Canada north of 60° and preserve what amounts to a sub-continent in its original state for future and presumably for the benefit of generations to come. On the other hand, this is a hungry world. Frightening forecasts are made of the size of its population just 20 years from today. Man, it appears, must consume more and more merely to subsist. He consumes raw materials, food, manufactured goods and, unavoidably, land and all it contains. This is inescapable and unless and until man is willing and able to control the population explosion, he will continue in this direction. The only way to avoid disturbing the northern environment would be to cease all further activity. However, this seems to be wildly impracticable. Vast resources needed by man for survival, are simply not going to be permitted to lie fallow in a world of have-not nations. Thus, we must face up to the inevitability of disturbance of the environment, except in national parks and other specially reserved areas. The main task confronting us all is to reduce to acceptable levels the bad effects of the exploitation of our natural resources and an expanding population.

This task is one which calls for the enlightened cooperation of the industrialist and the conservationist. Indeed, if I judge the public temper correctly, it will accept nothing less. For much too long the conservationist has been ignored in the headlong rush and almost universal dedication to development. But this situation is changing rapidly. In my own country within a very short time a major hydro-electric development has been blocked on the dual grounds of its likely damaging consequences for the economy of a small Indian group and the ecological implications. The largest Canadian province has become the first to ban the general use of DDT. The Federal government has recently announced tough policies with respect to water pollution. A new cheap process for the treatment of effluent which, it is claimed, will remove 97% of the phosphate nutrients has been announced. It seems clear that the warnings of the ecologists and the frightful evidence of environmental destruction have finally convinced public opinion.

I suggest there is little profit for anyone in extreme positions. Resource development *must* go on; otherwise we shall all starve. The environment *must* be protected; otherwise man and all living things will perish. The solution must lie in cooperation—in jointly discovering how we can avoid both perils and then to get on with the job. We all sit in the same boat which we have just recently discovered is not too seaworthy with some very ominous storms on the horizon. It is no time for uncompromising attitudes, quarrelling and recriminations.

Mr. Gordon, in these extensive quotations, does expose the conflicts in policy, perspective and action which the polar regions exemplify—and which characterize the untouched areas of the globe where they are endowed with the natural resources man seeks and must use. He goes further, in his statement, to delineate the steps he conceives his and other governments must traverse to protect virgin environments:

(a) to establish regulations governing entry into northern lands for exploration and development purposes;
(b) to establish policies and regulations relating to water conservation, use and quality control;
(c) to sponsor a broad program of hydrological and ecological research.

THE CASE OF THE ROTTERDAM REGION

In contrast to the situation described above for polar lands, unopened, sparsely used, lightly populated, let us review the plans and programs of an old, sophisticated, developed region, also confronted with the whole spectrum of environmental restraints and hazards.

The Port of Rotterdam was the child of hydrologic good fortune. It sits along a sharp bend of the Rhine. The current still provides there a depth between 15 and 20 feet, ample for the ships of long past days—a value non-existent for other fishing villages along the coast.[6] As time went on the port grew in size and importance. In May, 1940, the old center of Rotterdam was completely destroyed by German bombers and in October, 1944, about 35 percent of the port facilities were destroyed by German mines. During the Second World War the port came to a complete standstill. Was this, after the War, an opportunity for change or a return to the original status quo? Under such or similar circumstances, either man-made or by natural catastrophe, cities and regions throughout the world chose both routes, with the return to anterior status quo in the majority. Nostalgia prevailed over vision, or economics over esthetics.

Rotterdam has chosen a middle course after catastrophe, albeit with magnificent imagination, tempered by geography, economics, technology and political acumen. A circle, about 310 miles around this core city, covers an area with a population of 160 million people. The same radius circle around New York City, for example, encompasses a population of 50 million people. The Dutch region seems destined to become the new industrial axis of Northwestern Europe. The whole industrial pattern is changing and Rotterdam's

---

6. These and subsequent observations on this area I owe to Comm. on Science and Astronautics, Rotterdam—Europort (U.S. House of Representatives, 1969).

evolution is geared to it. It is and will remain an engineer's haven of activity for years to come.

In preparing for present and future growth it deepens harbors to accommodate ships of over 250,000 tons deadweight, with a draught of about 80 to 85 feet. By the year 2000, it proposes to develop required land for industries to the extent of 43,960 hectares or some 110,000 acres. Much of this will result from the recapture of marsh or "wet lands." The acreage is to be used for refineries, chemical industries, metals, basic steel, ship cleaning and repairs, container and general cargo handling.

The officials show complete awareness that the pace of this project development is not only contingent upon political acceptance, money and skill, but a highly integrated infra-structure. Roads, highways, railroads, metro transit, pipe lines, power facilities, water supply and waste handling systems will need to be heroically expanded on a fairly rigid time schedule.

Does the development of the Rotterdam Region do ecological violence to the natural environment? Historically, public policy in Holland has always favored man-made change in nature. If this were not so, there would be no Holland. It would be worth an orderly doctorate thesis to assess the pros and cons of such a national policy—the results of which are clear and measurable throughout its history. Would the application of the legal doctrines, being pressed in the U.S. today for the protection of wet lands, the preservation of the dunes, the exclusion of human adjustment of the sea littoral, if applied to Holland, have been wise for nature or man? It is conceivable that the long history of concessions to man's necessities for space and industrial development has produced irrevocable damage to nature. The extent of these disabilities and the means of avoiding them in the future would certainly be worth exploration and assessment.

EFFORTS AT POLLUTION ABATEMENT IN VARIOUS COUNTRIES

In many of the European countries, as in most American States, statutory prohibition of water pollution has been on the books for decades. In almost all cases, standards of quality for receiving bodies of water have been promulgated. Within and without the Iron Curtain countries these restraints have been available for a long time. In spite of them, however, water degradation has not, with some important exceptions, been prevented. The reasons for failure to forestall objectionable consequences are not difficult to detect. The desire for industrial growth, the proliferation of people, the unavailability of money to make correctives promptly, were not matched by militant public interest and concern, by official administrative action, or by court implementation. Punitive action on the legislative books is not synonymous with prevention or correction. It might even be surmised that the public has priorities, inarticulately expressed, which do not come up to the hopes of the more articulate minority conservation groups.

The case for air pollution control may perhaps be a more optimistic one, particularly in England. In that country, with its extraordinary meteorologic situation, the drive for cleaner air appears to be succeeding. Some may claim that, even there, prohibitory statutes have had less impact than technology, in shifting fuel from coal to oil and still later to gas. Regardless of specific causes, progress is discernible in some places.

On the other hand, the rapidly increasing use of the automobile and its objectionable exhausts may substitute a new hazard for an old and disappearing one. The mobile society exacts a price in air quality degradation, which is technologically difficult to avoid. Progress is being made in the U.S. in the reduction of this hazard, again not to the satisfaction of more impatient members of our society.

International agreements among the countries of Europe, directed toward pollution abatement, have been singularly devoid of significant accomplishment. Like so many treaties and conventions, they generate high hopes and satisfactions in signators, largely because of the beauties of language therein. They bespeak laudable agreements on high principles. They omit implementary mechanisms and money—and the powers which these might enforce. In some instances, such agencies engage in data collection—laudable in purpose and sedative in producing correctives.

Even in international allocations of waters, permanent agreements are rare, because economic and political considerations are eternally in flux. This has been true, in the U.S., with respect to the Rio Grande, the Colorado and the Columbia Rivers. India and Pakistan have an uneasy truce on the Indus. The Jordan River, under scrutiny for more than a quarter of a century, still bears no international seal. The Rhine and the Danube understandings need both new crystallization and dynamic implementations.

On the Rhine, authorities of Germany, Holland, France, Switzerland and Luxembourg are periodically re-awakened by sudden excessive contaminations dramatically publicized, even in a milieu already heavily degraded over the years. The accidental discharge of a poisonous insecticide in mid 1969, bringing an unusually high mortality of fish, served such a purpose. Renewed pressures toward speeding up corrective measures were imposed upon the International Commission for the Protection of the Rhine. The Commission, created in 1963, was only the latest of a series of efforts to have upstream nations assume some real responsibility for protecting downstream nation users of Rhine River waters.[7]

As one might surmise, money required to prevent this pollution, either by removal at its source or by subsequent treatment, will exceed some four billion U.S. dollars by 1975. The stakes are high in degradation of quality and equally high in costs of alleviation. The experience perhaps justifies the dictum that the will to change must invigorate and activate the words of international agreements.

SOME MISCELLANEOUS, BUT IMPORTANT, PROBLEMS

No single paper could possibly encompass the totality of environmental impacts upon man. Some have more significance than others. Their significance may be accidental and temporary. Some may have subtle, long-term terminal effects. Some have strong subjective influences, while others lead almost to hysterical reflexes. Because of this very wide spectrum of impacts, every policy maker and administrator is confronted with the necessity of measurement, of quantification, and of assessment. Not only concentration, time, extent, and location must be evaluated, but priority of decision and action. In the real world, it is still true that some environmental influences are more objectionable than others. By a "blunderbuss" policy, one might generate political satisfaction, but not real prevention or correction. The doomsday prophet proclaims the necessity of zero risk—hardly attainable, rarely necessary and sometimes even harmful (as in the elimination of natural immunity). Differentiating between the important and the insignificant, between the known and the unknown, between the ideal and the possible, is the difficult task of the administrator. In general, he is helped most by science and technology, by economics and by social understanding. Crystallizations in law are perhaps less calculated to provide the wisdom, maturity and judgment he so badly needs.

The present acclaim accorded to peoples' confrontation in public decision making, resting as it does upon a laudable thesis, is due some emerging reservations. "Vox populi," historically, has had its ups and downs and its validities and errors.[8] It is questionable whether a plebiscite is the sensible way (even via congressional action) to deter-

7. The discussion of *Pollution as an International Issue* is elaborated by the author in 47 Foreign Affairs 164-75 (Oct. 1968).
8. G. Boas, Vox Populi—Essays in the History of an Idea (1969).

mine where and when an antibiotic or a contraceptive pill should be used. Confrontation loses value when it is clear that neither consensus nor decision is likely to ensue. Indecision and deferment have their risks, too. A few indications of the disparity between popular assumption and scientific verity are here noted.

A. Radiation

The sea disposal of radioactive wastes gives rise to many questions, perhaps because of the manner in which we are made aware of the power of nuclear energy, but it is significant that the working group of the Intergovernmental Oceanographic Commission, surveying the situation on a world-wide basis, noted that because of the rigid control exercised over the atomic energy industry since its inception, the working group has no examples of adverse effects brought about by the discharge into the sea of radioactive elements. They might also have noted that all the wastes so far discharged into the sea are insignificant in relation to the amount of radioactivity reaching it from bomb fall-out.[9]

The atoms industry, aside from weapons testing, is by far the safest in the world for those working in it or those so far living outside of its protected zones.

B. Air Contaminents

The health effects of air pollution are better understood today than 20 years ago. Laboratory and field research, coupled with the difficult epidemiologic inquiries, are providing increasing clarification of biological effects, while at the same time sharpening perspective regarding some alleged effects. The work going on in this field throughout the world will unravel the situation to provide more valid criteria and standards than are now available. The status of air monitoring is likewise undergoing scrutiny, first, because it is far less extensive than desired, secondly, because the appropriate parameters to be measured are under review and, third, because it is difficult and costly.

It is of interest to note that, of many pollutants measured, dust is now considered to be of little medical importance, since dust particles are too large to be inhaled by man. Dust, like exhaust gases from Diesel engines, arouses public disgust. Although these exhaust gases are often considered to be a major source of pollution, they have been shown repeatedly *not* to contain sufficient amounts of any toxic substance to produce harmful effects on the human body.

9. *Sea Pollution*, 89 Royal Soc'y of Health J. 116 (May-June 1969).

There are many good reasons, other than health effects, for removing particulates.

Sulphur oxides in air have been severely limited by agencies, at all levels of government, sometimes it would appear with tongue in cheek (as some officials phrased it: "Why not push it down beyond reason, regardless of cost—it's popular!"). The concentrations found in the 1952 London fog, by the Air Pollution Research Unit of the Medical Research Council, are considered insufficient to produce the harmful effects on man caused by air pollution. The concentration of these substances should be regarded mainly as an index of the general level of pollution.

Extensive studies in London, of both mortality and morbidity during fog periods from 1952 to 1962, make quite clear that sulphur dioxide is not the responsible agent of excess disease, and that the effects of acute pollution are complex. It is not sufficient merely to measure smoke and sulphur dioxide. Leonard Greenburg and Marvin Glasser, on the other hand, claim that 0.2-0.4 ppm of SO_2 do cause excess deaths in New York City.

Popular alarm was generated only a few years ago, by many official agencies, with respect to the effect of discharges of 3, 4 benzpyrene and other polycyclic hydrocarbons. These are undoubtedly carcinogenic. There is no evidence, however, that, in the amounts normally present in air, they have any detectable effect in causing lung cancer. It is not possible to exclude air pollution completely as a causal agent of the disease. Its effects, if any, are negligible in comparison with those of cigarette smoking.[10]

These comments have special pertinence in the consideration of the wisdom of rushing to national and international standards as a panacea for control. The maximum permissible concentrations adopted in different countries vary widely. Too often, these guides are not based on completely reliable evidence. More often than not, they are transferred in toto from one country to another, without regard to the fact that social conditions, administrative and legal systems, and stages of development differ markedly.

Too much emphasis has been placed in the U.S. and elsewhere on the subject of guides and standards. These actions result from an unwarranted faith in the corrective value of standards—a faith more often violated than observed. One great country, devoted to standards, meets this dilemma by a delightful distinction between "hygiene standards" (based on purely scientific, medical, or

10. All of the above observations on health effects of air pollution have their origin in the report of the deliberations of experts from some 40 countries. The official document is EURO-1143, 23 World Health Organization Chronicle, No. 6, at 264-74 (June 1969).

physiological criteria) and "sanitary standards" (which take into account practical difficulties in achieving the "hygiene standard" in any given area).

A more pragmatic approach has been followed in the United Kingdom, where statutory maximum limits are rarely laid down in air pollution, or, for that matter, in water pollution. The policy is to take energetic practical action to reduce pollution rather than to attempt, with scarce manpower, money and knowledge, to define the precise composition of what might ultimately be accepted as pure air.

C. Accidents

In a busy world, accidents occur in transport, on the ground, on the oceans, and in the air. The *Torrey Canyon,* the *African Queen,* the Santa Barbara and myriads of other episodes remind us of the hazards imposed by spills. In a given year, hundreds of such accidents occur. With modern communications systems, their dramatic aspects are fully exploited. Their disastrous consequences, real or imaginary, are loudly proclaimed hour by hour. And, of course, a law must be rapidly enacted to prevent, to punish or to assess and collect damages.

Virtually all of the accidents, whether on land or sea, are the result of a variety of causes—rarely due solely to carelessness. Many, after the event, disclose deficiencies in navigation aids, design of containment, defects in structural design or maintenance. Management of the consequences of an accident has demonstrated, particularly at sea, a great confusion among administrative agencies, and an even greater ignorance of scientific control to reduce evil effects. When these difficulties are compounded by no inconsiderable hysteria the control is likely to be less than good.

In spite of these confused demonstrations, the actual consequences of the dramatic episodes have been far less publicized. The orderly scientific findings of the biologic impacts rarely find their way into the television studios and the screens. This is particularly true in the case of the *Torrey Canyon, African Queen* or chlorine barge sinking in the Mississippi. Non-dramatic consequences have little Madison Avenue appeal.

Real values result from accidents. Improved methods of clean-up are learned. Agencies' responsibilities are coordinated. Scientific correctives are developed. Prevention is advanced by improved design and warning systems, by defining corporate responsibility and by providing methods of assessing damages and allocating costs.

All of these important consequences move in fact toward crystallization via either private agreements (as in oil spills), advances in technology and administrative practice or statutory underpinning, or all three. It is well to recall that international agreements on the prevention of and penalty for oil spills at sea have been on the books for some decades. They do not eliminate the problems.

SUMMARY

The impact of man upon his environment has existed since man himself walked the earth. Whatever man does changes the ecology of his surroundings for good or evil. As populations grow, as urbanization and industrialization move forward and as science and technology burgeon, the potentiality for ecologic disturbance and degradation increases. This is the history of the centuries and the impressive lesson of the last quarter of a century.

Man's desire to protect himself against his own actions has likewise primitive origins. Even when living space was great, he learned, always the hard way, that he must avoid his own human wastes and that he must husband his natural resources. These he always practiced with less than maximum success for himself and for nature. As these situations become more acute, as they now have, he searches for better and safer ways of life, for the preservation of rare wilderness areas, for raising the esthetic quality of life and for protecting values for his descendants.

All of these laudable objectives, however, come into competition with desires which science and technology increasingly satisfy. In their satisfaction, wastes occur, resources are tapped, wilderness areas are invaded and human rights are offended. The cycle is old and efforts to meet the attacks have produced partial, but not one hundred percent, success. It is doubtful whether man can survive within a formula which guarantees the attainment of all ecological balances. The hope is that, with increasing emphasis upon a high environmental ethic of quality and a vigilant eye on ecological equilibrium, we may do better in the future than in the past. This desire cannot be gainsaid, even though one does not accept the doomsday prophecies of today.

Given the thesis that man creates and modifies his environment for good and evil, what are the means available to him for avoiding the bad and multiplying the good consequences of his existence? The most valuable tool is in his better understanding of the environment and how his actions affect it. This awareness alone, however, does not guarantee that he will act militantly to take those measures to safeguard his surroundings. Motivation is the high ingredient necessary, followed by the availability of money and professional manpower.

Law alone, at least from past experience, does not produce the desired result of protecting human rights, when the above ingredients in policy and action are missing. This is because human behavior is complex, often selfish, often unpredictable and frequently ignores human rights. The underpinning provided by law obviously assists in the protection of man and nature, provided public intent, economic pressures, health and safety so validate the law.

The hope that our purposes may be accomplished by fiat is one long cherished by many. This hope has culminated in the Environmental Policy Act of 1969, recently signed by the President of the United States. It is described by Senator Henry M. Jackson, Chairman of the Senate Interior Committee, as "the most important and far reaching conservation measure ever enacted." Like so much legislation, it is essentially a statement of good intentions and, as such, might well push forward our equally good objectives. It remains to be seen.

THE INDIVIDUAL AND THE ENVIRONMENT

CHRISTIAN de LAET†
and
SUSAN SINGH††

Since pollution control first captured the public attention several years ago theoreticians and amateurs alike have been looking for a means whereby the individual would be encouraged to take greater cognizance of the health of the environment in his day-to-day activities. The range of these inquiries can be broken down into four areas: prohibition through law, manipulation through economic incentives and disincentives, control through institutional structures, and development of the public conscience.[1] The one area which appears to hold the key to all the others is the latter one, an attempt to have people reassume the burden of the individual and collective responsibility which forms the cornerstone of our jurisprudence.

In the area of pollution control it appears that little can be accomplished until the individual recognizes his role in the creation of the problem and modifies his behavior. At the moment, man does not extend to the environment the notion of good neighborhood. Laws are an imperfect control mechanism however attractive they may appear as a visible course of action demanding little from the public purse. Schemes to install a market mechanism for disposal rights are unwieldy and uncertain of success. Institutions mean more of the same pattern of faulty management of environmental problems. Therefore, the only conclusion when searching for mechanisms for improved environmental management is to look at the common denominator to all these areas, the individual.

There are several reasons to suppose that the individual can rise to these demands for personal responsibility when external forces have not led to change. This article will outline some of the current trends that seem to be pointing towards greater individual involvement. Among these are the changing values of society that have given a new perspective to environmental issues; a new sense of the immediacy of the environment; a recognition of the value of restraint by the individual; and the interest of governments in public input to policy planning. In short, cause and effect relationships are being perceived

---

† Secretary-General of the Canadian Council of Resource and Environment Ministers, an intergovernmental consultative body in the area of renewable resources development and environmental management.

†† Associate, Canadian Council of Resource and Environment Ministers.

1. A. R. Thompson, *Legal Responses to Pollution Problems—Their Strengths and Weaknesses* (Twelfth Pacific Science Congress unpublished manuscript, 1971).

on a more mundane plane, and people are responding with their own sense of strategy and place.

NEW GOALS

Currently society is in the midst of questioning its value system. One dimension of this review is the introduction of a new parameter into the range of goals of society—that of the well-being of the environment as the ultimate warrant to our continued dominance on the planet, if not survival. Gradually we are coming to consider that in addition to those traditional goals shaping our lives such as health, food, shelter and self-realization is the right of the individual to a healthy environment. This may well have arisen out of the fear that these other goals would not be attainable without this one, but nonetheless it is a beginning of a greater sense of responsibility by the individual towards his surroundings.

A FINITE WORLD

Questions of the environment have impinged very little upon our consciousness so far. Garbage and sewage disposal have long been delegated tasks in which the citizen takes little interest as to techniques or end results. In many cases, this is to be regretted since the tangible costs of these essential services are obscured by the distance which our ethics command we should maintain from these "unmentionables." Similarly, in industry the simple act of physically removing wastes beyond the factory fence has long been thought a sufficient form of management. Even personal nuisances such as litter, noise and automobile exhausts have not generally been perceived individually as a part of the overall environmental crisis.

But this is changing. Man is beginning to realize that his environment is finite. Large populations have been drawn into cities by urban and industrial forces which in combination have placed a great burden upon the immediate surroundings. The results are a strain upon the resource base and the destruction of the only physical outlet to the urban maze. We see that some form of reallocation of the environmental supply must take place. Although man first looks for outside sources to blame, he must inevitably return to the individual either in his corporate or private role. It is man, by his dereliction of responsibility, his unconcern for the finality of his actions and his irresponsibility towards the capital value of his physical and natural environment, who is the primary force. We have met the enemy and to quote Pogo, "he is us." What we must now look for is some means to exercise this new sense of individual responsibility first through self-restraint and then through a communality of action.

THE ROLE OF RESTRAINT

The individual accepts many constraints on his behavior in the interests of the common good. These are meted out in rewards and penalties to physical, social and economic well-being of which most people understand and to which most subscribe. In general, however, this code of behavior is based on directly observable interests such as home, property and business. It is part of the fabric of our life that in order to make rights tangible there must be countervailing obligations upon them.

As the environment becomes something in which the individual perceives a specific personal interest as part of the general public right, we can expect that he will seek means to exercise his claim. He will look for systems of regulations, penalties and payments which parallel those applied to private property rights to enforce responsibility toward the public good. This can already be observed in the recent turn to litigation on environmental issues, particularly in the United States. These endeavors have unfortunately met with only partial success as a device of environmental management, largely because a parallel situation has not been deemed to exist between private and public property. The claim of the individual to a voice in what has heretofore been regarded as a common issue has not generally been granted.

SOME LEGAL PROBLEMS

The legal system in the western world is largely based on a tradition of personal responsibility through private property rights. When a matter comes into dispute, the purpose of the ensuing legal proceedings is either to determine responsibility and thereby assign blame, or to speak from a position of right and obtain prohibition. Each of the two parties to the dispute has a status recognized by the court through private holdings. Should their rights be held in common property, however, the situation is viewed quite differently. The right to engage in a dispute is called into question on the grounds that being one of many with rights, the individual can claim no uniqueness of position in terms of the injury suffered. Furthermore, one person cannot generally act as a representative of an affected group even though its members may have suffered identifiable damage.

Some advance has been made in the question of standing before the courts in common property questions. Certain judgments have recognized the rights of a group by reason of a special concern with the issues of aesthetics and environmental management to be heard on an issue involving these considerations.[2] These cases are currently being judged individually, with no guarantee of parallel results for parallel claims. Rather, one can expect that given the apparent reluctance of the courts to open up the limitations on access, these precedents may be overlooked in future rulings.[3] What appears necessary is a concerted effort by the legal profession to review this situation and bring it up to date with current expectations and current views of justice.

As environmental issues appear more frequently for judgment in the courts, difficulties will become increasingly apparent in levying penalties in keeping with the social setting which led to the initiation of the action. The goal in environmental litigation is not merely the imposition of a penalty but an attempt to force a greater consciousness of our abuses of the environment. Fines or payments of damages, even when imposed at maximum levels, risk being viewed by the offenders as part of the cost of operation and do nothing to deter or to ameliorate environmental degradation. Injunctions, the other likely result of legal action, while they can work to obtain the cessation of a new or impending activity, are not likely to be as freely applied to an established activity because of the greater displacement of investment.[4]

In the whole area of sentencing, there are many innovations the courts could consider which would render more appropriate the penalties to the intention of the plaintiff. Where fines or injunctions are inadvisable the courts should follow the trend of certain recent judgments which offer the accused the opportunity of substitute action applied elsewhere within the jurisdiction to recondition a portion of the environment similarly degraded to that part named in the suit. This would have the beneficial result of forcing those involved into a full realization of the extent of man's transgression upon nature. Forcing a look at environmental consequences might lead ultimately to a modification of the original situation which produced the litigation.

In anticipation of this impending problem of appropriate conclusions to litigation, the courts should be looking for new weights in

---

2. H. R. Eddy, *Locus Standi and Environmental Control: A Policy for Comparison,* 6 U.B.C. L. Rev. 207 (1971).

3. *Id.* at 212.

4. J. C. Juergensmeyer, *Common Law Remedies and Protection of the Environment,* 6 U.B.C. L. Rev. 229 (1971).

order to balance the interests of those speaking on behalf of the environment and those taking traditional positions of paramountcy of economic endeavors. The apparent disservice of compulsory pollution control measures has in numerous cases led to new profits through more efficient processing or recovery of valuable by-products. The courts must therefore become more conscious of the true justice of the situation and not be influenced by vested interests. The danger of building a structure of decisions on precedence which overlooks the original intent of a law or the basic trends of social preference is nowhere more evident than in this new face of environmental litigation.

Legal action is only one area that can facilitate the development of individual responsibility towards the environment. Although it is very much in the public view at the moment, and has several strong advocates, it is possibly not the most important area. Litigation has the undeniable drawbacks of differential access, expense, slowness in resolution, resistance to change and, perhaps most important of all, a position after the fact, that lead one to look for other mechanisms. Furthermore, it is a substitute for direct action and reflects a certain breakdown in the transfer and dissemination of social goals.

PUBLIC PARTICIPATION

If the individual is to have this sense of responsibility towards the environment which seems so necessary if any real progress is to be made in safeguarding the environment, then the individual must be able to perceive his own involvement not merely with the environment as a retreat but in the routine activities that affect his surroundings. The public must become increasingly involved, through individual and group inputs, in the decision-making process both at the point when a development scheme first becomes a possibility and then during its formulation and implementation. In this way not only will the public become committed to the well-being of the environment, but also it will understand more fully the implications of environmental quality.

Governments seem increasingly interested in new ways of receiving expressions of the public view. They are aware of the inadequacy of the ballot box to voice public desires on specific issues. In Canada, for example, both the federal and provincial governments are searching for mechanisms to involve the public, knowing that this wider input will assist in clarifying the goals of society and give those taking part in this clarification a greater sense of commitment to the end results.

One of the difficulties governments have experienced in the recent shift in public preferences to a greater consideration of environmental issues has been an uncertainty as to how deeply these views run into the fabric of society. At first glance, the environmental issue has been espoused only by a minority of committed, outspoken individuals and groups. Since implicit to environmental issues are some very difficult questions of industrial development and job security, governments have had to be certain of the breadth of this view.

The mechanisms for determining the public view are by no means certain. Public hearings have been widely used but they have acquired a dubious reputation as a result of two notable areas of mismanagement. Because public hearings tend to be held after the details of a plan are sketched out they often result in a confrontation between the polarized viewpoints of supporters and attackers, precluding any constructive discussion or positive outcome. Hearings have also been used as a vehicle for public education which runs counter to their primary purpose of facilitating a flow of information from the public to the government and which tends to bias the eventual product.

Currently, governments are looking to more general inquiries with the public to define initial premises and to evaluate alternatives. The several instances that have been tried have been most productive and have successfully avoided a conflict between representatives of diverse opinions.[5] People appear to appreciate a situation of open inquiry and respond with constructive inputs of their own. Problems arise only when the inquiry is set up as a meaningless ritual apart from the process of planning and implementation.

The importance of this search for mechanisms for public input rests on the need for communality of view before joint assumption of responsibility to the environment can be workable. At times this may appear unattainable, particularly between persons with diametrically opposing interests each of whom views the other's stand as irresponsible. Often however, the two sides can bridge the gap between them when they realize more fully the factors influencing the position of the other.

In this respect, it must be recognized that there are several kinds of agreement possible between people: agreement on substance, agreement not to agree on substance, and agreement as to why there can be no agreement on substance. Until now we have generally been

5. Canadian Council of Resource Ministers, *Proceedings of Prairie Water Seminar* (unpublished manuscript, 1971); the program of public participation to determine the location of the terminus of highway 417, Ottawa, Canada.

satisfied with first order agreements on substance. In fact, it has often been convenient not to recognize that more than first order agreements are possible. But we can no longer be satisfied with this simple view, particularly in the face of growing social and environmental pressures which may render first order agreements impossible. It is only through creative approaches to the interaction between groups that a fuller exploration of issues is possible and a move beyond standard outlooks can be made. The goal towards which we must move cannot be obtained by legal coercion either prescriptive or punitive. It is not amenable to the marketplace and probably cannot be successfully institutionalized in the formal sense of that word. It must proceed with each event so that gradually under pressure from the public to advance, and with the willingness of the government to respond, there will emerge a general expectation for individual response to these issues and an understanding of the individual role.

CONCLUSION

The development of environmental procedures in contemporary society must rest on a cornerstone of public commitment and responsibility. This implies a public dialogue on current and changing values, doctrines and choices so that the response formulated may be characterized by relevance, clarity and finality. The role of the jurist and the administrator is to apply their traditional crafts in new ways to translate the emerging ethic into workable systems. The result must reflect the social sense of justice and not necessarily the view of clinical excellence held by these professions. Done in a creative way many of the apparently insoluble problems now facing us will resolve themselves. Anything less will reduce these professions to technicians patching up after the fact.

CHANCES AND PROBLEMS OF INTERNATIONAL AGREEMENTS ON ENVIRONMENTAL POLLUTION

DR. KLAUS BOISSERÉE†

International regulations on environmental protection are often deemed necessary. In government programs there prevails a conviction that the future task of fighting environmental pollution is going to lead to international agreements. This concept is supported by the increasing activity of international organizations in the field of environmental protection.[1]

This seeming "communis opinio" does not render superfluous a reflection on the real chances of "concerted actions" on an international level. The following argument regarding the chances and problems of international agreements on the sector of environmental protection is primarily based on the situation as it represents itself from the European point of view. Large parts of Europe belong to the areas with pronounced environmental protection problems. This is why an intensive and international discussion on questions concerning environmental conditions has come up between the European states both inside and outside the Common Market.

One of the obvious and most frequently discussed environmental problems is the pollution of the air. International agreements in this field are difficult since there is—in comparison to water pollution—no "canalization" of emissions. Discussion of international activities in respect to air pollution control may thus be representative of the general problems involved. This article concentrates mainly on this sector and on multilateral activities since they may be particularly symptomatic of the efforts made towards an international activity in other parts of the world.

There are numerous reasons which may lead to international cooperation in the field of environmental protection. The fact that environmental dangers are cropping up simultaneously in all states is no sufficient reason for an internationalization of the problems.

†Ministerium für Arbeit, Gesundheit und Soziales, Dusseldorf (Federal Republic of Germany) Dr. Jur.; Member, Committee of Experts on Air Pollution of the Council of Europe; Member, ICEL; Member, Institut International des Sciences Administretif.

1. The Council of Europe is an organization of 19 European countries under international law which was founded in 1947 upon the initiative of Winston Churchill with the aim of better cooperation on the political and humanitarian sector between all nations of Europe; the states of Eastern Europe do not belong to the Council of Europe; the Council of Europe has its head office in Strasbourg; its bodies are the committee of ministers, the consulting meeting, European committees and bodies of experts as well as the Secretary-General.

In addition there are the following reasons for international agreements on environmental protection:

1) As far as questions regarding air or water pollution control are concerned, it is pointed out that air and water pollution do not stop at national frontiers. Protective measures which are limited to state boundaries may fail to be effective if similar measures are not taken in the neighboring country. This is true not only of pollution problems in the immediate frontier area, but also of the transportation of dangerous substances in the air and in the water over large distances to more remotely situated countries or in the open sea, including the danger of regional or global changes of climate associated with it. The general limitation of emissions tainting the atmosphere to avoid global or regional damages caused by biozide or radioactive substances should also be mentioned as a basis for international action.

2) Another reason for "harmonizing" environmental protection is the fact that nearly all methods in reducing environmental pollution constitute an economic burden for owners or operators of installations, vehicles or equipment causing emissions. Different requirements, particularly within economic areas competing with one another, may result in distortions of competition.

3) A slightly deviating special problem arises for the European Common Market whereby trade obstructions may be the consequence of differing environmental protection requirements.

4) Finally, it is emphasized that the recognition and assessment of environmental problems and measures for control and abatement call for substantial research and development work today and in the future. This could be done more quickly and at less expense if, owing to international agreements, knowledge and experiences could be exchanged among the states.

The present stage of international considerations regarding environmental protection shows that regulations dealing with common problems (frontier problems) or regional or global dangers have a certain chance of being included in bilateral international agreements. An example of this is the international non-proliferation agreement. The European Common Market is also interested in avoiding trade obstacles, thus avoiding disadvantageous effects of environmental protection. Some efforts have been made towards the international exchange of experiences and the pooling of research results. Certain international organizations are particularly active in this field.

In defining common maximum values (limits) and other environmental protection activities for the prevention of distortions of competition, agreement appears to be a long way off. Opinions on the necessity and possibility of a "concerted" action are not undisputed. As an example of a "dissenting vote," the following may be quoted from the annual report 1969 of the British Alkali-Inspectorate (the British Air Pollution Control Authority):

> ...In theory, it is common sense to have agreed international standards of emission, air quality, criteria, and enforcement but in practice there are many obstacles ahead and many differences in viewpoint which are going to be difficult to resolve ...
>
> Although it would be wishful thinking to believe that unanimity on action and standard is close at hand, whatever can be agreed, flexibility must be left for each nation to assess its own special problems and to tackle them in the manner best suited to its own particular conditions of population, economy, topography, meteology, national character, law making and system of government ...

Despite this view and with the development towards a uniform European Economic Area, the need for harmonizing the requirements in restraint of competition has become urgent for the EEC-States within the frame of the Common Market but definitely not only for them alone. This particularly applies to the German economy which, owing to the concentration of its industry and its population density, appears to be particularly stressed by the requirements of air pollution control.

Although Article 100 *et seq.* of the EEC-Agreement offer formal possibilities for the unification of legislation, these powers, even if environment protection is considered to be part of the health and social policy, are passively based on the fact that competition and trade are restrained within the Common Market.[2] The problem is that the EEC-Instrument is (at least at the present stage of development in the six member states of the EEC) suitable for equalizing the existing regulations which are of a trade restraining nature. But with regard to competition, it is principally irrelevant in which way this is done. Seen from the viewpoint of the environmental and health policy of the individual states, it is possible only to "freeze" existing national regulations and impose them equally on other partners of the community of states. Even a reduction of environmental requirements is often accepted through an international compromise. An example of this is the European settlement regarding the consolidation of national provisions on the purification of exhaust gases of motor vehicles.

Thus there exists no European environmental policy within the

2. The provisions related to social policy in the EEC-Agreement, Article 117, do not refer to questions of environmental hygiene and reduction of emission.

EEC which is more than just a harmonization for the prevention of trade restraints. Recently, however, a program for comprehensive environmental activities within the "Community of the Six" was promulgated by the Commission of the European Communities. Such harmonized progressive standardization on a European level, however, requires a special mandate regarding environment and health policy which is neither included in the EEC-Agreement nor in the Contract on the European Community for Coal and Steel. In addition the Treaties of Rome do not constitute a basis for the solution of special frontier questions, particularly with regard to equal procedural treatment of the population on either side of national frontiers and with regard to administrative cooperation in view of the assessment of projects and installations near frontiers where emissions can be expected.

It was, therefore, obvious for these reasons that other international organizations, although of a weaker organizational and legal structure but with more comprehensive functions than the European Communities, took charge of the problems of air pollution control on a supra-national level.

The coordination of research projects and the control of special technical developments for the supervision and reduction of air pollution is mainly part of the working program of the OECD,[3] the WHO,[4] the WMO,[5] and also of the civilian sector of NATO (committee on questions concerning the challenge by modern society) and the ECE.[6] The official exchange of opinions and experiences between the experts is undertaken by associations of non-governmental organizations. The Council of Europe in Strasbourg has developed a program which is to serve the purpose of comparison and unification of legal provisions, technical standards as well as the practical and organizational operations.

The activity of the Council of Europe in the field of air pollution control has meanwhile reached an effective stage and has shown results.[7] The committee of ministers of the Council of Europe has included[8] the supra-national problems of air pollution control into its international working program.

3. European Organization for Economical Cooperation and Development.
4. World Health Organization of the United Nations.
5. Meteorological Organization of the United Nations.
6. Economic Council for Europe of the United Nations. Besides the European states (West and East), the U.S. is also a member of the Economic Council.
7. International Union of Air Pollution Prevention Associations (members are free organizations from Argentina, Australia, the Federal Republic of Germany, France, United Kingdom, United States).
8. Secretary-General, Council of Europe, Man in a European Society (1966/67 and 1968/69).

The European committee of experts entrusted with the preparation of decisions of official bodies of the Council of Europe—committee of ministers, consultant meeting—has consolidated[9] its work in the manner indicated by the 1965 European Conference on questions on air pollution. The committee has worked out a comprehensive comparative statement and analysis of all legislative provisions of the member states on air pollution control, published in a document of the Council of Europe.[10] Based on the results of the comparison of legislative provisions and the critical consideration of an optimal legislative solution, the expert committee has investigated the possibilities of harmonizing or approaching the various domestic provisions of the European states. This work was facilitated by the fact that the principles of the various national laws are more alike than was generally assumed. Not all member states, however, have an environmental protection law which is comprehensive in respect to the scope of application.

This work is reflected in the recommendation for a model of European legislation. On March 9, 1968 the committee of ministers of the Council of Europe unanimously adopted[11] a Declaration of Principles on Air Pollution Control and recommended that the governments of the member states[12] consider these principles when setting up programs for the prevention and reduction of air pollution. At the same time, governments were requested to draw the attention of the public to this declaration of principles and to report once every three years to the Council of Europe on the measures taken in accordance with the Declaration of Principles.

An attempt is made to explain the Declaration of Principles without anticipating a political valuation of the document in the following discussion:

1) The document of the Council of Europe includes, first of all, such principles on national legislation on air pollution control as a model for legislative acts in this field of all European states. It is of particular importance that this European model, which is in accordance with German legislation, is based on the principle of prevention and provides that each person causing air pollution be held responsible for the reduction or at least better dispersal of his emissions

---

9. The Conference was organized by the consultant meeting of the Council of Europe and was attended by members from overseas.

10. Council of Europe Doc. EXP/AIR at 1 (1968).

11. Comm. Ministers, Council of Europe, Res. 4/68, Declaration de Principes sur la Lutte Contre la Pollution de l'Air (Declaration of Principles on Air Pollution Control).

12. Member states are Belgium, the Federal Republic of Germany, Denmark, France, Ireland, Iceland, Italy, Luxembourg, Malta, the Netherlands, Norway, Austria, Sweden, Switzerland, Turkey, the United Kingdom (England), and Cyprus.

without the offended party having to furnish proof of damage. As far as the classification in the legal system is concerned, the Declaration of Principles by interpolating public authorities for the control and ordering of improvement measures clearly envisages an arrangement under public law.

2) The legal means are quite concretely described. The construction or modification of installations substantially contributing to air pollution shall be subject to approval. For the purpose of limiting emissions, approval procedures shall provide for requirements to be fixed as to the location, construction and operation. Special provision is also to be made for the improvement of existing installations. In the opinion of the Council of Europe, requirements as to the type of operation shall be primarily taken into consideration for installations which are (under the aspect of air pollution control) of minor significance, if a great number of such individually less significant sources results in a concentration of air pollution in certain areas. This is obviously meant in respect to heating installations of medium or smaller size as well as of commercial emission sources for which the introduction of individual approval procedures can scarcely be taken into consideration. With regard to motor vehicles and mass-produced appliances which are the subject of cross-frontier traffic or international trade respectively, the Declaration of Principles provides for the greatest possible uniformity in view of standards of construction and operation insofar as the requirements regarding the reduction of air pollution are concerned.

The Council of Europe requires (and this is probably the most important point from a practical standpoint) administrative bodies in all member states for the control of air pollution and the enforcement of legal provisions as well as for the introduction of improvement measures. Legislation and administration shall be designed in such a way that due account can be taken of new procedures, technical improvements and scientific progress. Mention is also made of the possibility of taking measures in regions requiring increased protection. This is obviously intended for the protection of recreational areas, natural parks and heavily polluted areas where smog alarm plans are necessary.

3) The Declaration of Principles provides for the cost incurred by measures taken to prevent or reduce air pollution to be principally borne by the person having caused it. It is, however, expressly stated that in this case contributions from public funds are not to be excluded. Government aid is expressly appealed to with regard to the promotion and encouragement of investigation and research into technical means for the improvement of air pollution control and for

studies on the distribution of air pollutants and their effects on man and his environment.

Attempting to make an analysis of the Declaration of Principles, it should be mentioned that the declaration is a recommendation only and not a binding European convention. This is a disadvantage of the document, although it cannot be denied that it is easier to pass a really progressive model for European legislation in the recommended form rather than in the form of a legal convention where there is the risk of only including such standards that can be agreed upon by all nations on the basis of existing legal provisions. In addition, it ought to be said that a binding standardization by convention and the unification of legislation goes hand in hand with a harmonization of administrative practices and technical knowledge provided that it is absolutely clear how air pollution control functions in the individual state. But apart from these reservations, there is no reason why the Declaration of Principles could not at a later date be the basis for a still more extensive supra-national action of the Council of Europe.

Analysis of European legislation revealed that in most states air pollution controls are not exhaustively set forth in laws or regulations that could, at least theoretically, be harmonized by a formal act. The taking advantage of procedural knowledge causes (at least to the same extent as do the differences in legislation) inequities within air pollution control in Europe.

A comparison with the objective of an optimal adaptation and unification is doubtlessly difficult although no less essential in this case where numerous individual questions concerning production as well as environment conditions are involved. As far as this is concerned, the Council of Europe is only at the beginning of its work; not only shall information be obtained and made available for practical use by means of examples selected from the field of significant lines of industry in our countries but also comparative criteria shall be found on the effects and possibilities of an actual harmonization. The question of a "Europe-wide" standardization of certain emissions has proved to present a special problem in respect of this part of the work (particularly air pollutions with sulfur content). The question of establishing uniform standards for the quality of raw materials and fuels to be used in all countries is also going to be considered.

The prevention of frontier conflicts caused by air pollution has from the very beginning played a significant role in the work of the Council of Europe. Here, the problem of equal treatment of the population and administrative bodies on either side of the frontier is involved as far as the installation or the effects of close to frontier air pollution sources are concerned.

The committee of ministers has passed a resolution on a consultation procedure for close to frontier problems in which, in order to prevent international problems through air pollution and guarantee equal treatment to the population along international frontiers, it is recommended that member states:

1) Ensure for the inhabitants of regions beyond their frontiers the same protection against air pollution in frontier areas as is provided for their own inhabitants.

2) To this end, they should ensure that the competent authorities should inform each other in good time about any project for installations liable to pollute the atmosphere beyond the frontier.

3) The competent authorities beyond the frontier should be able to make their comments on such projects. These comments should be given the same consideration and treatment as if they had been made by the inhabitants of the country where the plant is situated or proposed.

Recommendations of the Council of Europe concerning a limitation of emissions of sulfur and lead compounds are aimed[13] at a certain prevention of distortion of competition and a limitation of total emissions. Finally, the Council of Europe has passed principles on the coordination of efforts made in town and land planning and in air pollution control.[14]

Some of the work within the frame of the Council of Europe program, which has been described here, has not yet been completed. But not only has information material that can be used for documentary purposes been established but also a frame for a uniform European legislation on air pollution has been created.

The objectives of the environmental policy of the Council of Europe go far beyond this. There is, first of all, the integration of special problems of air pollution control into the comprehensive program of environmental protection which in the last two years has been felt everywhere.

The recommendations of the European Conservation Conference held Feb. 9-12, 1970, have called for:

> Measures for the setting up of internationally recognized standards for the European industry to be introduced,
> the harmonization of international legislation in the field of environ-

---

13. Res. 70/20, Control of Sulfur Dioxide Emissions into the Air. Res. 70/20, Limitation of Emissions of Lead Compounds in the Atmosphere by Motor Vehicles.

14. Res. 70/11, Coordination of Efforts Made in Town and Country Planning and in Air Pollution Control.

mental questions to be promoted by European agreements,

the question to be examined whether a European body can be created which can be entrusted with the supervision of environmental conditions in Europe,

the possibility of creating a European fund for the fight against pollution,

an additional protocol to the Convention on Human Rights to be drawn up guaranteeing everyone the right to a healthy and uninjured environment.

The materialization of these objectives, particularly the preparation of a European Environment Convention and of an information center for questions concerning environment, is an eminently political task interfering with the powers of national legislation and administration. It, therefore, appears to be doubtful whether more extensive results on a multilateral level can be achieved without the decisive influence of parliamentary bodies; this is true of the Council of Europe as well as of the EEC or the United Nations. It is, therefore, encouraging that the International Conference of Parliamentarians has just adopted a decision on questions concerning the environment by means of which a new phase of international cooperation in the field of environmental protection could be initiated.[15]

---

15. Decision of the International Conference of Parliamentarians (Bonn, June 4, 1971).

LEGAL RESPONSES TO POLLUTION PROBLEMS—THEIR STRENGTHS AND WEAKNESSES†

Scientists in many disciplines are conducting the research necessary to identify and describe the factors causing today's deterioration of the natural environment. In the Arctic regions of Alaska and northern Canada, for example, both industry and government are sponsoring research into basic matters such as tundra productivity and technological impacts such as the building of hot oil pipelines over permafrost. The scientists both contribute and respond to the public outcry that the environment be defended. As the news media learn about hazards from the scientists they stoke the firest of public concern. Political action ensues. If a technology for coping with environmental damage is known, lawyers and legislators are asked to devise the legal means for bringing this technology to bear on pollution problems. What can legal science do?

The law can respond in four ways. It can apply the coercive power of the state to the pollution offender; it can manipulate the incentives and disincentives of the economic system to bring pressure on the offender; it can organize the administrative and institutional structures of the state to control the offender; and it can contribute to the consciousness of citizens that the natural environment must not be abused.

COERCIVE POWERS OF THE STATE

Punish the polluter! If a fine is an insufficient deterrent, impose a prison sentence! Penalties for oil spills from tankers are prescribed as high as $100,000 per day for Arctic waters.[1] Fines in excess of $1,000,000 were levied on Chevron Oil Company last year for failure to install required down hole safety devices on 90 oil wells off the Louisiana coast in the United States. In addition to penalties, close down the offending operation! An Imperial Oil exploration near Tuktoyaktuk in northern Canada was closed down in the summer of 1971 by government order because of the company's failure to take steps to avoid surface disturbance at its equipment-staging areas.[2]

---

†Originally prepared for the Twelfth Pacific Science Congress, Section C 1.3, Legal and Political Problems of Environmental Management.

††Faculty of Law, University of British Columbia.

1. Arctic Waters Pollution Prevention Act, Can. Rev. Stat. c. 2 (1st Supp. 1970); Canada Shipping Act, Can. Rev. Stat. c. 38 (1970-71), *amending* Can. Rev. Stat. c. 38 (1st Supp. 1970).

2. The Sun (Vancouver, B.C.), Aug. 6, 1971.

The first demand of the alarmed citizen when a pollution crisis occurs is usually resort to the coercive powers of the state. Indeed, the layman often has only this simplistic model of prohibition and penalty in his mind when he thinks of the legal system in relation to the environment.

Nor is his model unrealistic, for modern statutes are replete with penalty provisions. More sophisticated legal measures are needed to cope with pollution problems. Penalties, after all, usually operate after the harm has been done. The initiation of prosecutions is usually sporadic and haphazard rather than planned and co-ordinated.[3] If money penalties are stated in inadequate amounts, they may serve only as cheaply priced licenses to pollute.[4] They require careful statement and definition because of the criminal law tradition requiring penal statutes be given a strict interpretation in favor of the accused person. Yet, the highly technical nature of pollution problems may preclude such precise and careful defini-tion.[5] Again, the criminal law tradition presumes in favor of innocence and requires strict proof of an offense. The difficulties of establishing cause and effect between deposits of wastes in a stream and injury to fish, and giving convincing demonstration of an accurate use of the Ringlemann opacity test for air pollution are two current Canadian illustrations of the resistance to successful criminal prosecution inherent in cases where the offense is based on highly complex processes.[6]

Before considering more sophisticated legal responses to pollution problems, something more must be said to place the role of the criminal sanction in proper perspective. While prohibitions and penalties, standing by themselves, can be downgraded as means of dealing with pollution problems, they in fact are incorporated into almost all types of legal responses to pollution whether these responses be manipulation of the economic system or reorganization of the administrative system, or whether they take some other form. In the economic type of response, such as the imposition of effluent charges through a permit system, a penalty is usually imposed for violation of the terms of the permit;[7] in an administrative response, such as a contingency plan for dealing with oil spills, it is made an offense to fail to report an oil spill to the authorities. The 1971

3. Good, *Anti-Pollution Legislation and Its Enforcement—An Empirical Study*, 6 U.B.C. L. Rev. 271 (1971).

4. *Id.*

5. Difficulties in defining standards for "pure" water and "clean" air are notorious.

6. Lucas, *Legal Techniques for Pollution Control: The Role of the Public*, 6 U.B.C. L. Rev. 167, 174 (1971).

7. Northern Inland Waters Act, Can. Rev. Stat. c. 28, § 32 (1st Supp. 1970).

amendments to the *Canada Shipping Act* contain an array of offenses supporting its scheme for controlling pollution from ships. These include failure to report an accidental spill or the sighting of an oil slick, failure to provide evidence of financial responsibility for clean-up costs and damages resulting from a spill, failure to assist pollution prevention officers in the performance of their duties, failure to have certificates of compliance for ships, failure to comply with regulations respecting ship construction, fittings and supplies, and so on. This profusion of offenses might suggest either a repressive society or a paucity of available legal techniques for gaining compliance with the control regime. In my view neither suggestion provides a full explanation. In a significant number of cases the penalty may be the only practical way of introducing an economic disincentive to harmful conduct. When you add the moral force that a prosecution brings to bear on the offender to the injury that his reputation suffers, the penalty can be an impressive deterrent particularly if the offender cultivates an image as a concerned and responsible citizen. But the chief reason for the pervasive use of the criminal sanction seems to be that it operates as a sort of "fail-safe" mechanism. When all other legal devices for gaining compliance with the control regime fail, there is always the prosecution of an offender to fall back on. Someone can be made to pay! The public conscience can be appeased!

ECONOMIC INCENTIVES AND DISINCENTIVES

A convincing number of experts in a variety of disciplines assert that the main responses to pollution problems must be economic ones.[8] In language an economist might use, the need is to introduce into entrepreneurial decision-making, whether private or public, some mechanism for costing the impact of decisions on common property resources such as air, water and the other components of the natural enviornment. A geographer, J. W. MacNeill, observes in a recent Canadian study that "Indeed, some experts view environmental management largely as a problem of 'internalizing' these external costs."[9] Allen V. Kneese, a well-known United States resource economist, argues that "our present environmental problems, at least their environmental pollution aspects, are primarily a result of failures in our system of economic incentives."[10]

The problem seems to be that our market system, to which we

---

8. *See, e.g.,* U.K. Royal Comm'n on Pollution, Rep. of Feb. 1971.

9. J. MacNeill, Environmental Management 16 (1971). Constitutional Study Prepared for the Government of Canada, Information Canada.

10. A. Kneese, Protecting Our Environment and Natural Resources in the 1970's, 191 (Resources for the Future Reprint No. 88, 1971).

normally entrust the allocation of natural resources, is not geared to giving recognition to the interest in maintaining a healthy and harmonious environment. In the market trade-off of our many competing and conflicting individual and corporate interests, no one is asserting the environmental interest. Further, even if environmental impacts are taken into account by concerned entrepreneurs, our economic system encourages a short-sighted approach. An adequate return on investment is usually the ultimate arbiter of the entrepreneurial decision, and, unfortunately, natural resource ventures are usually associated with high risks and therefore compel short pay-out periods. If a decision to undertake a venture must be based on a calculated pay-out of investment and profit in ten years (not an unusual period in mining and oil ventures), the entrepreneur cannot be expected to give serious weight to a prognosis that fifteen years from now, his project may have damaging environmental effects. It is a conundrum of our times that our ability to anticipate and plan for the future is in inverse ratio to the rate of technological change; the faster the rate of change, the shorter the future time period when technological circumstances can be predicted as a basis for decision-making today. Natural scientists and engineers may well ponder this conundrum when next they are tempted to berate social scientists and politicians for failing to keep the social system abreast of technological developments. In economic terms, this faster rate of technological change means increasing factors of uncertainty and risk, higher discounts for these factors, shorter investment pay-out periods, and therefore shorter forward planning.

Technology offers new aids to planning which may tend to offset this spiral of uncertainty; indeed, a whole new science of futurology is emerging. Techniques such as computer simulation give the planner the ability to manipulate masses of data, they provide him with probability rankings of the results of such manipulations, and they correct his interpretations of these results by feedback systems.[11] But they cannot foretell the future and they cannot by themselves change the time criteria for business investment decisions. Nevertheless, they give promise that decision-making may ultimately catch up with technology.

In a broader sense, the policy being advocated is that decision-making in the market system be given the kind of holistic input that the science of ecology, itself, demands—a consideration of the whole spectrum of internal and external effects over a long range of time.[12]

11. Systems science applications in environmental impact studies are advocated by Robert F. Scott, Effects of Ecology on Technological Change, Proceedings of the 20th Alaska Science Conference (1970).

12. It is chastening to note that in putting forward an ideal environmental management

How can this change be accomplished? How can these externalities be introduced into the investment decision? The very definition of the common property resource is that it is not "owned" and therefore no one is pricing it in the marketplace. In the context of pollution control, many suggestions for change have been advanced, from the creation of private property in pollution rights[13] to the introduction of effluent charges which would amount to publicly administered prices for waste discharge.[14] In terms of protection of elements in the natural environment, significant research work by economists is leading to the ability to place helpful price estimates on such common property resources as wildlife and recreation landscapes.[15] But, obviously, when benefits of an aesthetic nature such as a wilderness solitude or a scene of great natural beauty are bestowed by the environment, values become too subjective for anything but arbitrary pricing.[16]

Many scientists react with undisguised hostility to suggestions that economic answers should be sought for pollution problems. After all, it is argued, the main, underlying threat to the environment stems from preoccupation with the dollar and with the claimed necessity of annual increases in the Gross National Product. Such reaction is too simplistic and ascribes to economics that which the discipline denies—a value system. Rather, the concern of economics is to quantify benefits and detriments. It presumes that to the extent that benefits and detriments can be quantified, decision-making can be simplified and improved.

From a lawyer's viewpoint, with his long scan over the history of legal sanctioning of desirable human conduct, the manipulation of economic factors as an answer to pollution problems has one great advantage. This advantage is that the decision to pursue this course or that, to incur this environmental cost or gain that environmental benefit, is a decision by the doer himself, without external coercion, and within the dictates of his own conscience and self-interest. This preference for individual choice may be regarded as merely a reflec-

---

program, 30 years was considered almost impossibly remote for future planning, *supra* note 9, at 24.

13. J. Dale, Pollution, Property and Prices (1968).

14. A. Kneese, Protecting Our Environment and Natural Resources in the 1970's, at 195 (Resources for the Future Reprint No. 88, 1970). The Council on Environmental Quality in the United States has advocated pollution charges in its annual report, *see* The Sun (Vancouver, B.C.), Aug. 6, 1971.

15. M. Clawson, Methods of Measuring the Demand for and Value of Outdoor Recreation (Resources for the Future Reprint No. 10, 1959); Pearse, *Toward a Theory of Multiple Use: The Case of Recreation v. Agriculture,* 9 Natural Resources J. 561 (1969).

16. It should not be overlooked that individuals do commonly place money values on mainly aesthetic benefits, as where a fortune is paid for a painting or the owner of land refuses to sell it at a price substantially above the market.

tion of Judaic-Christian values, or it may be categorized as a defense of the so-called free-enterprise, capitalist system. But it should not be construed as either. A lawyer appreciates how difficult it is to regulate his fellow man in all his myriad manifestations of conduct and with all his complex motivations and stratagems to frustrate the regulatory system. Hence the lawyer respects any mechanism that reduces the burden on the legal system of gaining acceptable human conduct, in environmental concerns as in all others.

Nor is the desirability of internalizing environmental costs and benefits into decision-making applicable only to ventures in a private enterprise system. Public enterprises such as hydro-electric power generation are notorious in North America for their myopic vision of costs and benefits when making decisions such as where to locate a dam. They are as needful as private enterprise of mechanisms that will internalize a broader range of cost-benefit criteria in decision-making.[17]

What techniques are available to lawyers to manipulate the economic system in these desirable ways? Obvious ones are changes in tax laws to provide incentives for the use of pollution-abatement procedures.[18] Less obvious ones are changes in liability laws. The imposition of legal liability for injury internalizes the cost of the injury, forcing the actor to take into account possible damage claims, at least if he is prudent and has other courses of action. The new amendments in Canada's shipping laws deal with oil spill damage by imposing an absolute liability that cannot be evaded by contract clauses.[19] The more imaginative techniques range from the development of new legal theory that will transform the common property resource into some form of ownership, to the introduction of new administrative systems that will inject cost-benefit considerations of environmental impact into investment decisions.

The new ownership theories will emerge in North America either through legislation or through the evolution of new common law concepts. The Canadian Bar Association is currently studying legislative proposals that would, in effect, create public ownership rights in

---

17. The Bennett Dam in British Columbia is a classic case. The provincially owned hydroelectric company entirely ignored downstream effects which have resulted in imperilling a major river delta system. *See* Death of a Delta (1970).

18. Lucas, *Legal Techniques for Pollution Control: The Role of the Public,* 6 U.B.C. L. Rev. 167, 177 (1971).

19. Arctic Waters Pollution Prevention Act, Can. Rev. Stat. c. 2, § 6 (1st Supp. 1970); Canada Shipping Act, Can. Rev. Stat. c. 38 (1970-71), *amending* Can. Rev. Stat. c. 38 (1st Supp. 1970). To the extent that damage claims are not satisfied, a Pollution Claims Fund meets the deficiency.

unpolluted air and water by giving individual citizens the right to enforce quality standards through the courts.[20] A similar public right has already gained a foothold in the United States both under statute[21] and at common law.[22] Lawyers like Professor Joseph Sax of Michigan argue for a legal conceptualization of air and water as commodities held in trust for the benefit of the entire community of citizens.[23] In consequence, individual citizens, as beneficiaries of this trust, have the right through the courts to defend air and water against invasions by polluters.

A controversial proposal to convert air and water from common property resources into privately owned resources from a pollution standpoint has been made by University of Toronto economist J. H. Dale. He advocates that the pollution-carrying capacity of a drainage basin should be determined and quantified among various classes of pollutants, that these quantities should be divided into units each of which is equivalent to every other in terms of the treatment costs imposed by it on the drainage basins, and that these units should be bought and sold as pollution rights on a free market. One could discharge effluent into the drainage basin only to the extent of purchased pollution rights. The price of the pollution rights would increase as the carrying-capacity of the basin reached its permitted level, and this increase would operate to allocate the pollution rights to the most efficient users.[24]

A less imaginative, but probably more acceptable method of internalizing environmental impacts is the introduction of administrative systems that impose on resource users a cost reflecting other resource values foregone or environmental costs imposed, usually by requiring the resource user to acquire and pay for a permit or license for his undertaking. Insofar as a permit fee is charged which represents an attempt to preassess the value of other resource uses foregone or the cost of environmental damage done, the permit system constitutes an internalization of these costs. In effect, the resource user has to take the permit fee into account in doing his personal cost-benefit analysis of his proposed venture. Examples of such permit fees in Canada are to be found in the *Northern Inland Waters Act*[25] and in the new

---

20. Resolution of Civil Justice Subsection (B.C. Division) of the Canadian Bar Association, 1970-71.

21. Mich. Comp. Laws Ann. § 691.1202 (Supp. 1971).

22. Scenic Hudson Preservation Conference v. F.P.C., 354 F.2d 608 (2d Cir. 1965), *cert. denied*, 384 U.S. 941 (1966).

23. Sax, *The Public Trust Doctrine in Natural Resource Law: Effective Judicial Intervention*, 68 Mich. L. Rev. 473 (1970).

24. J. Dale, Pollution, Property and Prices (1968).

25. Can. Rev. Stat. c. 28, § 32 (1st Supp. 1970).

northern *Land Use Regulations.*[26] In the former case the fee is to represent a charge corresponding to the treatment cost imposed on the water system by the effluent discharge.[27] In the latter case, the fee is to represent the value of commercial timber that is destroyed by line-cutting for seismic surveys.

Something has already been said about the problems of valuing non-priced items such as wildlife or wilderness resources. But even if the pricing problem can somehow be solved or evaded, there are other flaws in the economic model we are building. The public ownership concept has the serious defect that self-interest is often highly diluted, resulting in only sporadic enforcement of the public trust. That is, no single member of the public may consider his personal interest as a beneficiary of the trust to be sufficient to justify the costs and stress of a law suit. The answer to the problem is said to be collective citizen action. North America is witnessing a phenomenal growth in its citizen conservation and anti-pollution organizations in defense of national parks, wilderness, wildlife, and other environmental values. Still, the response, being dependent on individual initiative in preponderantly unorganized situations, is mainly sporadic and uncoordinated. Despite this deficiency, the citizen lawsuit has many advocates as an environmental protection mechanism.[28] Perhaps its enduring justification will lie in its ombudsman-like function of spurring government officials to hold fast to the performance of their duties in defense of the environment.

The flaw in the user charge system is the absence of an automatic pricing mechanism such as is supplied by exchange in the market-place. Kneese has described the effluent charge as a "publicly-administered price" for the privilege of discharging wastes.[29] This description recognizes that some public administrative system is necessary to determine what standards of pollution are acceptable, what the costs of maintaining these standards will be and how these costs should be apportioned among the various users of the resource so that the proper charge can be levied. Consequently, this kind of manipulation of the market system does not produce the ideal model of a system operating entirely by the free play of self-interest. Before

26. Gazetted July, 1971. They are made pursuant to Territorial Lands Act, Can. Rev. Stat. c. 263, § § 12-13 (1952).

27. The President's Council on Environmental Quality in the United States recommends such effluent charges in its 1970 annual report. The Sun (Vancouver, B.C.), Aug. 6, 1971.

28. *See, e.g.,* Carroll, *Participatory Technology,* 171 Science 647, 650 (1971); Eddy, *Locus Standi and Environmental Control: A Policy for Comparison,* 6 U.B.C. L. Rev. 193, 214 (1971).

29. A. Kneese, *supra* note 10, at 195.

self-interest can be triggered, the device must be armed by the deployment by government of a complex administrative system.

This need for an administrative system leads into consideration of the third method by which the legal system can respond to pollution problems—and reveals, as did the study of the first method (the use of criminal sanctions), that these methods are interlinked and overlapping, and that a comprehensive legal response will maximize all four methods.

ADMINISTRATIVE AND INSTITUTIONAL RESPONSES

Those who do not elevate economic solutions to highest priority in dealing with environmental problems will probably have their solutions fixed on administrative and institutional responses. If, as many contend, the pollution problem can be met only by a new consciousness of man's relationship with nature, man's administrative and institutional arrangements must undergo radical change to reflect this new consciousness.[30] Even within the context of pragmatic and evolutionary change, as distinguished from radical change, quite profound administrative and institutional restructuring must take place if environmental considerations are to be given high ranking among today's concerns.

The very emergence of ecology, even as a half understood concept in the lay mind, forces a re-examination of existing administrative and institutional structures to discover how well they fit an ecological view of pollution problems, and the results are discouraging. On the administrative side in Canada we find a river basin system regulated, not as a river basin at all, but in fragments under a patchwork of incomplete, uncoordinated and often contradictory regimes imposed by local, regional and national levels of government.[31] On the institutional side, our examination of economic factors bearing on pollution has shown how inadequately the institution of the market takes account of environmental factors.

But the lesson is being learned, and the first steps are being taken in a number of key environmental issues. The federal parliament in Canada has enacted a *Canada Water Act*[32] and has introduced a *Canada Clean Air Bill,*[33] both aimed at coordinated federal-provincial management of water and air resources with proper regard for spatial and other ecological characteristics. The *Canada Water Act* envisages the management of a water basin such as the Fraser River

---

30. C. Reich, The Greening of America (1970).
31. J. MacNeill, *supra* note 9.
32. Can. Rev. Stat. c. 52 (1st Supp. 1970).
33. Bill C-224 (1971).

system in British Columbia under a management agency that would have delegated authority under the respective federal and provincial constitutional powers to enable the formulation and implementation of a fully comprehensive control regime. Both these statutes are enabling—that is, they lay the groundwork for the establishment of air and water quality management, and it remains to be seen whether the respective levels of government will in fact cooperate as envisioned, and, if they do, how soon and how effectively management authorities can be organized and become operational.[34]

That pollution problems require a holistic and ecological perspective is evidenced in an even more fundamental way by the basic reorganizations that are taking place both in government and in business in Canada to reflect an environmental concern. On the government side, one can cite the transformation of the federal Department of Forestry and Fisheries into the Department of the Environment, and of the Alberta Oil and Gas Conservation Board into the Energy Resources Conservation Board, with a new mandate to "control pollution and ensure environment conservation" in energy resource developments.[35] On the business side, one can note that large corporations are establishing environmental departments.[36] One consortium of natural gas companies is even sponsoring an independent Environmental Protection Board.[37]

It is obviously beyond the scope of this paper to mention all of the administrative and institutional reorganizations that are taking place in Canada. But it may be noted that international initiatives, too, are directed toward these kinds of changes. One Canadian legal expert on international waterways predicts that "existing customary international law on pollution of drainage basins will be largely ignored. It will be displaced by treaties providing for the management and control of international drainage basins by international joint agencies."[38]

What is a lawyer's perspective on these administrative changes? He normally views the administrative process in terms of its impact on the individual citizen. He is concerned to know whether all affected interests are represented in the process, and, if not, whether there is

34. For parallel U.S. developments, see Freeman & Haveman, Water Pollution Control, River Basin Authorities, and Economic Incentives (Resources for the Future Reprint No. 92, 1971).

35. Energy Resources Conservation Act, S.A. c. 30, § 2(4) (1971).

36. E.g., Imperial Oil Limited.

37. The consortium is the Gas Arctic System Study Group, comprising five Canadian and United States natural gas distribution companies interested in pipelining Prudhoe Bay gas to United States markets.

38. Bourne, International Law and Pollution of International Rivers and Lakes, 6 U.B.C. L. Rev. 115, 136 (1971).

just cause for exclusions. He will ask what kind of participation in the process is afforded to the affected individual and will examine this participation for its fairness according to long established legal standards of just procedures.

Examined from this lawyer's perspective, protection of the environment is seen as an interest that is entitled to representation in the administrative process, as much as, from the economist's perspective, environmental protection is an interest that must be accounted for in the marketplace. The new insight for the lawyer is that this interest is now being recognized as an interest of individual citizens and groups of citizens, and not merely as the concern of resource users and governments. It is a parallel development to the newly-emerging citizen's interest under the public trust doctrine.[39] The argument is that the protection of the public interest exclusively by government agencies, departments and officials is no longer adequate. This inadequacy signifies the tendency of government bureaucracies to become narrow and partisan in discharge of their responsibilities, and to lose sight of broader public goals and aspirations. The argument is that a mines department becomes a captive of the mining interests, an oil and gas conservation board of the oil and gas interests, and a food and drugs directorate of the food processing and chemical interests. Should this tendency be established, ombudsman-type procedures are necessary as correctives.

In the environmental context, a protected environment becomes an interest to be given representation in the administrative process and this representation is necessary because the role of government agencies, departments and officials in protecting the environment needs to be supplemented and fortified by a citizen ombudsman role.

Many problems are encountered in any attempt to open up representation procedures. At what stages in the administrative process should representation be permitted? How should the issues be defined? Who should be heard? What sources of information should be available to them? Should the state provide financial and organizational support?[40] What kinds of representations should be allowed,

---

39. See p. 232 supra.

40. The significance of these questions can be shown by many examples. In the case of the Alaska oil pipeline, it is generally recognized that the heavy commitment of planning and investment prior to the environmental impact hearings by the Secretary of the Interior foreclosed from the beginning the possibility of an adverse decision. In British Columbia, the investment of $14,000,000 in mine mill facilities before pollution control hearings on the tailings and effluent disposal plans of Utah Mining Co. Ltd. was acknowledged by the pollution control authority as preventing rejection of the company's application for a discharge permit and as limiting the hearing to a consideration of conditions that would be attached to the permit. In this case, the issues before the hearing tribunal were defined by the application made by the company. Other issues which environmentalists and commercial

having in mind the necessities of an efficient hearing process and a timely decision?

Nor can these questions be answered in an "across the board" fashion, for it soon appears that each kind of environmental impact arises in its own set of circumstances with its own special requirements.

A proper representation procedure is illusory without a proper decision-making authority and executive follow-up. Who should comprise the authority? By what criteria should it decide as between competing interests? Should there be a hierarchy of decision-making for administrative efficiency and appeals? What kind of agency should carry out the decisions? What kind of feedback control should give warning when decisions are not being carried out or are producing different results from those intended? Should the right of representation include the right to monitor the carrying out of decisions and their effects?

These questions are posed to show the scope and complexity of the problems that preoccupy lawyers when administrative responses to pollution problems are proposed. In the United States these problems have, at least in part, been confronted in a bold way, even if answers are left to be determined in the flux of experience. The *National Environmental Policy Act of 1969*[41] requires all federal agencies, with respect to every legislative proposal or other federal action significantly affecting the quality of the human environment, to prepare advance statements describing the environmental impact of the action, any adverse environmental effects which cannot be avoided, alternatives to the proposed action, the relationship between the local short-term effects and long-term productivity, and any irreversible and irretrievable commitment of resources involved in the action. The significance of this requirement of impact statements is that they will initiate the process of representation, even if only in terms of letters to congressmen. In many cases federal agencies are, by their internal requirements, bound by law to hold

---

fishermen desired to raise were precluded. The statutory provisions which defined the hearing procedures denied the right to be heard to many organizations and individuals who obviously had interests that would be affected by the hearing process (commercial fishermen, for example). As to state assistance in providing information to affected parties and granting financial support, an Australian example can be cited for its constructive approach. Public hearings on the question whether oil exploration should be permitted in the region of the Great Barrier Reef are being conducted by joint federal-state commissions which can compel the attendance of government witnesses and the disclosure of government reports. Conservation interests are represented by counsel whose fees and expenses are being paid by the government.

41. 43 U.S.C. § 4321 (1970). *See* Vannacone, *National Environmental Policy Act of 1969,* 1 Environmental L. 8 (1970).

public hearings on such statements. To North Americans, the impact statement hearings by the Department of the Interior on the proposed authorization of a trans-Alaska pipeline system has already established the importance of this procedure in the fabric of United States political and constitutional life. The state legislatures are following suit.[42] The next five years will demonstrate whether or not the environmental interest has been securely anchored in the policy of the nation.

In Canada, the idea of representation remains relatively undeveloped in the administrative process, being largely confined to the traditional common law review by the courts when administrators abuse their jurisdiction. There is as yet no system for representation in the enactment of delegated legislation (*i.e.* rule-making by departments of government),[43] and representation in the case of departmental tribunals is not on any systematic basis. Nor is representation usually available in the early stages of the administrative process.

The Canadian weaknesses are all too apparent. At the present time the regulations which control the issue of oil and gas permits and leases in the vast Canadian northern and offshore regions, and thereby determine the pace and impact of northern development, are under revision by the responsible government departments, but no public participation is contemplated (or welcomed!) other than discussions with the two oil and gas industry associations.[44] The *Canada Clean Air Act*[45] provides for "consultation" with an advisory committee established under the Act, but such consultation is in the Minister's discretion. There is a provision for 60 days notice in the Canada Gazette of proposed national quality standards and of specific emission standards for federal industries, but no procedures for public representation are specified. A similar notice requirement with respect to the new *Land Use Regulations*[46] has given citizens the opportunity to make written representations to the government department, but Gazette notices frequently pass unobserved. In addition, there is no system for presenting submissions, no indication of

---

42. *E.g.,* Cal. Pub. Res. Code § 21000-150 (West Supp. 1971).

43. The Department of Indian Affairs and Northern Development experimented with the representation of affected interests when preparing the new Land Use Regulations, but the experiment was ad hoc, was without adequate forethought as to procedures, and left the writer, as one involved, with the conviction that such representation is needed but must be given a formal structure with procedures and responsibilities spelled out in advance.

44. The Canada Oil and Gas Land Regulations, SOR/61-252, administered by the Department of Indian Affairs and Northern Development as to the north, including offshore, and by the Department of Energy, Mines and Resources as to the east and west coast offshore regions and as to Hudson's Bay.

45. Bill C-224 (1971).

46. *See* note 43 *supra.*

who will study them, no opportunity to hear and rebut other submissions, and no decision or report to finalize the process other than the promulgation after 60 days of a binding set of regulations.

Pipeline proposals which will have an impact on the Canadian north equally as momentous as that which the oil pipeline will have in Alaska are now under feasibility studies by four or five major oil and natural gas consortiums. Such pipelines in Canada will require the issue of permits of different kinds, the major permit being a certificate of public convenience issued by the National Energy Board.[47] This Board has traditionally performed its certifying function in terms of the availability of reserves of oil or gas, the economic consequences of the location of the pipeline, and its design and engineering. There is yet no clear indication in Canada how the ecological impact of a pipeline proposal is to be assessed. Requests have been made for the issue by the government of impact statements and for public hearings before steps are taken that set the proposals on inevitable courses toward completion,[48] but no government response to these requests has yet been announced.

It is clear that just as new administrative and institutional changes have much to offer in the way of answers to pollution problems, they also pose difficult questions, the legal ones being as complex as any others. What the lawyer foresees are clearly established procedures whereby a citizen who has a substantive environmental interest in any proposed government decision or action affecting the enviornment will have an effective opportunity to present his reasons and arguments for or against the proposal for consideration by those who will be deciding or acting. The ingredients of the procedure must include liberal definition of those citizens who can show a substantive environmental interest, full disclosure of all relevant data, government cooperation and assistance in carrying out necessary investigations and tests, the opportunity to present the case at the appropriate decision-making level and in the appropriate time and sequence, the opportunity to see and, if desired, rebut opposing arguments, and the means of knowing what decision has been made. Such procedural requirements can be further elaborated, and are subject to the caveat that pragmatism and flexibility in the administrative process require that they be tailored to fit each decision-making role.

What he also foresees are legal and institutional changes that will inject the citizen interest in the environment into private decision-

---

47. National Energy Board, Can. Rev. Stat. c. N-6, § 46 (1970).
48. Anderson, *Government and the Environment: A Need for Public Participation,* 6 U.B.C. L. Rev. 111 (1971).

making as well. Normally, these changes will involve government regulation of private decision-making through controls such as licenses and permits, but other possibilities include institutional changes in the structure of private enterprise, itself, such as requirements that environmental interests be represented in the management of corporations.

What the environmental lawyer believes when he places such emphasis on the representation process is that, no matter how well the economic system is manipulated, there will remain substantial environmental concerns that are not reflected in the market place unless individual citizens and groups of citizens are recognized as having the legal right to be heard. He believes that the benefits of citizen participation will, in the long run, outweigh the costs imposed on entrepreneurs by such representation requirements.

CONTRIBUTION TO CONSCIOUSNESS
ABOUT POLLUTION PROBLEMS

Most students of juridical science see law as shaping values as well as reflecting them, and as contributing to consciousness as well as answering to its dictates. If, as Charles Reich maintains, a Consciousness III is emerging in North America that is more mindful and considerate of the natural world,[49] the law will both respond and contribute to this new consciousness as the legal system begins to deal with environmental problems. Contribute it must, for legal stratagems are mere gossamer webs if there is no consciousness and no ethic to give them sinew. Impact statements can be mere bureaucratic exercises and public hearings mere playacting after decisions have been irreversibly made. Advisory committees can become captives of the administration or neutralized by the withholding of essential information. In the field of private enterprise, environmental departments can be mere excrescences of public relations departments; the relatively few, qualified independent experts can be disarmed by research contracts or retainer fees. Given the most perfectly fashioned and functioning system of environmental protection, its mainspring must be a new consciousness of concern and respect for the natural world—a new "land ethic."[50]

49. *See* note 30 *supra*.
50. A. Leopold, A Sand County Almanac 217-20 (1966).

NATIONAL SOVEREIGNTY IN INTERNATIONAL ENVIRONMENTAL DECISIONS†

CHARLES R. ROSS††

The negotiations leading to the Boundary Waters Treaty of 1909[1] provide much food for thought for those who are currently attempting to resolve international environmental problems. The key figures in the negotiations were George Clinton, a Buffalo lawyer and a member of the International Waterways Commission, and George C. Gibbons, a lawyer from London, Ontario, a member of the Canadian section. These two individuals, particularly the latter, together with Elihu Root, the Secretary of State, and Chandler P. Anderson, his legal advisor, were generally considered the architects for the Boundary Waters Treaty of 1909.

The negotiations leading to the ultimate adoption at such an early date of the "Thou shalt not pollute" commandment of the treaty is quite interesting. For example, Article IV provides:

> The High Contracting Parties agree that, except in cases provided for by special agreement between them, they will not permit the construction or maintenance on their respective sides of the boundary of any remedial or protective works or any dams or other obstructions in waters flowing from boundary waters or in waters at a lower level than the boundary in rivers flowing across the boundary, the effect of which is to raise the natural level of waters on the other side of the boundary unless the construction or maintenance thereof is approved by the aforesaid International Joint Commission.
>
> *It is further agreed that the waters herein defined as boundary waters and waters flowing across the boundary shall not be polluted on either side to the injury of health or property on the other.*[2]
> (Emphasis added.)

Clinton and Gibbons, in preparing an early draft for submission on September 24, 1907, had drafted language which stated that:

---

†The author wishes to acknowledge his use of an unpublished Annotated Digest of materials relating to the establishment of the International Joint Commission prepared by F. J. E. Jordan, Dep't of Public Law, Carleton University, Ottawa, Canada, for use as a reference volume by the IJC, the U.S. Dept. of State, and the Canadian Dept. of External Affairs.

††M.B.A., LL.B., University of Michigan, 1948; Attorney at Law, Hinesburg, Vt.; Member, IJC.

1. Treaty with Great Britain Relating to Boundary Waters Between the United States and Canada, Jan. 11, 1909, 36 Stat. 2448 (1910) (effective May 13, 1910), often referred to as The Boundary Waters Treaty.

2. *Id.*

6. The said waters must not be polluted in one country to the injury of health or property in the other.[3]

Clinton, in explaining the draft to Secretary Root, stated that the clause

was inserted to take care of cases which are likely to arise in the future when the Northwest becomes more densely populated; perhaps the language is too strong.[4]

As it turned out, the language was almost too strong, though it did ultimately survive. At first it failed to attract too much attention as it survived in succeeding drafts proposed by Canada. It was eliminated together with all specific principles in a later draft by Secretary Root, who, at that time, was interested solely in the creation of a Commission of Inquiry. However, the so-called Anderson-Gibbons draft of December 1908 did include the prohibition against pollution.[5] This provision aroused the ire of Senator K. Nelson of Minnesota who, during the Senate hearings, objected on the grounds that Article IV created a police power over water pollution at the federal and international levels. Each of these was an invasion of state's rights and should be amended to preserve the rights of the states in dealing with their waters.[6]

Senator Nelson's problem with Article IV did not prove insurmountable, though, during passage in the Senate, Anderson was ready to strike the pollution clause if it would make the treaty more acceptable. Gibbons replied that the clause should remain "but only be enforced in more serious cases."[7] Apparently, because of more serious problems regarding diversion, the clause was retained. Citizens in both countries should give thanks that such was the case because it has served as a springboard to launch a slow and tedious counterattack against pollution.

Before discussing the development of the different pollution control philosophies which have arisen between the two countries in recent years and exemplified during the hearings on the problem of

---

3. Dep't of State, Numerical File 1906-10, 484 Nat'l Archives 5934, 5936-7 (proposed treaty clauses submitted by Clinton to Root, Sep. 25, 1907).

4. Dep't of State Numerical File 1906-10, 484 Nat'l Archives 5934, 5936-7 (letter from Clinton to Root, Sep. 25, 1907).

5. Letter from Anderson to Root, Nov. 24, 1908 (Anderson Papers, box 68); International Waterways Treaty: Revised Draft, Nov. 27, 1908; Treaty Relating to Boundary Waters and Questions Arising Along the Boundary Between the United States and Canada (Revised Draft), Dec. 2, 1908.

6. Letter from Sen. K. Nelson to Chairman Sen. S. M. Cullom, Jan. 29, 1909 (Anderson Papers, box 69).

7. Telegram from Gibbons to Anderson (confidential), Feb. 1, 1909 (Gibbons Papers, 8 Letterbook No. 1 at 507).

pollution control in the Great Lakes, a brief description of the IJC is in order. As the preamble to the Treaty states, the IJC was formed:

> ... to prevent disputes regarding the use of boundary waters and to settle all questions which are now pending between the United States and the Dominion of Canada involving the rights, obligations, or interests either ... along their common frontier, and to make provision for the adjustment and settlement of all such questions as may hereafter arise. ...[8]

The Commission consists of six members, three from each country. The United States Commissioners are appointed by and serve at the pleasure of the President. The Canadian Commissioners are appointed by Order in Council of the Canadian Government and serve at the pleasure of the Government.

The High Contracting Parties have used both Article IV and Article IX[9] frequently throughout the history of the IJC as a means to provide an orderly solution to a number of vexing problems involving matters of water pollution as well as a host of other problems, such as air pollution, water supply problems, navigation, power development, irrigation, recreation and scenic beauty.

These problems have been dealt with in a unique fashion under the Treaty. The Commission was to act as a Unit. Decisions were to be made by a majority of the Commissioners irrespective of nationality and it was believed and hoped that the Commissioners could act in

---

8. Boundary Waters Treaty.
9. Article IX states:

> The High Contracting Parties further agree that any other questions or matters of difference arising between them involving the rights, obligations, or interests of either in relation to the other or to the inhabitants of the other, along the common frontier between the United States and the Dominion of Canada, shall be referred from time to time to the International Joint Commission for examination and report, whenever either the Government of the United States or the Government of the Dominion of Canada shall request that such questions or matters of difference be so referred.
>
> The International Joint Commission is authorized in each case so referred to examine into and report upon the facts and circumstances of the particular questions and matters referred, together with such conclusions and recommendations as may be appropriate, subject, however, to any restrictions or exceptions which may be imposed with respect thereto by the terms of the reference.
>
> Such reports of the Commission shall not be regarded as decisions of the questions or matters so submitted either on the facts or the law, and shall in no way have the charater of an arbitral award.
>
> The Commission shall make a joint report to both Governments in all cases in which all or a majority of the Commissioners agree, and in case of disagreement the minority may make a joint report to both Governments, or separate reports to their respective Governments. In case the Commission is evenly divided upon any question or matter referred to it for report, separate reports shall be made by the Commissioners on each side to their own Government.

unison to achieve the best solution in the common interest of the two countries. Thus, in the words of former Chairman Heeney, we "act, not as delegates striving for national advantages under instructions from their respective governments, but as members of a single body."[10] In the whole history of the Commission there have been only three instances out of eighty-odd cases upon which the Commissioners have divided or failed to reach an agreement. It is true that this unanimity has not been easily won. Tempers have flared occasionally, but more often than not, it has been a case of controlled desire to find the facts and the recognition of the necessity to find a fair and equitable solution. The philosophy underlying the Treaty has served primarily to bring out the best in the Commissioners, the Staff, and the members of the invaluable boards.

Administratively, the Commission is to be noted for its lack of size. It really is only a skeleton organization. The Canadians have a Legal Advisor and an Environmental Engineer in addition to the Secretary, while the United States has only recently added an Environmental Advisor to its long-standing position of Secretary. This scarcity of manpower is more than compensated for by the power under the usual term of reference to call upon any department in either country for technical assistance. Invariably this is done and the usual procedure is to establish specific boards of advisors to handle each reference, thus attempting to take advantage of the expertise at all levels, the federal, state, provincial and even the local level.

Casting aside administrative details, the records of the IJC in pollution problems has not been without criticism, a good deal of which the Commission agrees with. A review of the deteriorating condition of the Great Lakes will highlight this.

On August 1, 1912, the Governments referred to the Commission for examination and report the following questions:

> 1. To what extent and by what causes and in what localities have the boundary waters between the U.S. and Canada been polluted so as to be injurious to the public health and unfit for domestic or other uses?
>
> 2. *In what way or manner,* whether by the construction and operation of suitable drainage canals or plants at convenient points or otherwise, *is it possible and advisable to remedy or prevent the pollution of these waters,* and by what means or arrangement can the proper construction or operation of remedial or preventive works, or a system or method of rendering these waters sanitary and suitable for domestic and other uses, be best secured and maintained

---

10. Heeney, *Diplomacy With a Difference* 3 (International Nickel Company, Inc. Reprint, 1966).

in order to insure the adequate protection and development of all interests involved on both sides of the boundary *and fulfill the obligations undertaken in Article IV of the Waterways Treaty* of January 11, 1909, between the United States and Great Britain, in which it is agreed that the waters therein defined as boundary waters and waters flowing across the boundary shall not be polluted on either side to the injury of health or property on the other?[11] (Emphasis added.)

This study was limited to the Great Lakes, the connecting channels, the St. Lawrence from Lake Ontario "to a point as far below the international boundary as should be thought necessary," the Rainy River and the St. John River from Grand Falls to Edmundston.

In 1918 the Commission reported back to the Governments that:

the lakes themselves beyond their shore waters and their polluted areas at the mouths of the rivers that flow into them, were pure but that the "entire stretch of boundary waters, including Rainy River, St. Mary's River, St. Clair River, Detroit River, Niagara River, St. Lawrence River from Lake Ontario to Cornwall, and the St. John River from Grand Falls to Edmundston is polluted to an extent which renders the water in its unpurified state unfit for drinking purposes."

Following this, in March 1919, the two Governments requested the Commission to prepare a draft convention granting the Commission the necessary authority to remedy existing conditions of pollution. About eighteen months later on October 6, 1920, the Commission submitted its draft and stated, in a covering letter, among other things, that:

The Commission is firmly of the view that the method best adapted to avoid the evils which the Treaty is designed to correct is to take proper steps to prevent dangerous pollution crossing the boundary line rather than wait until it is manifest that such pollution has actually physically crossed, to the injury of health or property on the other side; and that to this end the *Convention should clothe the Commission with authority and power,* subject to all proper limitation and restrictions and to give such directions as may be proper and necessary *to maintain boundary waters in as healthful a condition as practicable* in view of conditions already created, and should contain proper provisions for the enforcement of such orders, rules and directions. (Emphasis added.)

For a number of reasons too long to detail here, there was no action taken upon this Convention even though both Governments

---

11. Int'l Joint Comm., Pollution of Boundary Waters (Docket No. 4, Aug. 1, 1912).

had reached substantial agreement by 1926. In fact, according to a letter written to the Canadian Minister to the United States by N. A. Robertson for the Secretary of State for External Affairs, negotiations came to "an untimely end in 1929."[12] This attempt to improve the machinery of the Commission is of critical importance when one considers what has happened to the Great Lakes in the interim. Despite the warning of the Commission as long ago as 1918, the Great Lakes are subjected to ever increasing despoilation until now Lake Erie has become the household word for the ultimate in man's disregard for the impact of his activities on his environment. A "cess pool" and words of similar nature recall to all the failure of our two nations to heed the warnings of the IJC.

It is true that during this period the Governments did show some interest. In fact, on April 1, 1946, at the initiative of the Canadian Government another reference was made under Article IX (Docket No. 54) as a result of representations of persons in the Detroit River area. It is interesting to note in passing that at that time there were again suggestions to the effect that the best solution might well be the draft Convention. However, that was not to be the case, and the Commission, still earnestly striving to find another acceptable solution, recommended the adoption of "Objectives For Boundary Waters Quality Control," which were criteria to be met in maintaining the boundary waters in satisfactory condition. This was one of the very early attempts to establish specific water quality criteria in connection with effluent limitations.[13] Had these Objectives been complied with, the Great Lakes would be in much better condition than they are. However, though it did not seem possible at the time, the quality of the waters went from bad to worse. Eutrophication became the "in" word. It became necessary to institute yet another reference to cover Lake Erie and Lake Ontario and the international portions of the St. Lawrence.[14]

On December 9, 1970, after a long and exhaustive study and investigation, the IJC made a number of recommendations "as the minimum basis for programs to achieve and maintain waters in satisfactory condition as contemplated by Article IV." A series of twenty-two specific recommendations were made. Certain water quality objectives and schedules for phosphorus control were proposed and the Governments were urged to agree to put them into effect as set forth. Last but not least, the Governments were urged to confer

---

12. Canada, Department of External Affairs, Letter No. 1618, Dec. 19, 1941.
13. Int'l Joint Comm., Pollution of Boundary Waters (Docket No. 54, Apr. 1, 1946).
14. Int'l Joint Comm., Great Lakes Pollution (Docket No. 83, Oct. 7, 1964).

upon this Commission the authority, responsibility and means for coordination, surveillance, monitoring, implementation, reporting, making recommendations to governments, all as outlined in Chapter XIII of this Report, and such other duties related to preservation and improvement of the quality of the boundary waters of the Great Lakes—St. Lawrence System as may be agreed by the said Governments; the Commission to be authorized to establish, in consultation with the Governments, an international board or boards to assist it in carrying out these duties and to delegate to said board or boards such authority and responsibility as the Commission may deem appropriate.[15]

Since the issuance of the report there have been several meetings at the ministerial level in an attempt to implement recommendation twenty-two. This is highly encouraging. Contrasted to this progress, however, is the diverging viewpoints of the two countries on pollution control which surfaced during the course of the hearings held by the IJC. To those who participated throughout the investigation, it was no particular surprise, particularly in light of the history of industrial and residential development in the Great Lakes Basin by the two adjoining nations.

The investigation indicated clearly that in terms of gross volumes of pollutants, the United States was contributing and had contributed by far the larger share. In fact, in terms of assimilative capacity, as our recommendations indicate, a reduction in the quantities of several pollutants was in order immediately. The Canadians, who have watched with a certain degree of envy as our industries prospered and our standard of living rose, became concerned that the assimilative capacity of the Lakes, Erie in particular, was being preempted by the United States. Thus Canada would be left with no alternative but to adopt a closed cycle, or no discharge philosophy at a possibly very high economic cost. To them it could well appear to be a question of the "fustest with mostest."

Being somewhat behind the United States in economic development and wishing to maximize the use of all its resources, Canada is reluctant to allocate resources for what it considers to be unnecessary pollution control. This attitude is best illustrated by the contrasting positions of the State of Michigan and the Province of Ontario. Time and time again, the Ontario Water Resources Board took the position that standard effluent criteria such as secondary waste treatment made no sense by itself. It was and is their position that it is a waste of their resources to require this degree of treatment

---

15. Pollution of Lake Erie, Lake Ontario, and the Int'l Section of the St. Lawrence River, Final Report to the Two Governments, Dec. 9, 1970, at 92.

if the receiving waters can withstand a lower degree of treatment. This position is to be contrasted to that adopted by a number of States and encouraged by the Environmental Protection Agency that secondary treatment be the goal regardless of the assimilative capacity.

The contrasting positions of the two countries is even more clearly reflected when one compares the underlying philosophy of the so-called Muskie Act, S.2770 with the philosophy set forth in a joint report by the Ontario Water Resources Board and the Quebec Water Board entitled "Water Quality and its Control in the Ottawa River", Volume 1, issued June 11, 1971.

In the former case, the United States Senate unanimously departed from a long-standing policy of water quality standards control in the United States in favor of a no discharge policy by 1985. While, at the time this paper is being prepared, the House of Representatives has not acted, nevertheless, it seems reasonably certain that there is a significant shift underway in the United States to effluent standards as the primary means of control, partly because of the difficulty of relating the impact of any one or more discharges on the quality of a particular receiving body of water, and partly, I suspect, because of the feeling that most of the pollutants end up in the oceans where the accumulations may be building up to a dangerous level.[16]

As a matter of international environmental relations, S. 2770, Section 310, retains a hearing procedure to handle situations where pollution of United States waters endangers the health and welfare of persons in a foreign country. This is comparable to existing legislation and was not joyously received by Canadians. This feeling results, I believe, because the Act seems to place a foreign country in the position of a complaining party in the courts of the United States and also because it requires such foreign country to give the United States essentially the same rights.

There are those in the developing nations who will term the type of approach under S. 2770 as "Environmental Imperialism" or "Environmental Elitism." At times during the Lake Erie hearings it was apparent that there was some resentment against the United States for seeking to require other nations to adopt certain effluent limitations without particular regard to the alternative means and the costs and benefits thereof, especially in view of the fact that much of the United States prosperity may well have been at the cost of using up this public good. Some indicated, "Well, now, you can afford it, but we can't." The United States position became even harder to

16. An Act to Amend the Federal Water Pollution Control Act, S. 2770, 92nd Cong., 1st Sess. (Nov. 2, 1971).

understand for the Canadians when the United States refused to adopt the recommendations of the IJC as to limitations on the phosphorous content of detergents even though Canada instituted certain controls on a federal level, despite the fact it is often alleged that Canadian federal-provincial problems usually prevent coordinated national action. Throw in the recommendations of the United States Surgeon General, and everything becomes confused.

In the Ottawa River situation previously referred to, there is a much different approach adopted which should be examined closely. Here the two provinces, after an exhaustive investigation of the water quality of the Basin, were able to establish existing BOD loadings, for example, and calculate on the basis of mathematical models permissible BOD loadings.

> [A] reserve portion of these loadings (were) set aside to provide: 1) an adequate margin of protection in recognition of the limitations of water management theory and practice; 2) the maintenance of adequate water quality in the face of population and industrial growth, urbanization and technological change. Approximately one-third of the receiving capacity of the river was maintained in reserve.[17]

In the judgment of the two Boards, water quality control can be classified in terms of cycles which would be the time necessary to analyze problems, establish a basis for treatment, design and build and operate the facilities so as to utilize an appropriate proportion of the receiving capacity of the water course. Such a cycle was considered to be twenty years and during this time no user could discharge more than was permitted him and the treatment plant specified would be capable of the highest practicable degree consistent with current technology. The report calls for a reasoned approach to the use of the river with social and economic pressures dictating future uses. In the latter case, limitations of future industrial development as well as possible relocation of existing industries is forecast. In conclusion, the report discusses additional studies which might be required and states that:

> The changes in water quality as anti-pollution programs are implemented must be carefully documented. This will provide a basis for rationally evaluating the expected benefits in relation to the cost of future water quality programs. As the country continues to develop, greater pressures will be placed on all water resources and cost of maintaing the quality of all waters at desirable levels for all uses will,

---

17. Ontario Water Resources Comm. (jointly with) Quebec Water Board, 1 Ottawa River Basin Water Quality and Its Control in the Ottawa River 45 (1971).

even if attainable, require such a large committment of our economic resources that it may no longer be justifiable solely on the basis of pollution control.[18]

What lessons can we draw from this? First of all, it was fortunate that Elihu Root failed to persist in his position to limit the IJC to an advisory body on ad hoc resource matters. While the IJC may not have solved the problem of the pollution of the Great Lakes, nevertheless, it has been the conscience of the two nations some sixty-three years and an organization to which citizens can turn for support.

Secondly, by making the most expert manpower available to the Commission, it not only enables the Commission to speak with authority but also has resulted in a unique but extremely valuable international environmental esprit de corps. The proper and correct solution becomes the goal, not which nation has the most clout. National sovereignty becomes lost in the shuffle. The experts dedicate themselves to solving the riddle of how man and our nations can have, in the words of Lewis Mumford, "the right quantity of the right quality at the right time and the right place for the right purpose."[19] Whether to resort to water quality criteria or to use effluent standards is the type of question, as we have seen, which is hammered out together in an atmosphere of mutual respect.

A third feature is that slowly but surely the independence and stature of a body, which concentrates on its principle role of recommending what is best but not necessarily what is the easiest to get accepted, begins to carry weight of its own. The force of public opinion is not a force to be ignored, as the original supporters recognized.[20] It must be nurtured it is true, but it is a resource that is to be treasured.

A fourth point concerns the composition of this body. It does not require representation on the basis of one man, one vote. Rather, it requires the acceptance of the fact that the dominant power must always rely upon the force of its technical and moral position rather than upon economic imperialism. Issues seen through the eyes of the smaller power may appear to be far different than issues seen through the eyes of those "who have made it good".

The fifth point is that it is absolutely imperative that water resource development not be done in the abstract. It must be done in light of the realities of economics and politics. National pride should be used constructively, not destructively. I am convinced beyond

18. *Id.* at 49.
19. Mumford, R.D. #1, Amenia, New York (source of direct quote unknown).
20. Reader is referred to documentation in first six pages of this paper.

question that the Canadian action on detergents, particularly being the less wealthy nation, has had a tremendous impact in the United States, particularly in the local community and at the state level.

In conclusion, the case histories seem to suggest that some declaration of principle is needed as to our long range environmental goals. One goal would be to seek to affirm the ultimate necessity of imposing absolute limitations on the right to discharge waste materials. As the IJC pointed out in 1918, the time to correct the problem is before the waters are polluted to the degree that one country's action endangers the health and welfare of another country. Furthermore, the determination of the exact time when a certain build-up of wastes in any receiving body of water becomes detrimental is most difficult. The gradual accumulation of nutrients in Lake Erie with no obvious harm in the early years misled both nations into failing to realize that a specific rate of discharge of waste material may have an entirely different impact depending upon the particular history of the receiving water. Who knows for certain when the assimilated capacity is reached? It was apparently for this reason that Ontario and Quebec very properly established a reserve margin.

While our attention should be directed to the ultimate limitation of discharges, it would be most beneficial to have both nations continue to concentrate upon seeking to determine the impact of the discharge of any pollutant upon the waters. This is necessary because of economic reasons. No one sovereign nation, or even a combination of sovereign nations, can afford unnecessary allocation of its resources for unessential purposes. There must be a continuous monitoring, together with constant assessments, of the damage done, cost incurred and benefits received. If this is not done, no individual nation can long look for public support of its programs, nor can a sovereign nation look to support from the international community.

As Secretary Root pointed out, there is a very different attitude depending upon whether you are Big Brother or Little Brother, a strong or weak nation, a rich or poor country, a developed or developing nation.

Big Brother, who is usually strong, rich and a developed nation, is much more apt to act as some cost-plus utility might act. In other words, "Let's stop all discharges now, why worry about costs; after all, we were initially responsible for most of it anyway. Moreover, since other nations are dependent upon our good will, we can force them to comply. Furthermore, we obviously know best, otherwise we would not be such a successful nation."

Little Brother, on the other hand, is equally righteous. Such a nation, whose natural resources are coveted by those who do not want to exploit their own, is eager to compete in the International GNP (Gross National Product) Grand Prix. It is urged that, "You have had yours, now let us have ours. There is no valid reason why we are not entitled to a fair share of the assimilative capacity of any receiving body to use as we see fit." The very essence of assimilative capacity suggests certain rights or equitable entitlements. Moreover, it is oftentimes alleged that technology can come up with the answer to any problem, "so why get all worked up?". When such positions are set forth by underdog nations and the sympathies of the world are enlisted to support a nation's right to pollute, the confrontation becomes a very serious matter indeed.

In fact, both positions can be most appealing, depending upon where you sit. Too frequently one's position may be influenced by the ability of one party to predict more dire consequences than the other.

Fortunate for all of us, however, is the fact that, for those who urge the right to pollute their own share of the world, there has to be established some competent, credible body to determine the particular method of sharing—unless we continue to resort to war for solutions. It can start off on an ad hoc basis as did Ontario and Quebec, but ultimately, as Secretary Root discovered, the adoption of an international body, "a practical tribunal" in his words, based upon some agreed principles is required.

It is also fortunate that those who would ignore the laws of economics invariably find out that this is impossible. Moreover, those nations who try to do so cannot help but suffer the same fate as those nations who have sought to practice colonialism or economic imperialism. Environmental imperialism is no better, for those who practice it will ultimately find to their sorrow that an environmental dictator is as arbitrary and unreasonable as is a military or economic dictator. Freedom of any nature obviously will be more limited as man seeks to survive. Any restrictions on one's freedom, however, must be based upon sound social and scientific reasoning.

Disheartened as I am at times, I am encouraged, however, by the example of Canada and the United States, two great nations which, over the years, have mobilized the best brains in each country in a common effort to improve the quality of life of their citizens. That two nations situated next to each other can understand that political boundaries and nationalistic fervor must be laid aside speaks well for man's survival.

Nations, no more than man himself, cannot expect to subjugate the natural world to their wishes without understanding the relationship of living things to their environment. With the growing awareness that geographical proximity is no longer a necessary condition precedent to environmental damage, it is not unreasonable to believe that nations facing one another across an "Iron Curtain" may well join hands in the most important war of all—the war to insure man's survival—a survival dependent upon the recognition of the utter necessity of accomplishing that delicate balancing task required within a total ecosystem for the survival of the entire system. If it can be done, we may have taken the most important step of all towards "Peace With Freedom".

THE DEVELOPMENT OF INTERNATIONAL ENVIRONMENTAL LAW AND POLICY IN AFRICA†

J. D. OGUNDERE††

The beginnings of international environmental law and policy in Africa can be traced to the General Act of the Conference of Berlin,[1] signed on February 26, 1885, and ratified by most signatories on April 19, 1886, at which thirteen European states, and the United States of America were represented. The aims and purposes of the Conference were set down in the preamble:

> [W]ishing, in a spirit of good and mutual accord, to regulate the conditions most favourable to the development of trade and civilization in certain regions of Africa, and to assure to all nations the advantages of free navigation on the two chief rivers of Africa flowing into the Atlantic Ocean; being desirous, on the other hand, to obviate the misunderstanding and disputes which might in future arise from new acts of occupation ("prises de possession") on the coast of Africa; and concerned, at the same time, as to the means of furthering the moral and material well-being of the native populations. . . .

The declaration of purpose in the last clause which is the most significant for this article was solidified into an international obligation in Article VI of the General Act which, *inter alia,* provides as follows:

> Preservation and Improvement of Native
> Tribes; Slavery, and the Slave Trade
>
> All the Powers exercising sovereign rights or influence in the aforesaid territories bind themselves to watch over the preservation of the native tribes, and to care for the improvement of the conditions of their moral and material well-being, and to help in suppressing slavery, and especially the slave trade.
>
> Religious and other Institutions
> Civilization of Natives

†The author is indebted to Dr. T. O. Elias, the Attorney-General and Commissioner for Justice of the Federal Republic of Nigeria, and Dean of the Law Faculty of Lagos University for his helpful criticism of the manuscript.

††LL.B. (Lond); B.L. (Lincoln's Inn) 1957; LL.B. (Hons)(Cantab) 1961; Deputy Solicitor-General of the Federal Republic of Nigeria; Member of the International Council of Environmental Law; Council Member of UNIDROIT; Representative of Nigeria on UNCITRAL; Representative of Nigeria in the Sixth Committee of the U.N., 1966-1969; Deputy Leader of the Nigerian Delegation to the U.N. Conference on the Law of Treaties, Vienna 1968-1969; Member, Nigerian Institute of International Affairs; Life Member and Current Treasurer of the Nigerian Society of International Law.

1. Sir E. Hertslet, The Map of Africa by Treaty 468-87 (3d ed. 1967).

They shall, without distinction of creed or nation, protect and favour all religions, scientific, or charitable institutions, and undertakings created and organized for the above ends, or which aim at instructing the natives and bringing home to them the blessings of civilization.

Thus the moral and material well-being of Africans, which would seem to embrace their integration with the totality of their environment, and which were to be promoted by scientific institutions with the aim of bringing home to them the blessings of civilization, constitute the nucleus of international environmental law and policy in Africa.

The happy integration of man with and the maintenance of the ecological balance between man and his environment motivated the Conference[2] held in London in 1933 on the African Environment which culminated in the Conclusion of the 1933 London Convention Relative to the Preservation of Fauna and Flora in their Natural State.[3] The philosophy behind this Convention, which was the first fundamental Treaty[4] on which the protection of nature in African environment is based under international law, was the preservation of fauna and flora in Africa against the excesses of European hunters and farmers who had introduced the use of firearms and ploughs, particularly into the savannah areas of East and Central Africa.

The aims and purposes of the 1933 London Convention were to promote by international action, the establishment of Nature Reserves and National Parks[5] in the territories of the Contracting Governments where strict measures would be taken to control all white or native settlements in national parks with a view to ensuring that as little disturbance as possible is occasioned to the natural fauna and flora; and to establish round the borders of natural parks and strict nature reserves intermediate zones within which the hunting, killing and capturing of animals may take place under the control of the authorities of the park or reserve.[6] The Contracting Governments were under an obligation to notify the Government of the United Kingdom of legislative and administrative measures taken by each Contracting Government to implement the provisions of the

---

2. Proceedings of the Third Int'l Conference for the Protection of the Fauna and Flora in Africa, Oct. 26-31, 1953 (Bukavu, Belgian Congo, CCTA Pub. (hereinafter cited as Third Int'l Conference).

3. An Annex to the Recommendations and Resolutions of the London Convention 1933, *id.* at 161-85.

4. The nine signatory governments were: The Union of South Africa, Belgium, The United Kingdom of Great Britain and Northern Ireland, Egypt, Spain, France, Italy, Portugal and Anglo-Egyptian Sudan.

5. London Convention, arts. 3 and 6 (1933).

6. *Id.* at art. 4.

Convention. The Government of the United Kingdom had the duty to circulate the information received to other Contracting Governments.[7]

Under the Convention, the Contracting Governments also agreed to set aside game reserves in which the hunting, killing or capturing of any part of the natural fauna (exclusive of fish) shall be prohibited save by permission given for scientific or administrative purposes. The natural flora in such reserves were also protected and in addition forest reserves were to be created where the best indigenous forest species were to be preserved.[8]

The Convention also regulated the traffic in trophies,[9] prohibited certain hunting methods,[10] and approved the protection to be granted to some threatened species which were listed under class A and class B in the Annex[11] to the official document. In the Protocol[12] to the Convention, it was agreed that meetings were to take place periodically to facilitate co-operation for the purpose of preventing extinction of natural fauna and flora and to examine the workings of the Convention with a view to making improvements thereon. The first meeting held to review the workings of the Convention took place in London in 1938 in which Contracting Governments reported on measures they had taken in their respective territories in the implementation of the Convention.

In 1949, the Second International Conference[13] for the protection of nature was held at Lake Success under the joint sponsorship of UNESCO and the International Union for Conservation of Nature and Natural Resources (IUCN). That Conference passed a resolution stressing the need to hold a further meeting of the signatories of the London Convention. The Commission for Technical Co-operation in Africa South of the Sahara (CCTA) in collaboration with the government of Belgium and with support from UNESCO adopted the suggestion to call a further meeting as resolved at Lake Success in 1949, and called the Third International Conference for the Protection of Fauna and Flora in Africa which was held in Bukavu, Belgium Congo in 1953.[14] Although various amendments were proposed to the 1937 London Convention, these were not incorporated into the Con-

---

7. *Id.* at arts. 5 and 12.
8. *Id.* at art. 7.
9. *Id.* at art. 9.
10. *Id.* at art. 10.
11. Third Int'l Conference, *supra* note 2, at 185-93.
12. *Id.* at 194-95.
13. The Foreword of Jean-Paul Harnoy, Rapporteur General of the Conference. *Id.* at 7-13.
14. *See* the various recommendations and Resolutions of the Conference. *Id.*

vention.[15] However, several countries incorporated the proposals into their legislation just as they enacted legislation for implementation of the 1933 London Convention. In this period, the environmental question was the preservation of African fauna and flora, and greater emphasis was placed on the fauna.

The Charter of the United Nations signed at San Francisco on June 26, 1945, and which entered into force on October 24, 1945, has positive effects on the development of international environmental law and policy in Africa. The fourth and eighth preambular paragraphs to the Charter state:

> We the peoples of the United Nations determined
>> to promote social progress and better standards of life in larger freedom; . . .
>
> And To These Ends
>> to employ International machinery for the promotion of the economic and social advancement of all peoples.

The declaration of intention of the Organization contained in those preambular clauses with regard to the promotion of the economic and social advancement of all peoples is reinforced by Article 55 of the Charter which enjoins the Organization, *inter alia,* to promote:

> (a) higher standards of living, full employment and conditions of economic and social progress and development;
> (b) solutions of international economic, social, health and related problems; and international cultural and educational co-operation. . . .

There is no denying the fact that the obligations assumed by members of the United Nations in Article 55 constitute an inspiration to specialized agencies of the United Nations, in particular the United Nations Educational Scientific and Cultural Organization (UNESCO), in helping to promote the development of environmental policy in the world in general and in Africa in particular as we shall see later.

The decade commencing in 1960 witnessed the emancipation of several African states from colonialism, the high water-mark of which was the creation of the Organization of African Unity (OAU) in 1963. One should also mention that the period 1960-69 was declared the "Development Decade" by the General Assembly of the United Nations.[16] The Charter[17] of the OAU gave added impetus to the

---

15. W. Burhenne, *The African Convention for the Conservation of Nature and Natural Resources,* II Ecological Conservation J. 105 (Jan. 1970); Kai-Curry Lindahl, *The New African Convention,* 2 J. Fauna Preservation Soc'y (ORYX) 116 (Sep. 1969).

16. G. A. Res. 1710 (XVI) (Dec. 19, 1961).

17. Nigeria's Treaties in Force for the period 1st October, 1960 to 20th June, 1968 (Federal Ministry of Information Printing Division, Lagos, 1969) (hereinafter cited as

concerted efforts of the newly emancipated states of Africa in the development of their environment. Under Article 2(1)(b) of the Charter, one of the purposes of the Organization was to coordinate and intensify the cooperation and efforts of African states towards the achievement of a better life for the peoples of Africa; and under Article 2(2), the member states were under an obligation to co-ordinate and harmonize their general policies especially in the fields of economic cooperation including transport and communication, health, sanitation and nutritional cooperation and scientific and technical cooperation.

Pursuant to Article Twenty of the Charter, the Summit Conference[18] of Independent African States meeting in Addis Ababa, Ethiopia, from May 22-25, 1963, adopted the International Agreement establishing the Commission for Technical Co-operation in Africa South of the Sahara (CCTA) signed in London on January 18, 1954.[19] The CCTA was later merged with the Scientific Technical and Research Commission (STRC) of the OAU. Under Article VI(2) of the Agreement, the power and functions of the Commission, *inter alia,* are:

(a) to concern itself with all matters affecting technical co-operation between the member governments and their territories within the territorial scope of the Commission;

(b) to recommend to member Goverments measures for achieving such co-operation.

At the first session of the STRC in Algiers in February 1964, the Commission adopted its Rules of Procedure.[20] Rule 3 provides that within the framework of the Charter of the OAU, the Commission should promote and organize inter-African co-operation among member states in scientific, technical and research matters in accordance with the directives of the Assembly and the Council of Ministers; and that the Commission should encourage collaboration with other international organizations active in the field of science and research.

The newly independent African states were also brought into closer contact with international organizations which have shown serious concern in the past with the African environment, par-

---

Nigeria's Treaties in Force). *See also* T. Elias, *The Charter of the OAU,* 59 A.J.I.L. 243 (1965).

18. The Organization of African Unity, Basic Documents and Resolutions, Published by the Provisional Secretariat of the Organization of African Unity 23 (1963).

19. Int'l Agreement for the Establishment of the Comm. for Technical Cooperation in Africa South of the Sahara 2-13 (CCTA Pub. 61, Jan. 18, 1954).

20. Rules of Procedure of the Scientific, Technical and Research Commission of the OAU STR/2/Rev 1, (Scientific, Technical and Research Comm'n, First Sess., Algiers, Feb. 1964).

ticularly the International Union for the Conservation of Nature and Natural Resources (IUCN), the Food and Agricultural Organization of the United Nations (FAO), the International Council for Bird Preservation (ICBP), the International Council of Environmental Law (ICEL) and UNESCO.

As the decade advanced, African states, slowly at first and later increasingly, felt the need for the coordination of their activities in the conservation and management of their natural resources including the maintenance of the ecological balance of their environment. This was reflected, as we shall show later, in the creation of specialized inter-state organizations and commissions.

In 1960, the African Forestry Commission of the FAO created an ad hoc Working Party on Wildlife Management, charged with drafting an African convention for the conservation, control and exploitation of the wild fauna. During the first four years of the Working Party's life, it was not convened.[21] In September, 1961, a symposium was organized by the CCTA and IUCN under the auspices of the FAO and UNESCO in Arusha, Tanganyika on the Conservation of Nature and Natural Resources in Modern African States.[22] The plan for the Arusha Symposium was conceived by the IUCN at its General Assembly and technical meetings held in June, 1960 at Warsaw and Cracow in Poland. The IUCN then appreciated that the accelerated rate of destruction of wild fauna, flora and habitat in Africa, without adequate regard to its value as a continuing economic and cultural resource, constituted the most urgent ecological problem of the day in Africa.[23] The Arusha Conference made recommendations relating, *inter alia,* to the subject of international aid for education and training in conservation of water, soils, vegetation and wild life; land use policies which should aim at avoiding the intensive occupation of land unsuited for such use in the long term; and to the need for greater attention to the economics of resource development programs.[24]

In February 1963, at the joint session of the CCTA and the Scientific Council of Africa (CSA) held in Dar-es-Salaam, an African Charter for the Protection and Conservation of Nature[25] was adopted. In Article 1, nature in Africa is recognized as a sacred trust for the benefit of posterity. Article 2 recognizes that nature's mani-

21. Lindahl, *supra* note 15, at 117.

22. *Report of a Symposium on Conservation of Nature and Natural Resources in Modern African States,* organized by CCTA and IUCN under the auspices of FAO and UNESCO at Arusha, Tanganyika, Sep. 1961 (IUCN Pub. New Series No. 1, 1963).

23. *Id.* at 9.

24. *Id.* at 15, 69-72.

25. African Charter for the Protection and Conservation of Nature, CCTA 18th Sess., Feb. 4-9, 1963, Dar-es-Salaam (CCTA–CSA Pub.).

fold riches—economic, scientific, cultural and aesthetic—are an ir-replaceable capital which must be administered wisely and carefully by rational exploitation based on specific and well-proved scientific rules. In Article 4, African states are urged to relate the utilization and exploitation of water, soils, animals or plants to the rate of renewal or maintenance of the reserve in question. In Article 5, African states are advised that, while considering major projects like a hydro-electric scheme, they should make use of specialists includ-ing biologists so that the probable effect on natural conditions may be accurately assessed. Article 8 urges states to entrust the conserva-tion of nature and natural resources in their domain to a specialized organization. Here again, the 1963 African Charter embraces the totality of the human environment.

In September 1963, at Nairobi, the IUCN held its 9th Technical Meeting in conjunction with its 8th General Assembly. The theme of that meeting was The Ecology of Man in the Tropical Environ-ment.[26] That theme was inspired by an increasing realization that rational land-use programs either for an area, a nation or a region should be based on adequate scientific studies if a new balance were to be maintained between man and his ecological environment with a view to achieving a higher level of productivity and economic well-being.

Learned papers which were contributed by scientists and adminis-trators, including Africans, were divided into four parts. Part One dealt with "Pre-industrial Man in the Tropical Environment," that is, man as a hunter of food, gatherer of fruits, fisherman, pastoralist and cultivator. Part Two covered "Ecosystems and Biological Pro-ductivity," that is, the total complex of living things along with the physical conditions of soil, climate, and physiography that occur in a given situation, particularly the ecosystem of forests, savannah, desert, mountain, water areas and wetlands. The primary question for each ecosystem was its potentiality to support over a period of time plants, animals and man who are adapted to it. Part Three was devoted to "The Impact of Man on the Tropical Environment," particularly the effect of the introduction of non-indigenous plants and animals, shifting cultivation, fire, grazing and water control. Part Four dealt with "Ecological Research and Development" and covered the ways and means of evaluating environments and of pro-viding an ecological basis for living with them; it also dealt with case studies of development programs.[27]

Another important development in environmental policy in Africa

26. The Ecology of Man in the Tropical Environment, Ninth Technical Meeting, Nairobi, Sep. 1963 (IUCN Pub. New Series No. 4, 1964).
27. *Id.* at 19-22.

occurred under the recommendations of the International Conference on the Organization of Research and Training in Africa in Relation to the Study, Conservation, and Utilization of Natural Resources[28] which was held in Lagos, Nigeria, from July 28 to August 6, 1964, under the aegis of UNESCO in association with the United Nations Economic Commission for Africa, and in consultation with other specialized agencies of the United Nations. Twenty-seven independent African states attended the Conference and several international organizations including the specialized agencies sent representatives and observers to the conference. Three commissions were set up to study the organization of research, scientific and technical personnel, finances and research economics. The Conference considered the following agenda items and made recommendations thereon: National Scientific Policies With Regard to Research on Natural Resources; Preparation and Implementation of Policies of Research on Natural Resources; Scientific and Technical Personnel; Finances and Research Economics; and International Cooperation in Research on Natural Resources.

With regard to National Scientific Policies concerning research into Natural Resources,[29] the Conference appreciated that a scientific study of natural resources and their potentiality is essential for the economic and social development of African countries. In this regard the Conference reviewed the report and recommendations of the United Nations Conference on the Application of Science and Technology for the Benefit of Less Developed Areas, held at Geneva in February 1963. That Conference recognized that the process of development depended on the mobilization of a nation's entire resources and by the application of principles and coordination of scientific activities in the natural sciences, in technology and in social and human sciences.

In its concluding resolutions, the Conference proclaimed, *inter alia*, its conviction that the extension of scientific and technological research on natural resources, constitutes a factor essential to such development. The Conference recommended,[30] *inter alia*, that the governments should devote continued and very large-scale efforts to the promotion of scientific and technological research; that campaigns should be systematically organized in each country with a view to drawing the attention of the population to the essential role

28. Final Report of the Lagos Conference on the Organization of Research and Training in Africa in Relation to the Study, Conservation and Utilization of Natural Resources, July 28 to Aug. 16, 1964 (UNESCO/ECA Pub.).
    29. *Id.* at 13-25.
    30. *Id.* at 24-25.

which science and technology can play in solving the social and economic problems which hinder the development efforts of African countries. It also recommended that the plans for the wise exploitation and utilization of natural resources, renewable resources in particular, should not use up more than the capital which they can produce.

The Conference also considered preparation and implementation of policies of research on natural resources.[31] It recommended,[32] *inter alia,* that national research organizations be set up to coordinate the elaboration and implementation of programs of research on natural resources and that effective links be instituted between social organizations and planning commissions; and that a scientific and technical committee on natural resources in Africa be set up to carry out the task listed for action at a continental level. The Conference also recommended that the attention of African states should be drawn to the resolution on the conservation of natural resources, fauna and flora, in the developing countries, adopted by the UNESCO General Conference at its 12th Session in December 1962, "The African Charter" adopted by certain African countries in 1962, the resolution of the General Assembly of the IUCN adopted in Nairobi in 1963; that the 1933 Convention on the flora and fauna of Africa be revised in order to bring it up to date and to extend the scope of its application; and that the OAU should entrust the preparatory work to the IUCN assisted by UNESCO and FAO.

On the item Scientific and Technical Personnel,[33] the Conference recommended a list of categories and numbers of personnel needed. It also recommended co-operation between existing universities and research institutes of Africa and that African nationals trained abroad should be given incentives to return home.

The Conference made two important recommendations on Finance and Research Economics:[34] that a national scientific research council be set up in each country and that a research budget be established for that body.

A number of useful recommendations on the subject International Cooperation in Research on Natural Resources[35] were made including the one that UNESCO as well as other international organizations should give technical and other support to the projects of the Scientific Commission of the OAU; that a network of national

---

31. *Id.* at 26-40.
32. *Id.* at 38-40.
33. *Id.* at 48-50.
34. *Id.* at 55-58.
35. *Id.* at 62-64.

and international scientific institutions of the highest possible standard in training and researching in natural resources in Africa should be established or developed; and that UNESCO, ECA and other U.N. agencies and organizations, other inter-governmental and non-governmental bodies, and member states of UNESCO outside Africa should continue and expand their collaboration with the African countries in scientific research and training.

In 1965, in response to the recommendations of the 1964 Lagos Conference, the OAU requested the IUCN to prepare a draft of a revised 1933 London Convention on the flora and fauna of Africa which would cover the entire field of renewable natural resources and which would deal, not only with the protection of such resources, but also emphasize their conservation and sound management.[36] The ad hoc sub-committee of IUCN composed of experts and administrators from African states and including observers from FAO, UNESCO, and ECA met in Morges in December 1965 and examined the IUCN draft proposal which was later forwarded to the OAU by the President of the IUCN in December 1966. In September 1967, the Assembly of Heads of State and Government of the OAU, after a preliminary discussion, referred the draft and the comments of member states to a committee of five states who were requested to finalize the draft. In the meantime, in February 1966, the FAO distributed the draft of African Convention of Conservation and Management of Wildlife and Its Habitat to member governments and organizations. In February 1967, the FAO Working Party held the Second Session[37] in Fort Lamy in Chad to finalize its draft convention. Twenty-eight African countries and representatives of the United Nations including UNESCO and IUCN were present. In September 1967, the OAU heads of state and governments at its Kinshasa meeting unanimously resolved that only one general convention was required on the conservation, preservation and exploitation of nature and of natural resources in Africa, and appointed a committee consisting of Ethiopia, Chad, Liberia, Uganda and Tanzania to look into it. Early in 1968, representatives of the FAO, UNESCO and IUCN met in Rome to consolidate the two draft conventions; the consolidated draft convention was submitted to the committee of five which met in Addis Ababa in February 1968, which draft was finally approved at the OAU Summit meeting in Algiers in September 1968. The new Convention entitled "The African Convention for the Conservation of Nature and Natural Re-

---

36. Burhenne, *supra* note 15, at 105.
37. Lindahl, *supra* note 15, at 118.

sources" was signed by 38 African heads of state and governments and came into effect in July 1969.

The preamble to the Convention[38] emphasized that soil, water, flora and fauna resources constitute a capital of vital importance to mankind; that utilization of these natural resources must aim at satisfying the needs of man according to the carrying capacity of the environment; and expressed the desire of African states to undertake individual and joint action for the conservation, utilization and development of these assets by establishing and maintaining their rational utilization for the present and future welfare of mankind. Article Two stated the fundamental principle of the Convention: contracting states should undertake to adopt the measures necessary to ensure conservation, utilization and development of soil, water, flora and fauna resources, in accordance with scientific principles and with due regard to the best interest of the people. Article Four deals with the conservation of soil within the framework of land-use plans based on scientific investigations. Article Five deals with conservation, utilization and development of underground and surface water with special regard, *inter alia,* to the prevention and control of water pollution. Article Six deals with the protection of flora and its best utilization and development. Article Seven sets out the obligation of contracting states on the conservation, wise use and development of fauna resources and their environment, within the framework of land-use planning and of economic and social development. Article Eight deals with protected species of flora and fauna. Article Nine regulates traffic in specimen and trophies. Article Ten deals with conservation areas for the protection of ecosystems and conservation of all species listed in the annex to the convention. Article Eleven deals with reconciliation of customary rights with the provision of the convention. Article Twelve obligated contracting states to encourage and promote research in conservation, utilization and management of natural resources. Article Thirteen concerns conservation education. Under Article Fourteen, contracting states are under an obligation to ensure that conservation and management of natural resources are treated as an integral part of national and regional development plans.

Environmental policy is distinguishable from natural resources policy, although there is a close affinity and significant substantive overlap between the two.[39] International environmental policies can

38. Burhenne, *supra* note 15, at 106-114.
39. Lynton K. Caldwell and Irving K. Fox, Research on Policy and Administration in Environmental Quality Programs 15-50 (Indiana Univ. Institute of Pub. Ad., Mar. 30, 1967).

be said to be public policies which influence the way the physical and non-physical environment is used and which are co-ordinated or integrated on the international level. It includes the rational planning and use of air, water, land, fauna and flora, with a view to achieving an equilibrium of beneficial and adverse consequences. Natural resources policy, on the other hand, consists of ways and means of exploiting the natural resources of any given state with a view to deriving optimum benefits to the members of the community concerned.

African states, in the last decade, have tended to put environmental policy and natural resources policy in the same category in order to develop them in international agreements. Examples can be found in the International Agreements on the Niger and the Senegal Rivers and on Lake Chad. Article Two of the Agreement Concerning the River Niger Commission and the Navigation and Transport of the River Niger, Niamey, November 1964,[40] which states the functions of the Commission provides, *inter alia,* that the Commission shall collect, evaluate and disseminate basic data on the whole of the basin, examine the projects prepared by the riparian states and recommend to the governments of the riparian states plans for common studies and works for the judicious utilization and development of the resources of the basin. Under Article Twelve, the contracting states undertake to abstain from carrying out, on the portion of the river, its tributaries and sub-tributaries subject to their jurisdiction, any works likely to *pollute* the waters, or any modification likely to affect the biological characteristics of its fauna and flora, without adequate notice to, and prior consultation with, the Commission.

In the Convention and Statute Relating to the Development of the Chad Basin, Fort Lamy, May 22, 1964,[41] a preambular paragraph recognized the need to formulate principles for the utilization of the resources of the Chad Basin for economic purposes including the harnessing of the water. In Article Five of the statute, the member states agreed to consult with the Commission before adopting any measure likely to have an appreciable effect either on the extent of the loss of water or on the nature of the yearly hydrogramme and limnigramme and certain other features of the basin, the conditions subject to which other riparian states may utilize the water in the basin, the sanitary conditions of the water or the biological characteristics of its fauna and flora. There is also an agreement under

40. Nigeria's Treaties in Force, *supra* note 17, at 212-16. *See also* T. Elias, *Berlin Treaty and River Niger Commission,* 57 A.J.I.L. 873 (1963).
41. Nigeria's Treaties in Force, *supra* note 17, at 212-24. *See also* I. Agoro, *The Establishment of The Chad Basin Comm'n,* Int'l & Comp. L. Q. 642 (Apr. 1966).

negotiation on water utilization and conservation including pollution control in the Lake Chad Basin by the riparians: Cameroon, Chad, Nigeria and Niger.

The same mixture of environmental and natural resources policies also can be found in the Convention Concerning the Statute of the Senegal River, 1964.[42] Article Three provides that the contracting states[43] shall consult each other on any proposed works likely to modify appreciably certain characteristics of the river regime, including navigation, or its agricultural and industrial exploitation, the sanitary conditions of its water, and biological characteristics of its fauna and flora. In Article Four, the contracting states are obliged to ensure conservation of the water resources of the basin, maintain their natural flow and quality, and prevent their misuse, waste or pollution.

Other international agreements on environmental policy include the Convention on the African Migratory Locust, May 25, 1962.[44] The sole aim of the Convention is to take surveillance and preventive control of the African migratory locusts which in the past have devastated hundreds of square miles of both cultivated vegetation and of natural growth. There is also the Phytosanitary Convention for Africa South of the Sahara completed in London, April 29, 1954,[45] as amended by protocol at London on October 11, 1961, and substantially re-enacted by the OAU as the Phytosanitary Convention for Africa, 1967. The aim of the Convention is to prevent any new disastrous introduction of plant diseases and pests into Africa on the scale of the potato and vine diseases which ravaged Europe during the first part of the 20th century. One should also mention the Organization Communne de Lutte Anticridienne et de Lutte Antiquiaire (OCLALAV) or Convention for the Joint Organization for Locust and Bird Pest Control held at Fort Lamy May 29, 1965. The purpose of the Convention is to organize a joint eradication of locust and quella birds which do extensive damage to food crops across the savannahs and semi-desert of West Africa.

Population control as an environmental problem has not attracted concerted international action by African states. Africa embraces approximately a quarter of the land surface of the globe. In 1960, it had 9.1 per cent of the world's total population, 5 per cent of the

---

42. *Convention Concerning the Statute of the Senegal River,* 19 Revue Juridique et Politique 302 (1965).

43. Contracting states are Senegal, Mauritania, Mali and Guinea.

44. Nigeria's Treaties in Force, *supra* note 17, at 200-208.

45. A memorandum for Phytosanitary Procedure in Africa 173-84 (CCTA Pub. 8). *See also* U.K. Treaty Series No. 16 (1954) cmd 9077 and OAU CM/Res. 119 (IX) Sep. 13, 1967.

world's urban population and 11.2 per cent of the world's rural population.[46] It had 273 million out of 2,991 million of the world's population.[47] Thus Africa is the least urbanized of the major continents of the world. But its urban population growth rate is among the highest in the world.[48]

Also in Africa, there is a tendency towards concentration of the urban population in the large cities. Arising from this galloping urbanization are the dangers of air and water pollution as a result of industrialization, the increasing use or misuse of fertilizers and pesticides, and oil contamination of the rivers and seas. So far, there is no international convention among African states on the problems of urbanization or over-population. Africa's lukewarm attitude to over-population is understandable as generally speaking over-population is a relative term. A country which is unable to produce sufficient food on its own territory to feed its people is said to be over-populated; the type of farming is therefore important.

On this basis, Britain, which produces only fifty-five per cent of the food it consumes, is over-populated. In tropical Africa, an acre of land can produce the limited food needs of the average African. But the type of farming is generally "shifting cultivation"; six acres are required for the rotational cultivation of one acre to allow five years fallow. On this basis many African states may be said to be over-populated.[49] On the other hand, when mechanized farming becomes the predominant type of farming in Africa and better use is made of fertilizers, seemingly over-populated countries may gradually become under-populated.

Also most African states are not yet fully concerned with environmental pollution problems because their infant manufacturing industries are still few, and heavy rainfall in many countries dilutes and carries away liquid industrial waste, while ample sunshine dry them up quickly. This is in marked contrast to the tremendous public and government concern with problems of environmental pollution in highly developed industrialized countries.[50]

---

46. U.N. Growth of the World's Urban and Rural Population, 1920-2000, Sales No. E.69. XIII3, ST/SOA/Ser. A/44 at 13 (1969).

47. *Id.* at 12.

48. *UN/ECA Size and Growth of Urban Population in Africa,* Sixth Conference of African Statisticians, E/CN.14/CAS.6/3. (Addis Ababa, 1968).

49. D. Stamp, Land for Tomorrow, Our Developing World 105-125 (1969).

50. E. Bryan, *Water Supply and Pollution Control Aspects of Urbanisation,* 30 Law & Contemp. Prob. 176-92 (1965); R. Ayres and A. Kneese, *Production Consumption, and Externalities,* Am. Econ. Rev. 282-89 (1969); *International Aspect of the 1971 Environmental Program,* H.R. Doc. No. 92-46, 92d Cong., 1st Sess. 253-56 (1971).

The African Regional Seminar on Human Environment[51] held under the aegis of the Economic Commission for Africa in Addis Ababa, August 23-28, 1971, is a step in the right direction. It afforded African experts in the several disciplines connected with environmental problems to exchange ideas and views in preparation of the U.N. Conference on the Human Environment,[52] scheduled to take place in Stockholm in 1972. The seminar also made a number of recommendations.

In discussing the Founex Report,[53] the seminar shared the view that the major environmental problems of developing countries arose, firstly, out of lack of development and, secondly, out of the process of the development itself, through mis-management of natural resources. It also recognized that environmental policies needed to become one of the dimensions of development policies and should be integrated with the latter as part of a more unified approach to development.[54] The point was also made that lending and financing agencies should revise the guidelines of project appraisal taking into account environmental considerations.[55]

On the topic of human settlements, the seminar recommended the development of regional co-operation in such matters as environmental health, sanitation, health education, training and exchange of experiences in the management of the environment.[56]

In discussing the conservation of natural resources, the Conferences made an important recommendation regarding the establishment of Institutes of Environmental Study,[57] and on "Development and Industrialization," the seminar recommended that governments should adopt an inter-disciplinary approach in the planning of new industries or the expansion of the existing ones, having due regard to environmental considerations.[58]

On manpower and the environment, the seminar recommended a reformation of the curriculum in order to emphasize environmental education at all levels, and that environmental conservation and improvement should be the basic philosophy of public environmental education.[59] In relation to industrial development, it recommended

51. Rep. of the All-Africa Seminar on the Human Environment, U.N. Doc.E/CN:14/53 (Aug. 23-28, 1971).
52. U.N. Res. 2398 (XIII) (Dec. 3, 1968).
53. Rep. of the All-Africa Seminar, *supra* note 51, at para. 23.
54. *Id*. at para. 29.
55. *Id*. at para. 32.
56. *Id*. at para. 40.
57. *Id*. at para. 50.
58. *Id*. at para. 51.
59. *Id*. at para. 53.

that an inter-regional research institution be set up to study the effects of pollutive industries in the African region.[60]

In conclusion, Africa has taken rapid strides in the last decade to develop, on the international level, solutions to certain environmental problems, mainly relating to fauna, flora and water resources. In the next decade, Africa should concentrate on the problems of over-population, urbanization and pollution.

---

60. *Id*. at para. 56.

THE CONSERVATION OF MIGRATORY ANIMALS THROUGH INTERNATIONAL LAW

CYRILLE DE KLEMM†

Wildlife is an integral part of the natural resources of a nation. Full sovereign rights over all natural resources under present conditions of international law leave states free to use or misuse their wildlife as they wish, subject only to any international agreements that may have been concluded on the matter.

The misuse of sedentary animal populations in the absence of adequate conservation measures and regulations will not normally affect other sedentary populations of the same species in other countries.

Migratory animals present a completely different problem. Migration can be defined as the periodic movement of animals between alternate areas which they inhabit at different times, one area being that in which they breed. Many species perform such migrations over considerable distances and cross international borders in the course of their journey.

For legal purposes, migratory animals can be divided into two groups: interstate migrants—birds and certain species of fish which are at all times during their life cycle under the jurisdiction of at least one of the states in their range;[1] and international migrants—marine animals such as seals, turtles and some fish, which migrate from the high seas to the territory of a coastal state to breed.

It is obvious that if conservation measures are to be effective they must be over the whole range of a migratory species, requiring agreement between all the countries concerned; an international problem whose solution must be found through international law.

INTERSTATE MIGRATIONS

Many species of birds are migratory, but there may be a great difference from one species to another in the extent of the migration. Some species migrate several thousand miles. This is particularly true of species of the northern hemisphere which winter in temperate countries in the southern hemisphere. Each species has its own migration pattern, the dates of migration for a particular species being

---

†J.D.; L.L.M.; IUCN Legislation Commission member; ICEL Board of Governors; UNESCO consultant.

1. Many birds cross the open sea in the course of their migration. They are obviously not under the jurisdiction of any state at that time. Since they are not likely to be hunted either, this situation for practical purposes can be disregarded.

remarkably constant. Birds tend generally to migrate in flocks, halting on their way in suitable habitats from one to several days at a time. Ducks and geese will stop for several weeks during autumn migration while they shed their feathers and molt.

Some striking examples of long-distance migration are the Tahiti curlew which breeds in the northeastern United States and winters in the South Pacific; the European swallows which winter in southern Africa; and the many Siberian birds that cross the Himalayas on their way to India, while waders from eastern Siberia winter in Australia.

Certain species of fish which have spent their adult life in the sea go up the rivers to spawn. These are salmon, sturgeon, and shad. When they go up an international river such as the Rhine[2] or the Danube, they find themselves in a situation identical, legally speaking, to that of migratory birds since, as they proceed on their journey, they come under the jurisdiction of several successive states. Their conservation will, therefore, require an agreement between all the states concerned, as well as additional measures in the high seas.

Migratory birds and anadromous fish can be considered the objects of successive ownership on the part of all states exercising jurisdiction along their migration route, which means that when the migrants are on its territory, each one of the states concerned is free to collect as many animals as it wishes without taking into consideration the interests of the other states. A state is quite entitled to destroy large areas of essential habitat of a migratory species, causing a distortion in the migration pattern or even the very extinction of that species, possibly causing major damage to other states. The principle of successive ownership[3] based on territoriality and national sovereignty over natural resources can not apply to migratory animals. No state will take the pains to carry out extensive conservation measures when such measures are likely to be nullified by the absence of similar action on the part of the other states concerned. No country will feel inclined to limit shooting or fishing of migratory birds or fish if other countries do not impose similar restrictions.

Migratory populations need to be considered as constituting a joint resource of all the states along the migration route, which those states would mutually conserve or exploit. This principle, which is already implied in some international agreements dealing with the

2. The Rhine was a salmon river. In 1885 a Convention between Germany, the Netherlands and Switzerland reproduced in Legislative Texts & Treaty Provisions, U.N. Legislative Series ST/Leg/Ser. B/12, was concluded in order to regulate salmon fishing. Because of pollution the salmon runs have disappeared from the Rhine.

3. Ownership must be understood here as title. True ownership exists in socialist countries when all wildlife is the property of the state.

conservation of migratory species such as the Fraser River Sockeye Convention[4] should become the basis for all future treaties of that kind. Joint ownership would mean that all states concerned would have an equal interest in the preservation and rational management of a species, with research and management costs as well as benefits being allocated among the various parties according to a formula arrived at by negotiation.

A distinction should be drawn here between species which are harvested for commercial purposes or by sportsmen, and all other species which are completely protected. For these completely protected species, treaties based on the principle of joint ownership would harmonize national regulations, organize and coordinate research, prohibit international trade of protected animals and their products, and establish along the migration routes adequate reserves of suitable habitat. In some cases, it may not be easy to persuade all the countries concerned to join such an agreement. Several European countries presently allow the killing of birds of prey and the netting of large numbers of small song birds during their migration. The very existence of an international convention may go a long way toward helping national public opinion to exercise enough pressure on the government concerned to make it adhere to the convention. Special attention would have to be devoted to species threatened with extinction as full cooperation between the different wildlife administrations concerned is essential if these species are to survive. An exemplary case is that of the American whooping crane where excellent collaboration, based on the 1916 Anglo-American Bird Treaty, has been long established. Another example, providing complete protection for certain species of sturgeon which are at present seriously threatened, can be found in the Danube Fisheries Convention.

Joint ownership of exploited animal populations should have as its primary objective the establishment of management practices designed to secure the maximum sustainable yield, which can be achieved by the conclusion of treaties setting up the appropriate machinery and organizing the allocation of the resource between the various partners. The best example of such a treaty is still the Fraser River Salmon Convention of 1940. Sockeye salmon from the North Pacific go up the Fraser River system in Canada where they spawn. Before they get into Canadian waters, they have to pass through American waters along the coast of the state of Washington. A joint commission set up under the Convention is empowered to

---

4. Convention between Canada and the U.S. for the Protection, Preservation, and Extension of the Sockeye Salmon Fisheries in the Fraser River System, *signed* May 26, 1930, CLXXXIV L.N.T.S. 305.

take regulatory action, including opening and closing of fishing periods and areas. It ensures that the catch is equally shared between the nationals of each country. It carries out the necessary research and makes recommendations on all matters which may affect the salmon runs, such as dams and other obstructions, as well as water pollution. The Sockeye Convention, which was extended in 1957 to another species, the pink salmon, has been a success. It must be realized, however, that it applies to two states only and to a relatively limited area. Similar treaties might be concluded with respect to other international resources such as migratory game birds. Such treaties would have to cope with situations which would be materially more complicated although, legally speaking, they would not differ much from that of the Sockeye. In addition to provisions on research, management, control of trade and setting up of reserves, these treaties would have to provide machinery for regulation of hunting, for deciding on open and closed seasons, and on the basis of research establish the total number of birds which may be harvested in a given year.

EXISTING BIRD TREATIES—NORTH AMERICA

The most successful bird treaty to date has been the Convention signed in 1916 between the United States and Great Britain (acting for Canada).[5] This treaty applies to migratory game birds, small insectivorous birds and other non-game birds mainly water birds, excluding birds of prey. The harvesting of non-game birds listed by the convention is prohibited at all times. A long closed season protects game birds. The taking of nests or eggs of all birds covered by the convention, game or non-game, is forbidden. The export or international traffic of protected birds during the closed season is prohibited. There is no provision, however, for the setting up of reserves or habitat preservation.

This treaty was supplemented in 1936 by another, signed between the United States and Mexico[6] which extended southward the protection already granted to North American birds. In the 1936 treaty there is an article providing for the establishment of reserves, making it an international obligation for the United States and Mexico, but exempting Canada.

---

5. Convention with Great Britain on the Protection of Migratory Birds, Aug. 16, 1916, T.S. 628.

6. Convention with Mexico on the Protection of Migratory Birds and Game Mammals, Feb. 7, 1936, T.S. 912.

These two treaties have constituted the basis for all the federal migratory bird legislation which has been enacted in the three countries concerned. The treaties do not provide for joint commissions of advisement and enforcement, but in spite of this shortcoming, excellent cooperation exists between the wildlife administrations concerned. A number of ad hoc arrangements have made it possible to bring into effect many sound conservation measures; for example, the bag limit imposed on duck shooting in the United States is dependent on duck production in the Canadian Prairie area. Bird counting in Canada is therefore essential to determine what the bag should be, it being obvious that conservation measures in Canada will affect directly the number of birds which can be harvested in the United States. Although the treaty did not contemplate such developments, it can be said that the present arrangements derived from the treaty, informal as they may be, provide for a determination of the maximum sustainable yield of duck stocks as well as for a certain allocation of the resource.

Successful as these arrangements have been, an up-dated revision of the treaty should provide for a "well-financed internationally coordinated action program built on a solid foundation."[7] A further extension southward of the area covered by the present agreements would be most desirable in order to give adequate protection to birds that migrate to Central or South America.

EXISTING BIRD TREATIES—EUROPE

Many birds in Europe and Northern Asia migrate to Southern Europe, Africa, India, Southeast Asia, and Australia. The majority of waterfowl breed in Scandinavia, Russia, and Siberia. In the winter, however, they move to the lakes and deltas of dozens of different countries. Bird conservation on the old continent should be an international matter.

As early as 1902 a first convention on the protection of birds was signed by a number of European nations. It applied to both migratory and non-migratory species, but only to those which were deemed to be "useful to agriculture." Birds of prey and other so-called "harmful" birds received no protection. The convention prohibited large scale destruction methods such as the netting of song birds, and set as a target the prohibition of all taking of "useful" species. Although still in force, this treaty has been largely ineffective. Netting is still going on in some of the signatory nations. A new

7. Evans, Beyond National Boundaries in Waterfowl Tomorrow 712 (USDI 1964).

and improved convention was signed in 1950.[8] It lays down the principle that all birds are to be protected, with certain exceptions; it regulates hunting methods and provides for a closed season which is designed to protect wildfowl during the breeding migration in the late winter and early spring. To date the treaty has been ratified by only seven states, having met with heavy opposition from many vested interests.

Presently there is no comprehensive system in Europe for the preservation of migratory birds. A new convention is desperately needed, but the difficulties seem enormous. One possibility might be to distinguish between game and non-game birds, providing for the non-game birds, which should be completely protected everywhere, the necessary harmonization of national legislation. The highly complex matter of game birds, geese, ducks and waders in particular, has hardly been considered by governments. A non-governmental organization, the International Wildfowl Research Bureau (IWRB), with headquarters in England, has been able through voluntary contributions to gather considerable information on the status of wildfowl populations along the various flyways, as well as on the numbers wintering in the wetlands of many countries. This could be the basis of future scientific management. On a purely tentative basis the following system could be suggested: each major flyway would be served by a committee composed of representatives of all states within that flyway. The committee would be empowered to coordinate research and to recommend or possibly even decide on the open and closed seasons in the various parts of the area under its jurisdiction as well as on the number of birds which it will allow to be shot at various stages of their migration. A central committee would have to be established to coordinate, when necessary, the activities of the various flyway committees, and perhaps also to make the most important decisions. Provision would have to be made for the setting up of wildfowl habitat reserves along the migration routes. These reserves being essential to the survival of the common resource, they would have to be considered as permanent reserves, and their ecological condition not altered except in very exceptional circumstances and then perhaps only with the assent of the central committee. Reserves would naturally remain under national sovereignty, but they would be subject to a servitude contracted for by international agreement. If a state enjoys a right over wild birds which merely cross its territory at a certain time of year, it seems

8. The International Convention for the Protection of Birds was signed in Paris on October 18, 1950.

logical that other states enjoying the same right should obtain from the first state a committment that it will preserve the habitat essential to the movements of these birds.[9]

It is hoped that the governments concerned will realize the need for concluding such agreements, for the future of many increasingly important open air leisure activities may well now be at stake.

---

9. A draft, Convention on Wetlands of International Importance Especially as Waterfowl Habitat, has been adopted by the International Conference on the Conservation of Wetlands and Waterfowl convened by IWRB at Ramzar, Iran, in February, 1971, and is now open for signature. Its main feature consists of the compiling of a list of wetlands which contracting parties would undertake to preserve. Unfortunately, this provision is drafted in terms which are so weak that this obligation is almost non-existent. The text of this draft can be found in IWRB Bulletin No. 31 (July 1971).

THE LAW SCHOOL AND THE ENVIRONMENT†

FRANCES IRWIN††

That the environment has a place in the law school curriculum is becoming increasingly evident. Sixty-four institutions replying to a recent survey of environmental programs at law schools listed 120 courses and seminars related to the environment and 122 faculty members teaching or performing research in the field.[1]

A few environmental courses were introduced in the late sixties at law schools such as Harvard, Indiana, Michigan, and Stanford. The number skyrocketed in 1970 and continues to increase rapidly. The Walter F. George School of Law at Mercer University in Georgia and Washburn University of Topeka School of Law are among those which offered their first environmental law courses last fall. Meanwhile, other schools are moving beyond a first experimental course. Rutgers this year added seminars on energy and transportation policies to its previous seminar in environmental problems.

While the most common forms of environmental law offered remain the single introductory semester survey or research seminar, other approaches range from day-long short courses to major programs. Environmental Law Societies at Chicago, George Washington, and Harvard have sponsored one or two day intensive courses. George Washington held its Second Annual Short Course in November with a focus on "Water Pollution: the Potomac, A Case in Point." At least a half dozen institutions, often with the help of outside funding, are establishing major programs. One example is the University of Southern California Law Center. As a participant in the Sea Grant Program, the Center is developing a capability for research, education, and advisory services relating to the institutional framework required for managing marine resources. The Center offers a local government course which includes materials on coastline man-

†The bulk of information for this article comes from replies to a letter sent to American law schools in June 1971 by Wolfgang R. Burhenne, Chairman of the Committee on Environmental Law of the International Union for Conservation of Nature and Natural Resources (IUCN). The original purpose of the letter was to elicit information about the programs and interests of professors at these law schools which might help IUCN carry out its work, which ranges from collecting and computerizing environmental laws to drafting international agreements. The responses proved so interesting that IUCN wanted to make them available to a wider audience. Similar surveys are being made of environmental law programs in European universities.

††Formerly with Commission on Environmental Policy, Law and Administration, International Union For Conservation of Nature and Natural Resources.

1. These figures reflect the opinions of faculty members answering the survey on which courses offered and research done at their schools have a primary environmental component.

agement. Its library of materials on legal problems of coastal zones and international waters serves local attorneys and other interested individuals. It has proposed research which would result in a draft international convention on allocation of income from oceanic resources.

Courses with environmental content are required of all students at only a few law schools including the Universities of Denver, Iowa, Kansas, and the State University of New York at Buffalo. At Denver the first-year students take an introductory course called Environment and Resources Law which explores both the legal and economic dimensions of the conflicting demands for resources and the quality of the environment. The course defines and evaluates probable effects of present policies and alternatives from the points of view of the individual, the enterprise, and the public. At Kansas the course is called Property II but deals with environmental questions.

Where environmental law is an elective or an extracurricular activity, it is affecting a significant number of students. Fordham has regularly scheduled two or three sections of 20 to 25 students each of its Law and the Environment seminar since it was first offered in the spring of 1970. At George Washington University, the National Law Center's Environmental Law I course, given for the first time in 1970-71, attracted 74 students the first semester and 70 the second, while Environmental Law II enrolled 43 second semester and 36 during the summer session. The University of Pennsylvania Law School reports that a quarter of the first-year students are participating in the extracurricular Environmental Law Group which works with state and city agencies.

Just what environmental law is and what its place in the law school should be are debated questions. Environmental *science* has been defined as:

> ... the study of all of the systems of air, land, water, energy and life that surround man. It includes all science directed to the system-level of understanding of the environment, drawing especially on such disciplines as meteorology, geophysics, oceanography, and ecology, and utilizing to the fullest the knowledge and techniques developed in such fields as physics, chemistry, biology, mathematics, and engineering. Included therefore are such diverse matters as climate, air turbulence, the air-sea interface, estuaries, forests, epidemics, earthquakes, and groundwater. These environmental systems contain the complex processes that must be mastered in the solution of such human problems as the maintenance of renewable resources (water, timber, fish), the conservation of non-renewable resources (fuel, metals, species), reducing the effects of natural

260

disasters (earthquakes, tornadoes, floods), alleviating chronic damage (erosion, drought, subsidence), abating pollution by man (smoke, pesticides, sewage), and coping with natural pollution (allergens, volcanic dust, electromagnetic "noise").[2]

Environmental *law* considers the role of law in man's relationship to these surrounding systems of air, land, water, energy and life. Just as environmental science looks to various disciplines and fields for knowledge and techniques, environmental law draws on many legal specialties including administrative law, civil procedure, constitutional law, property, torts, and urban government as well as perhaps its most direct predecessors—land use planning, natural resources, and law and technology.

Environmental law courses have been organized in different ways. One method is to limit the subject matter to one of the systems. The University of Southern California has offered a course in air pollution. Yale's catalog lists Environmental and Economic Regulation of Energy Sources. At Chicago and Michigan, water law courses have taken a resource planning approach. Land use planning courses have become standard fare at many schools. Population control is beginning to receive attention. Minnesota offers a seminar, and the Fletcher School of Law and Diplomacy started a Law and Population Program during the past year.

Rather than focusing on one of these systems, many of the courses take case studies from several systems. At Harvard the Environment Protection course uses automotive air pollution, water quality management, and the control of carcinogens as case studies to provide the context for discussing questions such as:

> How should choices be made among alternative forms of private litigation and public regulation as modes of social control? How can conflicting interests best be identified and represented in processes of lawmaking and administration? Whose responsibility should it be to consider the future and how much weight should such consideration be given? By what criteria should the factual and economic burdens of uncertainty be allocated among the prospective beneficiaries and victims of technological developments? How can the use of expertise and systematic analysis in decisionmaking be reconciled with the goals of pluralism and participation? Through what institutional arrangements, and under what assumptions, are competing values such as "economic progress" and "quality of life" best reconciled?[3]

---

2. Nat'l Science Bd., Environmental Science: Challenge for the Seventies (1971).
3. 1971/72 Harvard Law School Catalogue quoted in letter from Laurence H. Tribe to the Comm. on Environmental Law, Oct. 5, 1971.

At Michigan the emphasis in the course on Legal Problems of Environmental Quality is on the role of private citizens and organizations in using the legal processes, the need for legislative reform and problems in the use of administrative and regulatory agencies. The subject matter used in covering these themes includes air and water pollution, shoreline and estuarine regulation, acquisition and management of public lands, waste disposal, and pesticides.

In some instances the environment is the subject matter for teaching legal techniques. The environment is providing a "jet age" vehicle for considering an age-old set of relationships, Professor Harold W. Young says, describing its function for the legal process course at Oklahoma which studies the interactions of the courts, legislatures, and administrative agencies. The law revision seminar at Colorado, the law and social change course at the University of Southern California and the legislation seminar at Ohio State have all used environmental topics extensively. It is also a favorite subject for independent research. Stanford students have completed about 20 research projects related to environmental law under its independent study program.

At a quarter of the schools replying, environmental law is being used for experiments with clinical and interdisciplinary approaches to legal education. UCLA and Colorado both include environmental internships as part of their programs, funded by the Ford Foundation. The interns are selected from second year law students and placed in industry, government, public interest law firms, and private law firms all over the country. They take an environmental law course before the summer internship and then participate in a seminar in the fall semester to help evaluate their experience. Professor Donald M. Carmichael, one of the faculty supervisors of the Colorado program, explains: "Since the students actually do their research within the agencies, they get insiders' views of the recalcitrancies of putting regulatory environmental law into operation. Frequently their research yields suggestions on legal and operational matters which is of benefit to the host agencies."[4]

Professor A. Dan Tarlock is skeptical of the rapid increase of courses on environmental law. More important is for universities to train a new type specialist. "Persons trained in one discipline with the ability to synthesize and apply the insights of related fields are needed for future decision-making."[5] While the great majority of

4. Letter from Donald M. Carmichael to the Comm. on Environmental Law, June 16, 1971.

5. Tarlock, *Development of an Environmental Curriculum*, in Law and the Environment 336 (Baldwin & Page 1970).

environmental law courses recognize the interdisciplinary nature of the problem and then consider the legal aspect, 17 of the schools responding indicated specific efforts to create courses open to students from other disciplines or to use materials from other fields. Several have already planned or are planning joint programs with other schools within their universities. The law school at the University of Montana is developing a four-year program with the graduate school under which a student would receive a law degree and a Master of Science in Environmental Quality.

The Colorado Law School is experimenting with one of the broadest interdisciplinary projects. It is a Technology Evaluation Seminar, funded by the National Science Foundation. Faculty and students from the Law School are cooperating with participants from Engineering, Political Science, Psychology, and Economics. Through an interdisciplinary case study approach, they hope to "elucidate major causes of the chronic time lag between the introduction of new technology, the perception within the scientific community of untoward environmental consequences of the technology, the emergence of this scientific knowledge into political and legal spheres, and the generation of an appropriate legal or political response. Pesticides provide the classic example . . ."[6]

At Notre Dame the Environmental Law program is open to both law students and graduate students in other disciplines. A three hour survey course discussing various legal remedies to environmental problems is followed by a course in which students are given an actual pollution problem in the local area and asked to develop solutions which are technically feasible and legally acceptable. At the University of Pennsylvania last year, Professor Bruce A. Ackerman formed a seminar of six students each from the schools of law, economics, and engineering to study control of water pollution in the Delaware Valley.

While at Notre Dame and Pennsylvania, as in many other programs, the stress is on local problems, courses are being offered and research carried out on international problems as well. At Northwestern, Professor Anthony A. D'Amato offers a course on Law, Ecology and the Global Environment, a study of legal and environmental variables in a global system perspective. Professor Samuel A. Bleicher of the University of Toledo has prepared materials on Pollution and Political Boundaries which "examine the fundamental elements of a 'newly-discovered' world concern, regulation of pollution, and at the same time use the problem as a springboard to

---

6. Letter from Donald M. Carmichael, *supra* note 4.

consideration of the processes by which law and governmental institutions develop or fail to develop to satisfy newly-perceived human needs and concerns."[7] At Tulane, Professor Julian Juergensmeyer includes a section on comparative environmental law in his materials. Among others who combine international and environmental interests are Professor Thomas J. Schoenbaum of the University of North Carolina School of Law, who is studying the coordination and comparative approaches to environmental problems in the United States and in Common Market countries, Professor Ludwik A. Teclaff, who specializes in international water law at Fordham, and Professor Keith Rosenn of Ohio State, who includes environmental matters in his study of legal problems of developing economies.

While it is often assumed that environmental issues compete with urban and poverty programs or international studies for funds and student interest, the survey showed that such interests are frequently linked. Land use, public health, and consumer protection are issues in both urban and environmental programs. The State University of New York at Buffalo Law School calls its program Environmental and Urban Law. It lists such courses as Problems of Open Space Preservation and Rejuvenation in Metropolitan Communities and Interstate Cooperation, Regional Planning, and Federal Intervention in Water Resource Allocation. Cornell offers a course in Problems of Urban Development. At UCLA the National Legal Program on the Health Problems of the Poor engages in environmental litigation.

Environmental law has close relationships to urban law, but it is perhaps more often thought of as a revised version of courses previously taught as natural resources law. Usually a concern with quality and the decision-making process replaces the earlier concentration on exploitation. The catalog description for Nebraska's course in Natural Resources, Policy Planning, and Environmental Law reads:

> Contemporary issues in water resource management and legal problems arising from the regulation of a public resource within the private property system. Riparian, appropriative and prescriptive water rights, rights in ground water; issues of large-scale government economic planning, including cost-benefit analysis; problems of interstate and federal-state relations; and the effect of present policies on future generations. Attention is given to zoning, recreation, and urban water development problems. . . .[8]

---

7. Samuel A. Bleicher, Pollution and Political Boundaries: Cases and Materials (mimeograph 1971).

8. Letter from Richard S. Harnsberger to the Comm. on Environmental Law, June 9, 1971.

Ohio State has chosen to divide the subject into three different courses. Natural Resources Law covers the law of oil and gas and of water quantity; Conservation Law considers air and water quality and problems of the living environment; and Administration of Natural Resources deals with administrative problems of protecting and managing the environment. The Denver Natural Resources Program, established in 1965, requires a student emphasizing natural resources law to take the traditional courses in water rights, oil and gas, public land and mining, taxation, and securities regulation, but the student must also take the introductory environmental course and an additional seminar or land use planning course.

Technology assessment is another close relative of environmental law. The concern with evaluating and controlling the impact of technology on society is evident in several of the programs described above, particularly the Colorado Technology Evaluation Seminar and the Harvard Environmental Protection course. Cornell offered a course in Science, Technology, and Law for the first time this year. Air and water pollution and exhaustion of limited natural resources are among the subjects considered in discussing the problems and potential for solutions presented by the science and technology of affluence.

Whatever its roots in urban law, resources law, and technology assessment, spokesmen for environmental law see it as much more than old wine in new skins. Malcolm Baldwin, Legal Associate at the Conservation Foundation, finds a distinctive feature of environmental law in its concern for non-proprietary cases in contrast to a conservation law under which cases were brought by injured persons on their own behalf.[9] Professor Harrison C. Dunning describes environmental law as "the law we employ to govern the interaction between man and the environment."[10] He sees a need for new legal forms to evolve. ". . .[I]f the law of torts and the public regulatory agencies, which themselves sponsor the developmental activity that must be controlled, provide no solutions, what will? What new legal forms could evolve?"[11]

Professor Joseph L. Sax of the University of Michigan Law School believes that environmental lawyers must reach beyond traditional legal aspirations. In a keynote paper given at the Environmental Law Seminar sponsored by the Smithsonian Institution and the American Law Institute and American Bar Association, he noted:

In the most important sense, there is no body of environmental law

9. *Environmental Law Course*, 22 Harvard Law School Bulletin (1970).
10. Dunning, *Notes for an Environmental Law Course*, 55 Cornell L. Rev. 804 (1970).
11. *Id.* at 806.

today. The significant history is yet to be written by lawyers such as those sitting in this room; and their success will, in my judgment, be measured by the degree to which this history goes beyond traditional legal aspirations. While it would, of course, be foolish to suggest that the *problems* with which we must deal are unique to legal experience, I do suggest that they call for approaches which are sharply distinct from the legal milieu in which we are accustomed to working.[12]

He proposed that:

An environmental law problem is presented when there is a loss of effective control over the impact of human activity on natural communities. And the job of the environmental lawyer is to restore that control. ... [T]he first job ... is to move from a static function of rulemaking for conflict resolution upon facts accepted as given to a prod and force for innovation of new knowledge which alone permits conflict to be resolved rationally. Only in this way can human activity be brought under control.[13]

---

12. Sax, Introduction to Environmental Law, 117 Cong. Rec. S 551 (daily ed. Jan. 29, 1971).

13. *Id.* at S 552.

ABOUT THE EDITORS

ALBERT E. UTTON is a member of the International Council of Environmental Law, chairman of the World Peace through Law Committee of the New Mexico State Bar, and member of the board of the New Mexico Water Resources Research Institute, as well as a delegate to the Universities Council on Water Resources. He has contributed articles to numerous law reviews and edits the *Natural Resources Journal.* He is also the co-author of *Water and Water Rights, Vol. II* (Allen Smith, 1967) and editor of *National Petroleum Policy: A Critical Review* (University of New Mexico Press, 1970).

DANIEL H. HENNING is Associate Professor of Political Science at Eastern Montana College. During the 1970-71 academic year, he was Visiting Associate Professor in the Program for Advanced Study in Public Science and Administration at the University of New Mexico. He has served as a ranger with the U.S. Forest Service and the National Park Service and, with the International Union for Conservation of Nature and Natural Resources, as a researcher-writer for the *United Nations List of National Parks and Equivalent Areas.* Dr. Henning is a Trustee (environment) for the Northwest Scientific Association and a member of the International Council of Environmental Law. His articles on environmental affairs have appeared in the *Public Administration Review, Annals of Regional Science,* the *Idaho Law Review, BioScience,* and numerous other journals.